THE UNITY TREASURE CHEST

→ *THE*

UNITY

TREASURE CHEST

A SELECTION OF THE BEST
OF UNITY WRITING

COMPILED BY

LOWELL FILLMORE

HAWTHORN BOOKS, INC.

W. Clement Stone, Publisher

NEW YORK

THE UNITY TREASURE CHEST

Library of Congress Catalog Card Number: 56-6997
ISBN: 0–8015–8192–3

2 3 4 5 6 7 8 9 10

CONTENTS

4. God Is the Health of His People
(HOW TO BE HEALED)

5. Plenty Everywhere
(HOW TO BE PROSPEROUS)

6. Living the Life
(MEETING THE CHALLENGES OF EVERYDAY LIVING)

CONTENTS

7. Love Is the Magnet
(HOW TO LIVE IN HARMONY WITH OTHERS)

8. The Light Shines in the Darkness
(HOW TO BEGIN AGAIN)

9. The Only Bond That Endures
(HOW TO MEET BEREAVEMENT AND SORROW)

ABOUT THIS BOOK

THE PUBLISHERS of this book have asked me to select for it some of the best and most helpful articles that have appeared in the Unity periodicals and other Unity literature, so that it will provide for its readers a cross section of the teachings of Unity School of Christianity.

The contents of this book have been chosen out of a sincere desire to give persons who are not already familiar with Unity a comprehensive idea of its teachings in a concise and easy-to-read form, and to show those who read them how to receive practical benefit from them.

We at Unity think of our publications as being educational as well as religious. You will find that the articles in this book are designed to show the reader how Christian principles may be applied in a practical way by anyone, no matter to what church organization he may belong, or if he is not a member of any church.

The Unity teachings are based upon a metaphysical interpretation of the Bible. I have tried to select representative articles from the thousands that have appeared in the Unity periodicals and other Unity literature during the past sixty-five years.

The first periodical published by Unity came out in April, 1889. Its publication came about because two humble and devoted people desired to tell others how they had learned to apply Christian principles in their daily lives. Charles and Myrtle Fillmore, my father and mother, believed in the healing principles that Jesus Christ taught, and they proved that these principles can be used today and every day to heal, to prosper, and to guide all persons who will apply them with faith and understanding. This first periodical later became known as *Unity* magazine. It is still being published monthly, and contains, in addition to many other helpful articles, one article by Charles Fillmore in each issue, which is selected from the many manuscripts written and talks given by him during his active ministry.

Myrtle Fillmore was so much interested in children that in 1893 she created out of her love for little children a magazine just for them, which she named *Wee Wisdom*. She dedicated it to the constructive entertainment and spiritual guidance of little children. By means of it she helped them to live happier, healthier, and more harmonious lives through learning and using the simple teachings of Jesus Christ. This magazine is still being published, and today many grandparents who read it when they were little children are sending it to their grandchildren.

Weekly Unity, the next Unity periodical, began publication in 1909. It is a messenger of truth and uplift, and cheers its large family of readers by its weekly calls.

You magazine is a monthly periodical especially planned to guide, entertain, and inspire teen-agers. *Good Business*, another Unity monthly periodical, contains articles and true stories showing how Christian principles can be and are being applied successfully in solving business problems. *Daily Word*, a monthly manual of daily meditations, began its inspiring mission in 1924, and now has nearly a million subscribers. It is also published in six foreign languages. *Daily Word* prints a one-page prayer and meditation for each day in the month. Another Unity periodical is the *Unity Sunday-School Leaflet*, which is prepared for children so that each student receives fifty-two separate lessons during the year. These lessons, which are based on the International Sunday School Lessons, can be used in Sunday schools or in the home.

Daily Word, *You*, and *Wee Wisdom* are also published in Braille every month for the blind, and are sent free on request. Unity also publishes a bimonthly magazine, *El Sembrador*, in Spanish, which is sent to any Spanish reader without charge. In addition to its eight periodicals, which are circulated in almost every country in the world, Unity also publishes sixty bound volumes, including six books for children, and hundreds of booklets, leaflets, and prayer cards. More than seventy radio stations broadcast the Unity message.

There are some 240 Unity centers in various cities throughout the United States, Canada, and abroad. These centers provide direct spiritual help through devotional services and class instruction in the spiritual principles set forth in the Unity literature. These centers are open daily for prayer, spiritual counseling, and for the sale of Unity books and literature. While the Unity centers are locally organized and financed, the teachers are trained by Unity School and work in close co-operation with Unity School. Those who attend a Unity center or a Unity church are free to maintain their affiliation with any church of their choice. Through the ministry of these centers, thousands of people of every faith and in every walk of life are receiving new spiritual understanding.

This *Unity Treasure Chest* also contains a condensed story of the Unity organization, known as Unity School of Christianity, which grew out of the healing through prayer of Charles and Myrtle Fillmore. It also tells how a healing group, known as the Society of Silent Unity, was organized by Charles and Myrtle Fillmore many years ago. This group now ministers to countless numbers of persons who need prayer for healing, prosperity, harmony, and spiritual understanding. Workers in the Society of Silent Unity are on duty to receive and answer telegrams and telephone calls at all hours of the day and night, besides millions of letters asking for prayer. No charge is made for their prayer ministry. It is supported by free-will love offerings from those who wish to give in return for the service they receive.

Readers of Unity literature include many ministers and members of various denominations and religious organizations. Unity literature is designed to help all who desire spiritual help, and it does not condemn or depreciate the teachings of any other religious organizations.

I trust that the selection of articles I have made here will give the readers of *The Unity Treasure Chest* inspiration, and will help them to attain an ever happier, healthier, and more joyous outlook on life.

LOWELL FILLMORE

Publisher's Note

Because *The Unity Treasure Chest* was reprinted exactly as originally published, in 1956, the "Notes on Authors" and "List of Unity Books" are no longer applicable. Many of the authors are now in different positions; several of the book titles listed are now out of print; and the Unity book list now contains many new titles. (A complete listing of current Unity books will be sent on request to Unity Books, Unity Village, Missouri 64063.)

Although Lowell Fillmore's introduction, "About This Book," which appears on pages 9 through 11, still expresses the insight and dedication of the author, some of the facts included are no longer applicable. The Unity periodicals *Weekly Unity, You, Good Business,* and *Unity Sunday-school Leaflet* have been combined with other publications or discontinued. At present Unity publishes *Unity* magazine, *Wee Wisdom,* and *Daily Word.*

THE UNITY TREASURE CHEST

1. We Are One With You

"We want to co-operate with all true,
honest, faithful Christian workers and will
do any right thing to further the cause.
We are one with you in advocating the
doctrine of Jesus Christ and the only
title we need is 'Christian Teachers
and Healers.'"

—*Charles Fillmore*

LOWELL FILLMORE

THEY MADE A CONTRACT
WITH GOD

MY MEMORY carries me back to the time when I was a
little boy living with my mother, father, little brother, and grandmother in a house out on Wabash Avenue in Kansas City, Missouri. I did not realize then that my mother's health was in a very
critical condition. I knew that my father was lame and wore one
boot that had a lift some four or five inches high fastened to the
sole, because I used to put it on and hobble around just for fun.
I knew that Mother did not do much of the housework and that
my grandmother helped take care of us boys and did the cook-
ing. I have been told since that my mother was in the advanced
stages of tuberculosis and that the doctors had given her only a
few months to live.

Mother seemed always cheerful and helpful, but there came
a time when she seemed to grow more cheerful. People from the
neighborhood began coming in to see her. She explained to me
that she was praying for them. I remember one old gentleman,
who lived across the street, came several times using his crutches.
Then, one day I heard Mother tell him to lay down his crutches
and walk across the room. He said he couldn't do it, but she insisted that he go ahead and try it. He did try, and walked without his crutches, but it was difficult, for I heard his joints pop.
This man was soon healed, as were many others who came in for
Mother's help.

One day, a salesman with a grip full of picture frames called and spread his wares out on the floor to show Mother the beautiful samples of gilded picture frames, and I, a little boy of five or six, came up to see what he was doing. The man said to Mother: "I have a little boy about the size of yours, but he will never see again." Mother asked if they had ever prayed for the little fellow, and when he said, "No," she suggested that she visit the boy and try to help him. The salesman was quite willing. I remember her telling me that the second time she went to see the little boy he came to the door and let her in himself. His sight had improved enough for that. Later he was completely healed. He is still living in Kansas City.

Later Mother started writing children's stories and with the help of my father began a little magazine for children, which she called *Wee Wisdom*. Through it she taught the little ones to pray for healing and for everything that would make them better children. *Wee Wisdom* in 1956 reaches hundreds of thousands of children.

It was not until later that I understood what had happened to change Mother from a sickly person to one who was well and strong and able to help others. It seems that she had been the youngest member of a large family that lived in a little town in Ohio, and they were all devout church members. She had always been very religious but had believed that she inherited tuberculosis from her earthly parents, because several members of her family had succumbed to this disease. She thought that it was God's will for her to be resigned.

She and father attended a course of lectures given by an out-of-town speaker. This lecturer brought out the idea that God is a loving Father and that it is not His will that His children be sick or suffer. It became clear to her that if God was in truth her Father, she did not need to inherit disease from her earthly parents. She then remembered that Jesus had said: "Call no man your father on the earth: for one is your Father, even He who is in heaven." * Thus, a new hope and faith were inspired in her heart and she, being very sincere in her belief in prayer, began giving thanks to her loving Father for her heritage of health. She realized that she could not possibly have inherited tuberculosis

* All Scriptural references, unless otherwise indicated, are quoted from the American Standard Version of the Holy Bible.

from Him. This filled her with such a spirit of enthusiasm and understanding of God's life and love that she daily grew stronger. Although one of her lungs was supposed to have been utterly useless when the doctor examined her, she no longer worried about that condition. She lived happily for more than fifty years after that experience.

My father, Charles Fillmore, had not been particularly religious, but he was a very practical man. At the time of Mother's healing, he was in the real-estate business in Kansas City. The very fact that Mother had discovered a religion that was practical for daily use attracted his attention. He began to study the Bible and other religious writings, and attended lectures on metaphysics. He spent a great deal of time in prayer and silent meditation, and many things were revealed to him. By patient prayer and meditation, he was able to fill out and lengthen the withered leg, which had not grown since he was twelve years of age, so that he was able to wear an ordinary shoe on that foot, and he no longer needed to carry a cane. The leg trouble had begun with what was at first diagnosed as rheumatism and which gradually developed into tuberculosis of the hip. His health was now improved and he overcame a catarrhal condition that had been a handicap to him since childhood. He was aware of the presence of God with him as he worked and he decided to give up his real-estate business and give full time to God's work. He and my mother wrote out a covenant between themselves and God in which they agreed that they would devote themselves and all they possessed and ever expected to possess to God's work, and accept in return His love and backing. (A facsimile of this covenant in my father's handwriting appears on page 21.)

Before *Wee Wisdom* was started, Father began writing articles and publishing a magazine in order that he might help others to benefit by practical prayer as he was being helped. A group of devout workers, known as the Society of Silent Unity, was organized for the purpose of united prayers.

Because Mother and Father believed that God did the healing work, it was impossible for them to put a price on it, and they decided to give their prayers free of charge to all who asked and to accept love offerings for their service, and they gave whether such requests were accompanied by offerings or not.

The prayer and educational work begun by them has since encircled the globe, and although my father and mother are no longer with us in the flesh, the movement that they started is growing rapidly and is helping millions of persons.

This work is known as Unity and is described as practical Christianity. My father and mother never claimed to teach anything new. They simply applied the truths taught in the Bible, especially the teachings of Jesus, in a very practical way. Father and Mother believed that teachers are necessary only to help the student find his inner Christ so that the Spirit of Truth can reveal all Truth to him. "God is no respecter of persons," and each follower of Christ must ultimately find the Truth of God within himself.

THOUGHT, 48-page
Magazine, $1.00 per year.
UNITY, Monthly Paper,
50 cents per year.
Metaphysical Series,
15 cents per copy.

METAPHYSICAL
BOOK DEALERS
AND PUBLISHERS,
820 Walnut Street,
KANSAS CITY, MO.

Dedication and Covenant.

We, Charles Fillmore and Myrtle Fillmore, husband and wife, hereby dedicate ourselves, our time, our money, all we have and all we expect to have, to the Spirit of Truth, and through it, to the Society of Silent Unity.

It being understood and agreed that the Said Spirit of Truth shall render unto us an equivalent for this dedication, in peace of mind, health of body, wisdom, understanding, love and an abundant supply of all things necessary to meet every want without our making any of these things the object of our existence.

In the presence of the Conscious Mind of Christ Jesus, this 7th day of December A.D. 1892.

Charles Fillmore.
Myrtle Fillmore

JAMES DILLET FREEMAN

EXCERPTS FROM
THE STORY OF UNITY

CHARLES and Myrtle Fillmore worked together to build Unity. It was Myrtle Fillmore who first accepted the idea of divine healing; it was Charles Fillmore who edited the first magazine. It was Myrtle Fillmore who first led Silent Unity; it was Charles Fillmore who named the work Unity and developed it into the world-wide organization it is today. It was Myrtle Fillmore who led the people in meditation and prayer; it was Charles Fillmore who made speeches and wrote books. They worked together as heart and head work together, and from their united efforts grew the great movement that is Unity. If Mrs. Fillmore supplied the original impetus, it was her husband who supplied the greater part of the energy that carried it forward.

Charles and Myrtle Fillmore had a simplicity about them that endeared them to all who knew them. They soared, but they lived simply. They founded a faith that reaches around the world, yet their humility was as great as their accomplishments. It was Unity, not Charles and Myrtle Fillmore, whose success they worked to forward. There was no pretense about these two. They never took a title to themselves and they were such unassuming people that no one else felt like calling them by a title either. Among their workers and close friends, there was almost a family feeling and many of these called them "Papa Charley" and "Mama Myrtle." They were the kind of people who, when they went to the vegetarian cafeteria that Unity built on the cor-

[22]

ner of Ninth and Tracy in Kansas City, stood in line, took their turn, and paid for their meals just as everyone else did.

Charles and Myrtle Fillmore believed that the most important thing in their lives was their ideas and their works, the good they did for others; they were teachers. Those who came to Kansas City after 1906 and studied under them remember them always as they appeared on the platform at 913 Tracy Avenue before the congregation of the Unity Society of Practical Christianity on a Sunday morning. Myrtle Fillmore, wearing her white hair like a crown, gentle, smiling, sitting silent with a look not wholly of this world, and Charles Fillmore standing at the rostrum leaning slightly to one side with his hands braced before him and making in his calm, deliberate style some observation like the following:

"God is the health of His people. God is infinite life. Let us hold to the Spirit of God, demonstrating itself in life everywhere. That is what the scientific world is preaching today, and we cannot get away from this proposition of the omnipresence of the one life. There is nothing else to come but the Spirit of Truth. We do not look for another. We know that the Spirit of Truth is here. It has always been here, but we have turned our face in another direction. We have looked somewhere else rather than to the Spirit of Truth. The Spirit of Truth is in the midst of you. It is in you, and you will never have peace of mind, you will never have success in any way, you will never have health of body, you will never have anything satisfactory until you demonstrate its presence and its power in your life."

Charles and Myrtle Fillmore were more than teachers. They were healers. They were not content merely to have ideas or even to tell others of the ideas. They took the ideas and worked to demonstrate them in their own lives and bodies. The very heart of the Unity teaching has to do with healing the ills of mind, body, and affairs. Unity began with the healing of Myrtle Fillmore. Its first fruits were the healing of her friends and neighbors, accomplished by her realization of the Christ power within. The heart of Unity today is the Society of Silent Unity, which sends its message of healing to hundreds of thousands of persons throughout the world each year. In the anteroom outside the Fillmores' offices each day, people waited their turn to have these two teachers, who had touched God's power and whom God's power had touched, utter a healing prayer for them.

Charles and Myrtle Fillmore were builders, too. Go out to Unity School today and walk down the shady lanes or stand and gaze at the buildings that house Unity and you get a sense of what they built. It was their son Rickert who erected the buildings at Unity Farm, but it was they who envisioned such a spiritual center; and it was they who from nothing but an idea and faith in that idea, in half a century built the Unity work of which the buildings are but a visible expression.

Today the presses in the vast Unity printing building are rolling out literature in a dozen languages to be sent to millions of people in most of the countries of the earth. On the radio from scores of stations in the United States and other countries, the Jesus Christ message as interpreted by Charles and Myrtle Fillmore goes out to more than three million people. Teachers and Truth lecturers in hundreds of Unity centers are every day expounding the ideas of these two pioneers to thousands of eager students.

Charles and Myrtle Fillmore had many abilities. They were practical people: teachers, ministers, healers, builders. But they had vision, too. They worked to turn their ideas into magazines and buildings, into restored bodies and renewed minds and illumined lives. But their ideas soared even beyond their accomplishments. They had the vision of the perfect man in God, and this perfection was their goal. They aimed at the highest, and how high they mounted! They aimed at eternal life, and how much of life they won, not only for themselves but for how many others! Because they lived close in thought and aspiration to God, there was about them an atmosphere of spirituality that those who were near them felt.

Charles and Myrtle Fillmore followed the "visionary gleam." They were pioneers of mind and spirit. They were never bound by limited conceptions about life but were always striking out into the new. They were people with the courage to step out on faith. "Judge not according to appearance," said Jesus, and Charles and Myrtle Fillmore took Him at His word. Appearances might say, "You cannot do it," but Charles and Myrtle Fillmore did not believe in appearances. "If you need something," said Mr. Fillmore, "go ahead and get it, do something about it."

Charles and Myrtle Fillmore were a man and woman of faith. In the word faith is summed up the story of their life and works —and the story of Unity. They did their works through faith. They soared beyond their works through faith. They were teachers through faith. They were healers through faith. They were builders through faith. They were overcomers through faith.

Many, many times in the history of Unity they came to a place where it seemed that they could not go on, yet they went on through faith.

They taught that God is a help in every need and they prayed in this simple faith. Over and over when they were in need, they went to God to prove that what they taught is true. All that they thought and wrote and did they wrought through faith. Through faith, they turned to God in the beginning. Through faith, they healed their bodies. Through faith, they brought healing to others. Through faith, they founded Unity. Through faith, they persevered in their idea when everything seemed to say that they were destined for failure. Through faith, they built a work that rings the world around with faith and prayer.

They never lost faith.

Once Unity was in serious financial straits. Bills that had to be paid were piling up, and there did not seem to be money enough to meet the pay roll. The Fillmores called their staff together to pray about the matter. One of the staff said, "Let us pray that the money holds out."

"Oh, no," whispered Myrtle Fillmore, "let us pray that our faith holds out."

In the spring of 1891, Charles Fillmore and his wife and a few students met together one evening to pray. As they were sitting in the silence, suddenly into the mind of Charles Fillmore flashed the name UNITY. At the moment, he had not even been thinking about a name and when it came to him it startled him.

"That's it!" he cried out. "UNITY!" he told the others. "UNITY! that's the name for our work, the name we've been looking for."

Later he told friends the name came right out of the ether,

just as the voice of Jesus was heard by Paul in the heavens. "No one else heard it, but it was as clear to me as though somebody had spoken to me."

Then and there the name UNITY was adopted. It was an apt and fortunate choice. The Fillmores had borrowed the best from all the religions. Where the churches had put the emphasis on controversial doctrinal points that had caused division after division in the Christian world, Charles and Myrtle Fillmore were to put their emphasis on the things that are practical, the things that apply to everyday thinking and living. They were not to found a new religion but were to work within the framework of existing religions and appeal to church members without causing them to divorce themselves from their church. They were to propound a teaching that people of all faiths could study and apply to their lives. They were to be a force for unity in the world. The movement that Charles and Myrtle Fillmore had founded was to live and grow under the name UNITY.

"The world," said Charles Fillmore, "is governed by the law of mind action." It was through this belief that he came to Unity's unique concept of prayer—the use of affirmations and denials, spiritual decrees rather than petitions, in addressing God.

Affirmations and denials are statements that deny the reality of undesirable conditions and affirm the reality of God and His good, such as *"There is nothing in all the universe for me to fear, for greater is He that is in me than he that is in the world,"* and *"I am a radiant, all-wise, all-loving, all-conquering son of God."*

"Prayer," wrote Charles Fillmore, "is not the beseeching of a reluctant God. It is intercommunion with God. 'Ye ask, and receive not, because ye ask amiss.' Not that we ask for what God is not willing to give, nor what we, as His children, may not rightfully ask for and claim; but because we beseech and supplicate, as though God were not willing but possibly might be induced to change and grant our petition. This is a false notion.

"'For I, Jehovah, change not.' 'Jesus Christ *is* the same yesterday and today, yea and for ever.' If God ever did answer prayer, He always does, being the same God. Therefore, if there seems to be any lack of principle, it is in the one who prays.

Misunderstanding of the will and nature of our God prevents prayer from being answered.

"Prayer does not change God, the unchangeable, but it changes mortals and makes them receptive to that good which is being given without limit. 'God is Spirit: and they that worship him must worship in spirit and truth.' Translate material desires into their spiritual correspondents and then declare that in Truth and in Spirit you receive that which you desire, and then you will have it materially as well as spiritually. 'But seek ye first his kingdom, and his righteousness; and all these things shall be added unto you.' "

Fifty years before the inception of the science of psychosomatics, which treats of the relationship of the mind to bodily illness, Charles and Myrtle Fillmore were teaching that the ills of our body are the result of our wrong thinking, that disease has its origin in negative mental and emotional states. Over and over, in the early pages of *Unity*, they traced physical disturbances to mental causes. Many years ago, Myrtle was writing to a correspondent:

Perhaps it will help if I tell you that I suffered with a trouble similar to yours for years. And I prayed for healing, many times; and did all I knew to please the Lord; and still my healing did not come. I tried to look over all my faults, and to bring myself into harmony with Truth. After asking the Lord to show me just what was hindering, Spirit spoke to me very clearly, saying, "You have looked among your faults; now, suppose you look among your virtues." And I did; and there I found the cause of the deep-seated physical suffering and congestion!

I had considered it a virtue to control my feelings; to never give way to them, outwardly; to never let anyone know when I was hurt or angered. I kept a calm and pleasant exterior, but inside I sometimes grieved and resented and worried and rebelled. And, my secret thoughts and feelings were cutting and congesting and weakening my vital organs and the walls of my body. As I turned the light of Spirit upon these hidden things, and sought to have Divine Mind transform my very subconsciousness, so that I should work from an entirely new basis, I was healed and restored to harmony and strength. There were times, after the first revelation, when I would forget and give way to old ways of thinking, and there would come a physical warning. I have found that whatever thoughts I harbor do produce some sort of results in me or my environment; that if I want perfect health, I must let the law of God, the rules of harmony and health, come first, regardless of what they do to old habits and thoughts.

The Fillmores taught that the way for a man to change his physical condition is to change his thinking. "People come to me and they ask me for help," said Charles Fillmore. " 'Ask me to do anything,' they say, 'but don't ask me to change my thinking.' But they have to change their thinking if they want to be well."

Over and over, the Fillmores echoed the words of Paul, "Be ye transformed by the renewing of your mind."

"What can a man do with the thoughts of his mind?" Charles Fillmore wrote. "He can do everything with them. They are under his absolute control. He can direct them. He can coerce them. He can hush them or crush them. He can dissolve them and put others in their place. There is no other spot in the universe where man has mastery. The dominion that is his by divine right is over his own thoughts. When man apprehends this and commences to exercise that dominion, he has begun to open the way to God, the only door to God—through mind and thought."

"The purpose of prayer," the Fillmores taught, "is to change your thinking. God does not change; His will is always, only good. All that keeps you from your good is your failure to unify yourself in thought with the source of all good, God."

Following this line of thought, the Fillmores worked out a new technique of prayer, which they called the silence, using affirmations and denials. They instructed the student to relax in mind and body, to turn to God in his thoughts, to think not about his problem but about God, whose wisdom, love, and power are mighty to solve every problem. To enable him to keep his mind away from the problem and on God's presence and power, they taught the student to use affirmations and denials, repeating them over and over. The words themselves had no magic power, but continued concentration on them brought the student to realize the Truth in them. "Ye shall know the truth, and the truth shall make you free."

Jesus taught, "All things whatsoever ye pray and ask for, believe that ye receive them, and ye shall have them." The Fillmores' technique of prayer is based on this idea of Jesus—"be-

lieve that ye receive"—and those who apply this idea rediscover
what many churchmen have forgotten, that faithful prayer gets
results.

The Fillmores did not advance new teachings. All that they
taught is based on the Bible, and especially on the teachings of
Jesus. They saw Jesus as the Son of God, the Master, conscious
of His oneness with our Father, demonstrating His Sonship in
His life, the perfect channel of God's power and love. They felt
that Unity is a return to His original teachings, a return needed
for centuries. Before they decided to call it "practical Christianity," they had called their teaching "primitive Christianity."

The Fillmores went back to the original teachings of Jesus,
and came forth with a modern, seven-day-a-week religious teaching, expressed in up-to-date, easy-to-understand language. They
demonstrated that religion has practical value in helping people
handle today's problems.

Jesus taught that God is loving and accessible. "The kingdom
of God is within you," He said, and Paul told the Athenians, "In
Him we live, and move, and have our being." But through the
centuries, people had come to believe in God as a stern judge,
living in a far-off heaven to which people went after they died.

The Fillmores restated in modern language the great truths
that they found in the Bible: "God is within you. You can find
Him there. Heaven is a state of mind. You can enter into heaven
now."

"God is your loving Father and you are His beloved children,"
they taught, and repeated as had Jesus the words of the Psalmist,
" 'Ye are gods, And all of you sons of the Most High.' "

" 'Christ in you, the hope of glory,' " they declared. "The
Christ Spirit is in you, and the Christ power. Claim it now, use
it now to remake your life."

The Fillmores lived by the Bible. They studied the misunder-
stood teachings of Jesus—about the immanence of God, about the
love of God, about the power of believing prayer. Jubilantly in
their magazines, in their books, in their talks, they proclaimed
these teachings until thousands on thousands of people were putting the teachings into practice and proving with quickened
bodies, with minds set free, with lives renewed, that the teachings are true.

Charles and Myrtle Fillmore were people of vision. Their vision is expressed in Mrs. Fillmore's first affirmation, "*I am a child of God and therefore I do not inherit sickness.*" It was the vision of a way of life better than that which men have so long felt that they are heir to.

The teaching of Charles and Myrtle Fillmore was an affirmation of life. "Live!" they proclaimed. "Live free! Live whole! Live eternally!"

THE LIGHT THAT SHINES
FOR YOU

THERE IS a light that shines from a window in the Silent Unity building. In terms of candlepower this light is very small; it casts a faint golden glow on the tiles of the cloister roof on which it falls.

It is only in terms of spiritual power that this light has significance, for this is the light in the room where Silent Unity keeps the vigil of prayer.

Probably the gaslight shed but feeble illumination on the upstairs room of the house in Kansas City, where Charles and Myrtle Fillmore and a few friends met more than sixty years ago "in silent soul communion . . . all those who are in trouble, sickness, or poverty, and who sincerely desire the help of the Good Father."

But a light was lighted then far brighter than eyes have power to see, a light for minds to follow and for hearts to be warmed by. This is the light of Silent Unity's prayer. This light has never gone out.

For more than sixty-three years someone in Silent Unity has been in prayer. In the early morning, throughout the day, through the dark hours of the night, week in, week out, month following month, through years of war and peace, through depression and prosperity, for more than sixty-three years—prayer!

Today in the room at Unity Village where the light is kept burning this vigil of prayer goes on.

[31]

From the moment a message is received at Unity it is infolded in an atmosphere of prayer. All members of Silent Unity join in prayer at 8 a.m. every day, using the *Daily Word* lesson for the day. At 10:45 a.m. certain workers—those who through years of service have established a high sense of consecration—join in the prayer room for what is known in Silent Unity as the "healing meeting," where the needs of individuals are taken up in prayer. At noon the whole group joins again in prayer, and at 2:30 p.m. it unites in prayer once more. At 9 p.m. the night staff takes part in a healing meeting.

Yet these meetings are but a small part of the sum of prayer in Silent Unity. All day long as letters, telegrams, and telephone calls flow across the desks, every worker—the person who came to work yesterday and the one who has been in Silent Unity for many years, the one who first receives a message from a corre- spondent, the one who checks the address and does the necessary filing work, the one who addresses the envelope that carries Si- lent Unity's answer, the one who writes the letter and chooses the prayer and pamphlet to send, the one who puts the answer in the mail—blesses each request he handles. And every half hour throughout the day the workers, one after another, go into the prayer room to pray alone. With night, the spiritual vigil goes on in the room where the light is kept shining.

Yet even this does not complete the sum of prayers of which Silent Unity is the radiating center. All over the earth, constantly, there are hearts attuned to ours in Silent Unity, voices joined with ours in declaring the Unity affirmations of faith, hundreds of thousands speaking words of blessing, breathing prayers of love, adding to the spiritual force, the prayer force that is Silent Unity.

This is why the light that shines from the window, though to the eye it seems only a little light, lights the farthest corners of the earth. This is why "down under" in Australia, deep in darkest Africa, beyond the Arctic Circle, this light is shining. In these and other faraway places, hearts are warmed by it, minds are illumined by it.

This is a spiritual light. It is the spiritual light generated by sixty-three years of constant prayer, generated by the prayers that are continually going forth in Silent Unity today, going forth at the very moment you read these words, generated by prayers going forth all over the world.

"Where two or three are gathered together in my name, there am I in the midst of them." This is the ministry of Jesus Christ, who said: "I am the light of the world." "Ye are the light of the world." It is the light of His Spirit that radiates from our window, radiates through our prayers, the Christ light lit by many years of faith in Him, by many thoughts of love for Him, by many hearts and minds consecrated to serving Him.

The light of His Truth, like the light in the window, may seem only a little light; but if you are lost, you may find your way again by it.

Are you in need of help? Sit down and begin to write, "Dear Silent Unity . . ." Even as you write the words, you will feel the silent unity of love, the silent unity of those who pray together, the silent unity of God and man, the silent unity of Spirit that is Silent Unity. Even as you write the words, in your heart and mind the light will begin to glow.

Go to a telephone, wherever you may be, in any part of the earth, at any moment of the day or night, and call BAltimore 1-4720, Kansas City, Missouri. From the room where the light shines a voice will ring out for your heart to hear, "Silent Unity!" and the light that shines in this window will begin to shine for you.

If you cannot write a letter, if you cannot reach a telephone, heart speaks to heart across the silence of prayer. Let your heart cry out in faith and hope and love; turn in your mind to Silent Unity and utter a silent prayer for help; even as you turn, you step within the circle of the light.

Silent Unity is as a pool of light, an ever-widening pool of trust in God, forever being fed by continual affirmations of faith. Every word of prayer is as a loving hand stretched forth to help into the pool someone in need.

Though the world may fall asleep to spiritual truth, the faith of Silent Unity never sleeps, never slacks. Here always someone has his heart outreached in prayer to everyone who reaches out his heart. Here constantly we keep the vigil of faith, the watch of prayer. This is a spiritual trust we keep, a spiritual tryst, a trust we keep in God, a tryst we keep with anyone who may be in need.

All those who are in need we embrace with our prayers and draw them close to God, draw them into closer awareness of the good that is theirs in Him. We embrace them with our hearts and draw them into the light of Truth.

Are you in need of help?

There is a light that shines for you. Wherever you are, whatever your need, you can step into this light.

Do you need peace for your mind? The light floods your mind, the light of the Christ Mind. It penetrates into cobwebby corners; it unravels knotty tangles; it shows the way to go; it brings order and wisdom.

Do you need health for your body? The light shines in your body, the warm light of life, the vitalizing light of Spirit. It suffuses the cells, it bathes the tissues. In its life-giving glow your body is revealed as a temple of light, a temple of the living God.

Do you need prosperity for your affairs? The light illumines your affairs. It reveals new opportunities, invisible avenues of supply. It discloses rich ideas that you can use; it gives you a sense of security in which you have the courage to step forward; it lights the steps for you to take.

Do you need harmony in your life? The light radiates through every department of your life. It shines on misunderstandings, and they are dissolved. It shines on complications, and they are straightened out. It shines on seeming emptiness, which is filled with beauty and joy. This is the light of understanding, the light of "silent soul communion," the light of Christ compassion.

Do you have someone dear to you in need of help? Your love lifts him into the light. Your prayers lift him into the light. In the light of the omnipresence of God his needs are met.

Are you in need of help?

There is a light that shines for you.

You need never be alone—not even on the darkest night. Silent Unity is no farther from you than a prayer's length.

In a room of a building in Unity Village where a light is shining from a window someone is praying, someone with a spirit kindred to your own, someone whose thoughts reach out to you in faith, someone whose heart reaches out to you in love. The light in this window shines for you. The light in this heart shines for you.

Silent Unity is as the Christ light lit in the window of the world. If you are a traveler on the road of prayer, this light shines for you.

CHARLES FILLMORE

INVOCATION

I am now in the presence of pure Being, and immersed in the Holy Spirit of life, love, and wisdom.

I acknowledge Thy presence and Thy power, O blessed Spirit; in Thy divine wisdom now erase my mortal limitations, and from Thy pure substance of love bring into manifestation my world, according to Thy perfect law.

THE SEVENFOLD AFFIRMATION

I am a child of the living God.
I have within me the all-creating power of the
    Christ.
It radiates from me and blesses all whom I
    contact.
It is my life, my strength, my courage,
My patience, my peace, my poise,
My power, my wisdom, my understanding,
My joy, my inspiration, and my abundant supply.
Unto this great power I entrust all my problems,
Knowing they will be solved in love and justice.
O Lord Christ! I have laid all my desires upon
    Thine altar, and I rest in Thy graciousness.

2. Every Man Is King

"Every man is king in his own mental domain,
and his subjects are his thoughts. . . .
The body is the instrument of the mind, and
the mind looks to the Spirit for its
inspiration."

—*Charles Fillmore*

DANA GATLIN

WHERE I AM KING

I THINK it came to me as one of the profoundest realizations of my life that my mind is absolutely my own. What enters it and lodges in it and colors it is under my jurisdiction. My thoughts are really under my control, and likewise my moods and emotions, although I had previously thought that these were in the nature of powerful waves that washed up over a man from external conditions to bend him to their will.

One day I was wishing that there might be more peace, order, and beauty in my life, and suddenly the thought came to me "How about your mind—couldn't you improve conditions a little there?" So I stood off, as it were, and peered into my own mind, gazing at the thoughts milling around in a disordered fashion, and I was horrified by the first intentional inventory. There were grudges, grievances, doubts, worries, preoccupation with physical ailments. Everything in the world seemed to have gone wrong or threatened to go wrong. That day I had "the blues."

That day I also started setting my mind in order. I resolved sincerely to keep a closer watch over my thoughts. I resolved to honor my mind and guard it against unlovely thoughts. I set up a kind of mental signboard: "*My mind is a place of loveliness, and ugly visitors are not welcome.*" The sustaining thought came to me, "Keep your mind an open channel for God." I prayed to God to help me, and He did.

I have often thanked Him that He prompted me to look to my mind, to take an inventory of what is really harbored there, to

[41]

cherish what is desirable and to throw out what is not. This is something any of us, under any circumstances, can do. It is what we should do.

Your mind is your own. It is your own place. You have the absolute say-so as regards what shall enter and dwell there. This fact should be a source of renewed strength and joy to you. You are the absolute arbiter. Of course it will require watchfulness, alertness, fidelity, and sincere desire on your part. Yet it rests with you and is within your capacities. Any good gardener is on the lookout for weeds, wants to pull them up, and is perfectly able to pull them up. He gives his loving attention to the plants that will blossom into beauty. So with you. If you then encounter difficulties that seem too great for human control, you can always have recourse to God. You can turn to Him, ask His help, and put the tangled garden of your mind in His care. He will surely help you to get it back in order.

You will be surprised how much you can do for yourself, if only you set about it. You will be surprised at the number of weeds, at the many kinds already rooted, perhaps hidden, but ready to pop up at a moment's notice. Ugly, fearsome weeds. Thoughts of doubt and fear. Criticism and condemnation. Ranklings and bitternesses. Pain and sickness, sorrow, limitation, lack. Worry and anxiety, weakness and inertia. Disagreeable conditions and circumstances. Thoughts along these lines are weeds. They mar and foul the fair areas of your mind. Don't let them remain for a minute, don't nurture them. Get rid of them as quickly as possible. Pull them up and throw them out. Your mind is your own place, and you don't want ugly things in it. You want it filled with that which will, in turn, fill your life with joy, peace, love, order, harmony, and beauty.

You may think you have no power over the conditions that fill your life, the thoughts that fill your mind. Nothing is falser than this belief, which in itself is a destructive weed. You have the power, and you may exercise it in accordance with your desire, purpose, integrity, and perseverance.

The sorry fact is that we often really do not want to give up our error thoughts. It is very difficult to give up our grudges. We seem to like to cling to them. We like to exaggerate our ailments and troubles. We like to dramatize them and ourselves. We actually derive a certain morbid pleasure from our "organ recitals" and misfortunes. We want our sufferings to seem a bit worse than the other fellow's. We have had a harder time than most people, and we want everybody to realize just what a hard time we have had. All this is very human. We like sympathy. If other people won't feel properly sorry for us, we make up for it by feeling sorry for ourselves—one of the most debasing processes that can go on in the human organism. We hug our resentments.

If we indulge ourselves in this way, we shall have a fine harvest of weeds, a harvest that won't be pleasant. Sometimes our mind gets so choked with weeds that it is difficult to disentangle and clear it even when we earnestly wish to do so. Then is the time to pray, to cast off every thought pertaining to the outer, every personal conception, and turn to God; to turn the attention to His realm, which is "a realm of light and love, joy and supply, back of the sense world of limitation."

What a source of strength and help it is to realize and accept this truth! God's realm of love and peace and beauty that can never be marred or destroyed or taken away! Inexhaustible and unassailable! Always there, awaiting our recognition, there for us to think about to our fill! Peace, love, and joy flowing to us in an inexhaustible tide. Probably before this we had formed the very human habit of looking solely to outer circumstances for our happiness and in doing so had been cheated or betrayed. It is a wonderful experience when we realize that joy is a thing of the spirit, transcendent; that instead of being dependent on circumstances, it has itself the power to bring about happy circumstances. Train yourself therefore to acknowledge this spiritual gift, which is dependable, always at hand awaiting reception into your mind. Remember it and think of it. What a wonderful thought to let enter your mind! Say to yourself every morning and many times each day:

"Today I accept the peace, love, and joy of God."   ..

These gifts will surely flow into your thoughts, into your mind. They will transform your mind. They will transform your body, your life, your world.

God's joy is always at hand, yours for the taking. But you must take it yourself, give it a place in your thoughts. And you must make a place for it; that is, drop many other thoughts from your mind. Several years ago I read a statement that greatly impressed me. It was to the effect that as soon as we make and keep our thoughts fifty-one per cent constructive our battle is won. Our life will take an upswing.

Sometimes we meet people who seem to have lost all their energy, enthusiasm, aspiration, and their very capacity for caring. Perhaps you have reached that place yourself, or at least have days of weariness, boredom, futility, and depression. Most of us have known such days. Then if we are sincere in our desire to be uplifted, it is good for us to turn to the Father and pray:

"Father, help me to love life."

If we are sincere, He will help us. The way He usually helps is by helping us to weed out the thoughts that are choking our mind and to substitute for them thoughts that will grow and flourish to a happier and more beautiful fulfillment.

Love—we may think that we know all about love, that we have given proper attention to it. But to what degree do we really keep our mind filled with freeing, kind, tolerant, generous thoughts toward people, conditions, circumstances, even toward life? It comes to us with a shock to face the situation squarely and to discover that we really do not love life, that we are tired of it, bored with it, disgusted with it, defeated by it. In that case there is one prime thing for us to do. We must do it quickly. It is as important a thing as we shall ever find to do. We must somehow reawaken our friendly feeling for life, re-establish friendly relations with it. For life is God's supreme gift to us. In our dire straits the first and the best procedure is simply to throw ourselves on God. If you feel discouraged, if you feel tired, if you feel all out of sorts, if you do not know what to do, turn to Him with these words:

"Father, help me to love life."

The Father will hear you. He will answer you, He will help you. As soon as you face the matter and tell Him about it, you will begin to feel better. You will be relieved, rested, encouraged. You will find yourself getting a different slant on things, new ideas will present themselves, a new strength will arise in you, energy to carry on. You will think differently, speak differently, move differently, act differently. You will find yourself disposed to feel more patient, more tolerant—even cheerful. Unexpectedly you will run into a kindness; you will be appreciative of it, responsive. Life isn't so bad after all. You find your interest awakening, perhaps your enthusiasm, your confidence—you are expectant! Something pleasant and delightful happens—you are keyed to receive it. An opportunity presents itself—you catch at it eagerly. It's a good world after all—full of interest, activity, and promise. In the selfsame world—and perhaps under not greatly changed conditions—you feel like an entirely different person. Your thoughts have changed their color and trend. You are responsive to life again. God has answered your prayer.

In an orderly, harmonious, established mind there is no place for grudges and grievances. There must not be if it is to attain peace. Human relationships often offer the trickiest and most subtle obstructions, especially our private, unspoken thoughts. It doesn't do much good to refrain from angry or critical speech if we seethe inwardly with unspoken condemnations. They poison us within, and we throw off poison into the very air. So we must weed up those thoughts promptly and resolutely. By whatever process, we must rid ourselves of them. This is one of the most insidiously difficult tasks the human mind has to accomplish, requiring watchfulness and absolute sincerity. We must want to keep our mind clean, lovely, and harmonious, to harbor only thoughts that are freeing, generous, and kind. We must root out every lurking, secret impulse of criticism and condemnation. Yes, often it is difficult. The unwanted thoughts creep up on us unawares. It requires patience and perseverance, trying and trying again; but it can be done.

Sometimes it helps, when thinking of the person who arouses our secret criticism, to say in thought:

"You too are a child of God. You too are heir to His peace, love, joy, and illimitable bounty. You too are seeking to find and know your divine relationship. You want to be radiant and loving, kind and generous and happy, even as I do."

Sometimes it helps most just to put the matter in the hands of the Father, asking Him to take care of it for us, and then try to forget about it. I know a woman who accomplished marvelous results both within her own mind and in a discordant environment by quickly praying at every appearance of inharmony:

"Father, I thank Thee for Thine unseen presence and for the divine harmony that blesses this home."

Very often our human emotions cheat and betray us. The human way is to let them have sway. We think they can't be conquered, or else we do not bother to think about them and just give them their head. They can be mastered. They must be if our mind is to be peaceful. If our mind finds the way to peace, our life will become peaceful. Over and over I have found this prayer efficacious:

"Today I accept the peace, love, and joy of God."

If your mind and the conditions of your life are disordered, try it. Remember it the first thing when you wake in the morning. Remember it often during the day, under all kinds of outer conditions and circumstances:

"Today I accept the peace, love, and joy of God."

It helps!

It is a wonderful thought to reflect that your joy is from God. All your joy. It is. Nothing can affect it or take it away. Say to yourself:

"I am unified with all the joy there is."

Feel the universal joy flowing into you. You are attuned to the joy of the universe. You will grow responsive to this realization, you will learn to rely on it, you will expand under it and find poise and happiness. You will learn how to deal with your negative moods and emotions and find strength, wisdom, and courage.

It requires great courage and wisdom to deal with grief. Grief is utterly personal, it is very human, it all but overcomes us; but grief never helps. It is difficult, however we try to deal with it. It is apt to master us and often does. Often it seems heartless to try to master it; it seems heartless to try to let go of it. But what good do we achieve by clinging to it, either for ourselves or for anyone else? Is it not better to lift the human mind up toward God and give this load, too, into His care? "Cast thy burden upon Jehovah." The hour of grief is the time of times when we must turn to God, to His light, His enduring promises, His strength, security, and love. No human power or wisdom can help us then. Only God. Let Him through.

"I will fear no evil; for thou art with me." There is beauty and peace in fearlessness, and beauty and peace will reign in your mind when it is filled with fearless thoughts, thoughts of divine guidance and protection.

Do not allow yourself to become fearful and anxious even for the safety of your loved ones. Again, it requires courage to relinquish personal thoughts and fears. But be courageous in this way: Let the fear thoughts go and give your dear ones over to God. Remember who and what God is. Surely you can trust Him! Let your reliance on Him so fill your mind that it will blot out every thought of fear. Instead of worrying and fretting in the human way, lift your mind up until it can hold this thought for your dear ones:

God is taking care of you. The Spirit of the Lord watches over you and keeps you in perfect safety. His Spirit is now guarding, protecting, inspiring, and guiding you in all your ways.

This thought illumines and calms your mind. It gives comfort, brings peace. It produces tranquillity and strength. It helps you and helps your dear ones. Instead of holding over them the shadow of your worry and tension you are blessing them by your thought. Let your every thought be a blessing.

Watch your thoughts. Catch yourself up when you find yourself thinking unwholesome or unworthy thoughts. Say to yourself, "Would Jesus think this?" Try to imagine what Jesus would think in its stead; and try to think—dare to think—the Christ thought of love, wisdom, security, joy, and peace.

It requires patience, determination, imagination, faith, and sincere desire to build your mind toward loveliness. It requires perseverance. But it can be done. Almost at once your efforts begin producing results in the outer. Fifty-one per cent—get across the halfway mark in your percentage of constructive thought and your goal is won!

Like every other training enterprise it becomes easier with practice. Your mood is your response to conditions around you. If it is favorable to your peace, happiness, and achievement, make use of it. If it isn't favorable, drop it, change it. You can!— by changing your point of view, your trend of thought, your habits of mind, even by temporarily changing your occupation. Do something for a while that is entirely different, that interests you, that you enjoy doing. Shift the focus of your attention. If a thought disturbs you, drop it. Turn to something pleasanter. If you seem unable to find a pleasant thought, manufacture one. In fact you are not manufacturing it, for in reality there are plenty of pleasant thoughts divinely true. But you have to open your mind to them. Marvelously beneficial results have been attained by the simple process of making a list of pleasant, happy, desirable things and dwelling on these from time to time during the day.

The color and content of the mind are strictly up to the individual, regardless of outer circumstances. If your "frame of mind" and your thoughts are unsatisfactory you can change them. Sometimes it may seem difficult to do, but it can be done. Your mind is your own, and you are the sole arbiter. It is up to you.

Remind yourself that you are one with all peace and love and joy everywhere.

Coax your thoughts. Be kind to them. Give them a new impetus, fresh attention.

Your moods do not depend on outer circumstances. The reverse is true. Say to yourself:

Today I accept the peace, love, and joy of God.

There is a realm of light and love, joy and supply back of the limitations of the sense world.

My mind is an open channel for God. I think His thoughts after Him.

My mind is a place of loveliness. No ugly thought can enter there.

Father, let Thy kingdom come forth on earth as it is established in the realm of divine harmony.

H. EMILIE CADY

FINDING THE CHRIST
IN OURSELVES

THROUGHOUT all His teachings Jesus tried to show those who listened to Him how He was related to the Father, and to teach them that they were related to the same Father in exactly the same way. Over and over again He tried in different ways to explain to them that God lived within them, that He was "not the God of the dead, but of the living." And never once did He assume to do anything as of Himself, always saying: "I speak not from myself: but the Father abiding in me doeth his works." But it was very hard then for people to understand, just as it is very hard for us to understand today.

There were, in the person of Jesus, two distinct regions. There was the fleshly, mortal part which was Jesus, the son of man; then there was the central, living, real part which was Spirit, the Son of God—that was the Christ, the Anointed. So each one of us has two regions of being—one the fleshly, mortal part, which is always feeling its weakness and insufficiency in all things, always saying, "I can't"; and then at the very center of our being there is a something which, in our highest moments, knows itself more than conqueror over all things; it always says, "I can, and I will." It is the Christ Child, the Son of God, the Anointed in us. "Call no man your father on the earth:" said Jesus, "for one is your Father, even he who is in heaven."

He who created us did not make us and set us apart from Himself, as a workman makes a table or a chair and puts it away

[49]

as something completed and only to be returned to the maker when it needs repairing. Not at all. God not only created us in the beginning, but He is the very Fountain of Life ever abiding within us. From this fountain constantly springs new life to re-create these mortal bodies. He is the ever abiding Intelligence which fills and renews our minds. His creatures would not exist a moment were He to be, or could He be, separated from them. "We are a temple of the living God; even as God hath said, I will dwell in them, and walk in them."

Let us suppose that a beautiful fountain is supplied from some hidden but inexhaustible source. At its center it is full of strong, vigorous life, bubbling up continually with great activity; but at the outer edge the water is so nearly motionless as to have become impure and covered with scum. This exactly represents man. He is composed of a substance infinitely more subtle, more real than water. "We are also his offspring." Man is the off-spring—or the springing forth into visibility—of God the Father. At the center he is pure Spirit, made in the image and likeness of the Father, substance of the Father, one with the Father, fed and renewed continually from the inexhaustible Good, which is the Father. "In him we live, and move, and have our being." At the outer edge, where stagnation has taken place (which is man's body), there is not much that looks Godlike in any way. We get our eyes fixed on the circumference, or external of our being. We lose consciousness of the indwelling, ever active, unchanging God at the center, and we see ourselves sick, weak, and in every way miserable. It is not until we learn to live at the center and to know that we have power to radiate from that center this unceasing, abundant life, that we are well and strong.

Jesus kept His eyes away from the external altogether, and kept His thoughts at the central part of His being, which was the Christ. "Judge not according to appearance," He said; that is, according to the external, "but judge righteous judgment," according to the real truth, or from Spirit. In Jesus, the Christ, or the Central Spark which was God, the same that lives in each of us today, was drawn forth to show itself perfectly, over and above the body, or fleshly man. He did all His mighty works, not because He was given some greater or different power from that which God has given us—not because He was in some different

way a *Son* of God and we only *children* of God—but just because
this same Divine Spark, which the Father has implanted in every
child born, had been fanned into a bright flame by His prenatal
influences, early surroundings, and by His own later efforts in
holding Himself in constant, conscious communion with the
Father, the Source of all love, life, and power.

To be tempted does not mean to have things come to you
which, however much they may affect others, do not at all affect
you because of some superiority in you. It means to be tried, to
suffer, and to have to make effort to resist. Paul speaks of Jesus
as "one that hath been in all points tempted like as we are." And
Jesus Himself confessed to having been tempted when He said to
His disciples: "Ye are they that have continued with me in my
temptations." The humanity of the Nazarene "suffered being
tempted," or tried, just as much as you and I suffer today because
of temptations and trials, and in exactly the same way.

We know that during His public ministry Jesus spent hours
of every day alone with God; and none of us knows what He
went through in all the years of His early manhood—just as you
and I are doing today—in overcoming the mortal, His fleshly
desires, His doubts and fears, until He came into the perfect
recognition of this indwelling Presence, this "Father in me," to
whom He ascribed the credit for all His wonderful works. He had
to learn as we are having to learn; He had to hold fast as we are
having today to hold fast; He had to try over and over again to
overcome, as we are doing, or else He was not "in all points
tempted like as we are."

We all must recognize, I think, that it was the Christ within
which made Jesus what He was; and our power now to help ourselves and to help others lies in our comprehending the truth—
for it is a truth, whether we realize it or not—that this same Christ
lives within us that lived in Jesus. It is the part of Himself which
God has put within us, which ever lives there, with an inex-
pressible love and desire to spring to the circumference of our
being, or to our consciousness, as our sufficiency in all things.
"Jehovah thy God is in the midst of thee, a mighty one who will
save [or who *wills* to save]; He will rejoice over thee with joy;
He will rest in his love, he will joy over thee with singing." Christ
within us is the "beloved Son," the same as it was in Jesus. It is

the "I in them, and thou in me, that they may be perfected" of which Jesus spoke.

In all this explanation we would detract nothing from Jesus. He is still our Saviour, in that He went through suffering unutterable, through the perfect crucifixion of self, that He might lead us to God; that He might show us the way out of our sin, sickness, and trouble; that He might manifest the Father to us and teach us how this same Father loves us and lives in us. We love Jesus and must ever love Him with a love which is greater than all others, and to prove our love, we would follow His teachings and His life closely. In no way can we do this perfectly, except by trying to get at the real meaning of all that He said, and letting the Father work through us as He did through Jesus, our perfect Elder Brother and Saviour.

Jesus sometimes spoke from the mortal part of Himself, but He lived so almost wholly in the Christ part of Himself, so consciously in the center of His being, where the very essence of the Father was bubbling up in ceaseless activity, that He usually spoke from that part.

When He said, "Come unto me . . . and I will give you rest," He could not have meant to invite mankind to come unto His personal, mortal self, for He knew of the millions of men and women who could never reach Him. He was then speaking from the Christ self of Him, meaning not "Come unto me, Jesus," but "Come unto the Christ"; nor did He mean, "Come unto the Christ living in me," for comparatively few could ever do that. But He said, "The words that I say unto you I speak not from myself: but the Father abiding in me doeth his works." Then it was the Father saying not "Come unto Jesus," but "Come unto me"; that is, "Come up out of the mortal part of you where all is sickness and sorrow and trouble, into the Christ part where I dwell, and I will give you rest. Come up into the realization that you are one with the Father, that you are surrounded and filled with divine love, that there is nothing in the universe that is real but the good, and that all good is yours, and it will give you rest."

"No one cometh unto the Father, but by me" does not mean that God is a stern Father whom we must coax and conciliate by going to Him through Jesus, His kinder, more easily entreated

Son. Did not Jesus say, "He that hath seen me hath seen the Father," or in other words, "As I am in love and gentleness and accessibility, so is the Father"? These words mean that no man can come to the Father except through the Christ part of himself. You cannot come around through some other person or by any outside way. Another may teach you how to come, and assure you of all that is yours if you do come, but you must retire within your own soul, find the Christ there, and look to the Father through the Son, for whatever you want.

Jesus was always trying to get the minds of the people away from His personality, and to fix them on the Father in Him as the source of all His power. And when toward the last, they were clinging to His mortal self, because their eyes had not yet been opened to understand about the Christ within their own souls, He said, "It is expedient for you that I go away; for if I go not away, the Comforter will not come"; that is, if He remained where they could keep looking to His personality all the time, they would never know that the same Spirit of Truth and Power lived within themselves.

There is a great difference between a Christian life and a Christ life. To live a Christian life is to follow the teachings of Jesus, with the idea that God and Christ are wholly outside of man, to be called upon but not always to answer. To live a Christ life is to follow Jesus' teachings in the knowledge that God's indwelling presence, which is always life, love, and power within us, is now ready and waiting to flow forth abundantly, aye, lavishly into our consciousness, and through us to others, the moment we open ourselves to it, and trustfully expect it. One is a following after Christ, which is beautiful and good so far as it goes, but is always very imperfect, the other is a letting Christ, the perfect Son of God, be manifested through us. One is an expecting to be saved sometime from sin, sickness, and trouble; the other is a knowing that we are, in reality, saved now from all these errors by the indwelling Christ, and by faith affirming it, until the evidence is manifested in our bodies.

Simply believing that Jesus died on the cross to appease God's wrath never saved and never can save anyone from present sin, sickness, or want, and was not what Jesus taught. "The demons also believe and shudder," we are told, but they are not saved thereby. There must be something more than this—a living touch of some kind, a sort of intersphering of our own souls with the Divine Source of all good and giving. We are to have faith in the Christ, believe that the Christ lives in us, and is in us God's Son; that this indwelling One has power to save and make us whole; aye, more, that He has made us whole already. For did not the Master say, "All things whatsoever ye pray and ask for, believe that ye receive them [present tense], and ye shall have them?"

If, then, you are manifesting sickness, you are to ignore the seeming—which is the external, or circumference of the pool where the water is stagnant and the scum has arisen—and, speaking from the center of your being, say: *"This body is the temple of the living God; the Lord is now in His holy temple; Christ in me is my life, Christ is my health, Christ is my strength, and Christ is perfect; therefore, I am now perfect because He dwelleth in me as perfect life, health, strength."* Say the words with all earnestness, trying to realize what you are saying, and almost immediately the perennial Fountain of Life at the center of your being will begin to bubble up and continue with rapidly increasing activity, until new life will radiate through pain, sickness, sores, all diseases, to the surface, and your body will show forth the perfect life of Christ.

Suppose it is money that you need. Take the thought, *"Christ is my abundant supply* [not supplier]. *He is here within me now, and greatly desires to manifest Himself as my supply. His desires are fulfilled now."* Do not let your thoughts run off into how He is going to do it, but just hold steadily to the thought of the supply here and now, taking your eyes off all other sources, and He will surely honor your faith by manifesting Himself as your supply, a hundredfold more abundantly than you have asked or thought. So also with "whatsoever ye pray and ask for." But remember the earnest words of James, the apostle: "He that doubteth is like the surge of the sea driven by the wind and tossed. For let not that man think that he shall receive anything of the Lord."

Nowhere in the New Testament is the idea conveyed that Jesus Christ came that there might be, after death, a remission of the *penalty* for sin. That idea is a pure fiction of man's ignorant, carnal mind of later date. In many places in the Biblical record, reference is made to "remission of sins"; and Jesus Himself, according to Luke's record, said that "repentance and remission of sins should be preached in his name unto all the nations." "Sins," in the original text, does not mean crime deserving punishment. It means any mistake or failure which brings suffering. Christ came that there might be remission or cessation of sins, of wrongs, of mistakes, which were inevitably followed by suffering. He came to bring "good tidings of great joy which shall be to all the people." Tidings of what? Tidings of salvation. When? Where? Not salvation from punishment after death, but salvation from mistakes and failures here and now. He came to show us that God, our Creator and Father, longs with yearnings unutterable to be to us, through the Christ, the abundance of all things that we need or desire. But our part is to choose to have Him, and after we have chosen, to "hold fast" till He comes—not till He comes after death, but just to hold steadily to our faith until He manifests Himself. For instance, in thus looking to Him for health, when by an act of your will you stop looking to any material source (and this is not always easy to do), and declare the Christ in you to be the only life of the body, and it always perfect life, it needs but that you hold steadfastly, without wavering, to the thought, in order to become well.

When once you have put any matter into the hands of this indwelling, ever present Christ, in whom there is at all times an irrepressible desire to spring to our rescue and to do all things for us, do not dare to take it back into your mortal hands again to work out for yourself, for by so doing you simply put off the time of His bringing it to pass. All you have to do in the matter is to hold to the thought: *"It is done. It is manifest now."* This Divine Presence is our sufficiency in all things, and will materialize itself as such, in whatever we need or desire, if we but trustfully expect it.

This matter of trusting the Christ within to do all things for us—realizing that we are one with Him and that to Him is given all power—is not something which comes to any of us spontaneously. It comes by persistent effort on our part. We begin by determining that we will trust Him as our present deliverance, as our health, our riches, our wisdom, our all, and we keep on by a labored effort, until we form a kind of spiritual habit. No habit bursts full-grown into our lives, but every one comes from a succession of little acts. When you see anyone working the works of Christ, healing the sick, loosing the bound, and so forth, by the word of Truth spoken in faith, you may be sure that this faith did not jump to him from some outside source all at once. If you knew the facts, you would probably know of days and nights when with clenched fists and set teeth he held fast to the Christ within, "trusting where they could not trace," until he found himself possessing the very "faith of the Son of God."

If we want the Father within, which is the Christ, to manifest Himself as all things through us, we must learn to keep the mortal of us still, to still all its doubts and fears and false beliefs, and to hold rigidly to the "Christ only." In His name we may speak the words of healing, of peace, and of deliverance to others, but as Jesus said of Himself, so we must also say of ourselves: "I can of myself [that is, of the mortal] do nothing." "The Father abiding in me doeth his works." He is the ever present Power to overcome all errors, sickness, weakness, ignorance, or whatever they may be. We claim this Power, or bring it into our consciousness where it is of practical use, by declaring over and over again that it is ours already. Saying and trying to realize the truth, *"Christ is my wisdom, hence I know truth,"* will in a short time make us understand spiritual things better than months of study will do. Saying, *"Christ is my strength, I cannot be weak or frail,"* will make us strong enough to meet any emergency.

Remember, we do not begin by feeling these things at first, but by earnestly and faithfully saying them, and acting as though they were true—and this is the faith which brings the Power into manifestation.

The Christ lives in us always. God, the Creative Energy, sent His Son first, even before the body was formed, and He ever abides within, "the firstborn of all creation." But it is with us as it was with the ship on the tempestuous sea after the storm arose: Jesus' being in the vessel did not keep it from rocking, or the angry waves from beating against it, for He was asleep. It was only after He was awakened and brought out to manifest His power that the sea became still and the danger was over.

The Christ in us has been there all the time, but we have not

EVERY MAN IS KING

EVERY MAN IS KING

known it, and so our little ships have been tossed about by sickness and poverty and distrust, until we have seemed almost lost. I, the true spiritual self of me, am one with the Christ. You, the true spiritual self of you, are one with the Christ. The true self of every person is the child of God, made in His image. "Beloved, now are we children of God, and it is not yet made manifest what we shall be. We know that, if he shall be manifested, we shall be like him." Now, already, are we sons. When He shall appear—not when, sometime after the transition called death, He, some great, glorious Being, shall burst upon our view, but when we have learned to still the mortal of us, and let the Father manifest Himself at our surface, through the indwelling Christ—then we shall be like Him, for He only will be visible through us.

"Behold what manner of love the Father hath bestowed upon us, that we should be called children of God." We are not simply reflections or images of God, but expressions (from *ex*, out of, and *premere*, to press or force), hence a forcing out of God, the All-Good, the All-Perfect. We are projections of the Invisible Presence into visibility. God made man one with the Father, even as Jesus was; and just in proportion as we recognize this fact and claim our birthright, the Father in us will be manifested to the world.

Most of us have an innate shrinking from saying, "Thy will be done." Because of false teaching, and from associations, we have believed that this prayer, if answered, would take away from us all that gives us joy or happiness. Surely nothing could be further from the truth. Oh, how we have tried to crowd the broad love of God into the narrow limits of man's mind! The grandest, most generous, loving father that ever lived is but the least bit of God's fatherhood manifested through the flesh. God's will for us means more love, more purity, more power, more joy in our lives, every day.

No study of spiritual or material things, no effort, though it be superhuman on our part, could ever be as effectual in making grand, Godlike creatures, showing forth the same limitless soul which Jesus showed, as just praying continually the one prayer, "Thy will be done in me"; for the Father's will is to manifest His perfect Being through us. "Among the creatures, one is better than another, according as the Eternal Good manifesteth itself

and worketh more in one than in another. Now that creature in
which Eternal Good most manifesteth itself, shineth forth, worketh, is most known and loved, is the best; and that wherein the
Eternal Good is least manifested, is least of all creatures" (*Theologia Germanica*). "It was the good pleasure of the Father that
in him should all the fullness dwell"—fullness of love, fullness of
life, fullness of joy, of power, of All-Good. "In him are ye made
full." Christ is in us, one with us, so we may boldly and with
confidence say, "In Christ all things are mine." Declaring it will
make it manifest.

Above all things else, learn to keep to the Christ within yourself, not that within somebody else: let the Father manifest
through you in His own way, though His manifestation differ
from that in His other children. Heretofore even the most spiritually enlightened of us have been mere pygmies, because we
have, by the action of our conscious thought, limited the divine
manifestation to make it conform to the manifestation through
someone else. God will make of us spiritual giants if we will but
take away all limits and give Him an opportunity.

"Although it be good and profitable that we should learn and
know what great and good men have wrought and suffered, and
how God hath dealt with them, and wrought in them and
through them, yet it were a thousand times better that we should
in ourselves learn and perceive and understand who we are, how
and what our own life is, what God is doing in us, and what He
will have us do" (*Theologia Germanica*).

All the blessings promised in the twenty-eighth chapter of
Deuteronomy are to those who "harken diligently to the voice of
Jehovah thy God," those who seek the inner voice in their own
souls, and learn to listen to and obey what it says to them indi-
vidually, regardless of what it says to any other person, no matter
how far he or she may be advanced in spiritual understanding.
This voice will not lead you exactly as it leads any other in all
the wide world; but, in the infinite variety, there will be perfect
harmony, for there is but "One God and Father of all, who is
over all, and through all, and in all."

Emerson says: "Every soul is not only the inlet, but may become the outlet of all there is in God." We can only be this by
keeping ourselves consciously in open communication with God

without the intervention of any other soul between Him and us. "The anointing which ye received of him abideth in you, and ye need not that any one teach you." "But the Comforter, even the Holy Spirit, whom the Father will send in my name, he shall teach you all things." "Howbeit when he, the Spirit of truth, is come, he shall guide you into all the truth: for he shall not speak from himself; but what things soever he shall hear, *these* shall he speak: and he shall declare unto you all the things that are to come."

It needs but the one other little word "now," firmly and persistently held in the mind, to bring into manifestation through us the highest ideal that we are capable of forming; aye, far higher, for does it not say, "As the heavens are higher than the earth, so are my ways higher than your ways, and my thoughts than your thoughts?" This manifestation through us will be the fulfillment of God's ideal, instead of our limited, mortal ideal, when we learn to let Spirit lead and to hold our conscious minds to the *now*.

You want to manifest the perfect Christ. Affirm with all your heart and soul and strength that you do so manifest now; that you manifest health and strength and love and truth and power. Let go of the notion of being or doing anything in the future. God knows no time but the eternal Now. You can never know any other time, for there is no other. You cannot live an hour or ten minutes in the future. You cannot live it until you reach it, and then it becomes the Now. Saying or believing salvation and deliverance are to be, will forever, and through all the eternal ages, keep them, like a will-o'-the-wisp, just a little ahead of you, always to be reached but never quite realized.

"Now is the acceptable time; behold now is the day of salvation," said Paul. He said nothing about our being saved from our distresses after death, but always taught a present salvation. God's work is finished in us now. All the fullness abides in this indwelling Christ now. Whatever we persistently declare is done now, is manifested now, we shall see fulfilled.

WINFRED RHOADES

HOW DO YOU THINK OF GOD?

WHEN YOU THINK of God, in what manner do you think of Him?

Do you still have the childhood idea of God as something like a magnified man sitting on a throne somewhere in the far reaches of space, surrounded by cherubim and seraphim and angels and archangels who are perpetually hymning His praises?

No picture can be made of God. God cannot be defined. God cannot be explained. Because of that philosophers have spoken of God as the Absolute, or have used the words "the great First Cause" instead of the word "God." When you read the lives of the saints you find that some of the men and women who have most completely given themselves to God have been most impressed with the mystery of God. They have spoken of Him as the "Byss of the Abyss," and emphasized their relations with Him as relations with impenetrable darkness.

On the other hand, the exultant words of the First Epistle of John shine before our eyes as an offset to the idea of incomprehensibility, when we read that "God is light, and in him is no darkness at all." *

Both of the thoughts are true, the thought of darkness and the thought of light. One refers to man's effort to understand God; the other refers to what God is for the world. If you attempt to say what God is, you find it impossible to do so. When Moses

* All Scriptural references in this article are quoted from the English Revised Version of the Bible.

wanted to know what to tell the Children of Israel about his authority for speaking to them as he did he was told to say: "I AM
hath sent me unto you." "I AM THAT I AM" was all that could be
given him as to the nature of God. On the other hand, if you
open your mind to the thought of what that I AM must stand for
ultimately, and of what must come from God in eternity, you
know that it must be light.

Another of the great expressions is that God is love. But what
does that mean? Does it mean something personal or something
impersonal? Still another of the great expressions is that God is
spirit. And there again the same question arises. In both cases it
makes a difference whether you think of the word with a small
letter or a capital. If you use a small *l* or *s* you have the same
implication as when you speak of the "feeling of love" or the
"spirit of good will" as they are met with in everyday life. But
if you use the capital *L* and the capital *S* you suggest conscious
personality and purposeful activity. I AM, which stands for pri-
mordial Being, also implies Personality.

That idea of Personality is expressed in the lofty words used
by Isaiah when he speaks of God as "the Creator of the ends of
the earth"; and in the words used at the end of the Book of Revelation: "I am the Alpha and the Omega, the first and the last,
the beginning and the end." And it is gloriously expressed in the
104th Psalm:

Who coverest thyself with light as with a garment;
Who stretches out the heavens like a curtain:
Who layeth the beams of his chambers in the waters;
Who maketh the clouds his chariot;
Who walketh upon the wings of the wind:
Who maketh the winds his messengers;
His ministers a flaming fire:
Who laid the foundations of the earth,
That it should not be moved for ever.

There you have, in sublime poetry, the thought of God's ever-
nearness, and that is a very great thought to live with. It is the
thought that is given in the very first words of the Bible. You
read as you open the Book of Genesis, "In the beginning God."
And that is, I believe, the most impressive and most suggestive
introduction to a book that is to be found in all the world's vast

literature. Then immediately you read that "the Spirit of God was brooding upon the face of the waters." That is the reading which you will find in the margin, and seems to me more significant even than the more familiar reading, "moved upon the face of the waters." And after that the sublime poem of creation immediately says: "And God said, Let there be light: and there was light." God before all things. The Spirit of God brooding, always brooding, still brooding over all creation. Light as the result of the creative brooding. That is magnificent!

We are living in a period of darkness and bewilderment. But there is light back of all the darkness! As a newspaper editorial said at Easter time: "However hideous and flaming may yet be the death of our epoch, there is no death but has its resurrection. And even while our world, as we have known it, is dying, at the same time it is being born."

New creation always! That is what the everlasting brooding of the Spirit of God must lead to. It is true for the world. For the individual also, the continual brooding of God is true. The Spirit of God is always brooding over us to care for us, and to develop in us the life that needs to be.

Another way of expressing the idea of the relations between God and man is to say that God is the infinite ocean of life in which we live and move and have our being. All life exists as the result of God's creative fiat, but it makes a vast difference to what degree a man recognizes that he lives in God, and stimulates himself with the thought. Say to yourself: "God is with me; I am with God." Say it to yourself over and over throughout the day, and you can become possessed of a calmness and peace that you have not known before, a quietness and confidence that make over for you the living of life. You can become possessed of a strength and a wisdom hitherto unknown for dealing with the difficulties that are part of life's educational process. By frequent affirmation of the fact of God's presence you can help yourself to realize that life and wisdom are all the while available for your immediate needs, and you can build up in yourself a calmness and poise that will react upon your whole condition.

Jesus Christ called God the "heavenly Father," and there you have the thought of the fundamentally and essentially personal nature of God carried to its limit. "Your Father knoweth what things you have need of, before ye ask him," said Jesus, and by His own example put confidence in God into practice when it came to His darkest hours.

A great deal has been written in recent years about the way in which fears, frights, disappointments, defeats, resentments, hates, sorrows, and other such thoughts and emotions can live in the subconscious depths of the mind for years after they have been forgotten by the conscious mind, and produce unhappy results in the individual in whom they maintain their hidden power. But let this not be forgotten: radiant aspirations, lofty ideas, noble thoughts, high resolves of the soul, brave victories of the spirit, immortal confidences—these also can continue to function in the subconscious mind long after they have first found their way there. Drop down into your subconscious mind the thought of God as brooding, infolding, life-giving Spirit and presence, and you have latent within you powers that can mightily change for you the experience of life.

Such realization of God is not a matter of feeling. It is a matter of conviction. It may be accompanied by feeling. It may not be so accompanied. The wise man builds his life on convictions, and not on feelings.

Even then there is one thing more to be considered. That which counts most in one's life is not even a conviction. It is the practice of a conviction.

"God is my salvation; I will trust, and will not be afraid." You can read that and have a thrill of feeling come over you; but unless you then practice the great thought it will do you no good. Really cast fear out of your life and trust God absolutely for the final outcome of life. Live by a conviction instead of an emotional thrill. Then you put God in practice.

"Underneath are the everlasting arms." A very lovely idea. Perhaps you give it to some troubled friend as a thought to live with. But do you live with it yourself? Do you put it into practice every day, under all circumstances? Do that, and you can become possessed of the peace that passes all understanding.

"God is light, and in him is no darkness at all." "God is Spirit." When you sincerely seek for light from God for the government of your daily life in practical ways, when you endeavor to think and speak and act in accordance with divine light, when you try to manifest the Spirit of God in every way in your daily life and endeavor to live all the while as the agent and instrument of the Spirit of God—when you do these things you put God in practice.

To put God in practice makes you close to God.

"God is love"—another of the great words. The practice of love is the practice of God. You try to do to all people the things that love stands for. You may not like all people, you may not enjoy them, but you act in the way that divine love indicates, and thus you put God into practice in your life.

The way to get close to God is to practice God.

"My flesh and my heart faileth but God is the strength of my heart and my portion for ever."

When you deliberately take strength from God, when you invite the mind and Spirit of God into yourself for continual inspiration, you practice God and keep yourself in immediate relation with Him.

Take God into your consciousness in the great way. Invite increasingly into yourself what Paul speaks of as "all the fulness of God." Pray every day that you may know God's mind, and think God's thoughts, and manifest His nature, and express His life, and be a channel of His love, and live as the agent and instrument of His Spirit. Realize that you are surrounded by the sustaining life, the invigorating energy, the directive mind, the infolding presence, the empowering Spirit of the Infinite and Eternal. Then you add to your struggling selfhood a great plus of power for the living of life with its difficulties and all its challenges.

Whatever your experience of life may be, whatever it may entail, there is possible a reality of association with God intense and vivifying and exultant that can lift up for you the whole living of life. Cultivate the habit of living in realization of God's "hereness," and you can change the weakness of your life into strength.

CHARLES FILLMORE

JESUS CHRIST'S ATONEMENT

THERE MAY BE found, in the traditions of nearly all peoples, reference to a time when man was in a state of consciousness very much superior to that which he now manifests. In the Hebrew Scriptures that superior plane is symbolically described as the Edenic state, and the departure from that place in the divine economy is called the "fall of man." Of late years we have been taught in the new metaphysics that there never was a "fall of man"; that man never fell; that his creation was spiritual, and that he is just as spiritual today as he ever was or ever will be. Of man as an idea in Divine Mind, this is true; but that there is not a harmonious manifestation of that idea clearly indicates that there has somewhere been a lapse in man's evolution.

When by study of himself as "mind" and by studying his place in Being, man gets away from the sense consciousness, he rises into a mental atmosphere where he sees the relation of ideas in divine order. This perception can be attained by anyone who will detach his thinking ego from the world of phenomena and let this ego float out into the universe of causes. It has been attained by thousands in every age, and their testimony is worthy of careful consideration.

When man touches in mind this plane of causes, he sees that the discords of humanity, in body and affairs, are the direct result of disorder in his relation to creation. He sees that there has been, through man's power of free thought, a most vital and far-reaching departure from the divine idea of his being.

Man cannot thwart the divine plan, but by virtue of his own creative or formative power in that plan he can turn his part of the work out of its true course and impede the consummation of it. This has been done, and we exist today in a state of lapse, so far as our relation to God and the orderly movement of His idea in creation are concerned. So we have to admit that the "fall of man" is in a measure true. When we understand this "fall" we shall perceive more fully why certain conditions that prevail are so incongruous in a world where a good and perfect God is supposed to rule.

Material science says that evolution is the order of nature and that all the silent records of earth, as left by departed races, testify to a steady rise of man from lower to higher conditions.

A large number of metaphysical writers and teachers have fallen into this line of thought and have assumed that the records of man's evolution, as found in archeological and geological research, bear testimony to his mind evolution, and that the experiences through which he has passed are in the divine order of creation. We either must accept this testimony as true or expunge it altogether.

We accept the testimony, but we say that it is but the evolution of man out of a lapse from divine order in creation, and that it is no part of the original divine plan, any more than a fall into a muddy swamp would be a necessary part of a journey to a beautiful city. Man is the son of a God whose methods are harmonious in bringing forth His ideas. Man is His idea—a self-conscious entity, having in embryo all the faculties and powers of that from which it came forth. In following the orderly path of its unfoldment this man idea is in conscious mental communication with its source, and knows what to do and what not to do in bringing forth creation. "And Jehovah God commanded the man, saying, Of every tree of the garden thou mayest freely eat: but of the tree of the knowledge of good and evil, thou shalt not eat of it: for in the day that thou eatest thereof thou shalt surely die."

We see that the "fall of man" antedated the formation of this planet as we behold it geologically. Jesus recognized this when He said: "And now, Father, glorify thou me with thine own self with the glory which I had with thee before the world was."

We are by birth a spiritual race, and we should never have known matter or material conditions if we had followed the leadings of our higher consciousness.

It is the recognition of this higher consciousness and the recognition of our place in Being that we are seeking. We are emerging from the darkness of Egyptian bondage—we see the Promised Land, and we want to know the shortest way to it. That way is the Christ way. The demonstration of Jesus relates Him to us in a metaphysical sense, because it is only by a study of states of consciousness formed by thought that it can be understood.

We have been taught by the church that Jesus died for us—as an atonement for our sins. By human sense this belief has been materialized into a flesh-and-blood process, in which the death of the body on the cross played the important part. Herein has the sense consciousness led the church astray. That spiritual things must be spiritually discerned seems to have escaped the notice of the church in forming its scheme of atonement. At the root of the church's teaching is Truth; Jesus of Nazareth played an important part in opening the way for every one of us into the Father's kingdom. However, that way was not through His death on the cross, but through His overcoming death. "I am the resurrection, and the life."

To comprehend the atonement requires a deeper insight into creative processes than the average man and the average woman have attained; not because they lack the ability to understand, but because they have submerged their thinking power in a grosser thought stratum. So only those who study Being from the standpoint of pure mind can ever understand the atonement and the part that Jesus played in opening the way for humanity into the glory which was theirs before the world was formed.

We who have studied these creative processes through thought action know how states of consciousness are formed and how persistent a certain mental state is after it has once crystallized. The man ego seems to lose its identity in its own formations, and forgets for the time all its past experiences and powers. We see this in certain social states among the people. No matter how miserable and degraded the state, people get so accustomed to it that they do not aspire to anything higher. Reformers of the criminal classes in our large cities tell us that their most difficult problem is to awaken in these people a desire for better things. They are attached to their habits of thought and living, and they do not want to be reformed. The same is true in the history of civilizing the savage races. Just when they are about to reach the place where they will see the desirability of a better way of living, they suddenly fall back into the old life, and are satisfied. The tendency of thought emanation is to crystallize about the form that it has made and, in spite of the struggles of the man ego, to hold to it.

We can readily see how a whole race might be caught in the meshes of its own thought emanations and, through this drowsy ignorance of the man ego, remain there throughout eternity, unless a break were made in the structure and the light of a higher way let in. This is exactly what has happened to our race. In our journey back to the Father's house we became lost in our own thought emanations, and Jesus Christ broke through the crystallized thought strata and opened the way for all those who will follow Him.

By so doing He made a connection between our state of consciousness and the more interior one of the Father. He united them—made them a unit—a one, hence the at-one-ment or atonement through Him. He stands ready to pass over all who will accept His way. That which died upon the cross was the consciousness of all mortal beliefs that hold us in bondage—such as sin, evil, sickness, fleshly lusts, and death—which He overcame. "I have overcome the world." The "overcoming" by Jesus made a great rent in the sense consciousness, and opened a way by which all who desire may demonstrate easily and quickly.

But in order to receive the benefit of Jesus' work it is necessary for everyone to go to the place where He made the rent in the race beliefs. If you were held in the meshes of a great spider web, and someone made a hole through which you could pass, you would go where the hole was and would pass out that way. The same rule holds good with respect to this aperture that Jesus made in the limitations of sense that hold the race in bondage—we have to go where He is, mentally and spiritually. "I go to prepare a place for you." So we see that the church is not so far wrong in its call to "follow Jesus." The error lies in the belief that He was the only begotten Son of God, and that He overcame for us, and that by simply believing on Him we are saved.

In believing Him to be the only begotten Son of God, we have confounded His higher consciousness or Christ consciousness, which is the only begotten Son of God, with His lower or Jesus consciousness. He recognized His identity in God as the Christ, the Son of God; He also recognized His consciousness of self, the son of man. So each of us is a son of God. We shall come into conscious recognition of the Christ Mind, making the conjunction between our mind and God's mind, just as soon as we let go of the limitations of mortal sense. God has but one Son, the Christ, the one ideal man. This divine conjunction was accomplished by Jesus, and the Christ shone out through His mortal self and illumined it, until it lost its personality and disappeared into divine individuality.

By believing that Jesus was more divine than other men, the church has assumed that He had certain privileges that the Father does not extend to all; that in a superhuman way He made good all our shortcomings; that we are saved from suffering for our acts by simply believing on Him and accepting Him, in a perfunctory way, as our Saviour. Paul is responsible for a good share of this throwing of the whole burden upon the blood of Jesus—doubtless the result of an old mental tendency carried over from his Hebrew idea of the blood sacrifices of the priesthood. In order to show the parallel in the life of Christ, Paul preached to the Jews that He was the great once-for-all bloody sacrifice and that no other would ever be necessary.

But Jesus went further than this. He said: "Follow me." "Keep my word." He meant: Do as I do. I have overcome; now by following in my footsteps you shall overcome.

We all recognize the advantage of thought co-operation. It is much easier to hold ourselves in the true consciousness when we are associated with those who think as we do. It was the work of Jesus to establish in our race consciousness a spiritual center with which everyone might become associated mentally, regardless of geographical location. He said to His disciples, "I go to prepare a place for you . . . that where I am, *there* ye may be also." That place is a state of consciousness right here in our midst, and we can at any time connect ourselves with it by centering our minds upon Jesus and silently asking His help in our demonstrations. It is not the prayer of a "worm of the dust" to a god, but of one who is on the way, asking the guidance of one who has passed over the same road and who knows all the hard places and how to get through them.

This is in one sense the relation of Jesus Christ to each of us, and so far as our present demonstration is concerned, it is the most important relation. The road that we are traveling from the mortal plane of consciousness to the spiritual plane is beset with many obstructions, and we need the assistance of One stronger than any of those who yet dwell in flesh bodies. He who is still in the perception of the earthly is not always a safe guide, because he sees in a limited way. We want one who sees wholly in spirit, and such a one we find in Jesus Christ.

He has not left us or gone to some faraway heaven, but He may be reached by the humblest of us in a moment's time, if we really aspire in soul for His companionship and help.

This is a simple statement of the relation that Jesus of Nazareth bears to us. Yet He was more than Jesus of Nazareth, more than any other man who ever lived on the earth. He was more than man, as we understand the appellation in its everyday use, because there came into His manhood a factor to which most men are strangers. This factor was the Christ consciousness. The unfoldment of this consciousness by Jesus made Him God incarnate, because Christ is the mind of God individualized, and whoever so loses his personality as to be swallowed up in God becomes Christ Jesus or God man.

We cannot separate Jesus Christ from God, or tell where man leaves off and God begins in Him. To say that Jesus Christ was a man as we are men is not true, because He had dropped that personal consciousness by which we separate ourselves into men and women. He was consciously one with the absolute principle of Being. He had no consciousness separate from that Being, hence He was that Being to all intents and purposes.

Yet He attained no more than is expected of each of us. "That they may be one, even as we *are*" was His prayer.

It is all accomplished through the externalization of the Christ consciousness, which is omnipresent and ever ready to manifest itself through us as it did through Jesus.

This principle has been perceived by the spiritually wise in every age, but they have not known how to externalize it and to make it an abiding state of consciousness. Jesus accomplished this and His method is worthy of our adoption because, as far as we know, it is the only method that has been successful. It is set forth in the New Testament, and whoever adopts the life of purity and love and power there exemplified in the experiences of Jesus of Nazareth will in due course attain the place that He attained.

The way to do this is the way Jesus did it. He acknowledged Himself to be the Son of God. The attainment of the Christ consciousness calls for nothing less on our part than a definite recognition of ourselves as sons of God right here and now, regardless of appearances to the contrary. We know that we are sons of God—then why not acknowledge it and proceed to take possession of our God right? That is what Jesus did in the face of most adverse conditions. Conditions today are not so stolidly material as they were in Jesus' time. People now know more about themselves and their relation to God. They are familiar with thought processes and how an idea held in mind will make itself manifest in the body and in affairs; hence they take up this problem of spiritual realization under most favorable conditions. It must work out just as surely as a mathematical problem, because it is under immutable law. The factors are all in our possession and the rule that was demonstrated in one striking instance is before us. By following that rule and doing, day by day, the work that comes to us, we shall surely put on Christ as fully and completely as did Jesus of Nazareth.

The process of Jesus' evolving from sense to soul was first a recognition of the spiritual selfhood and a constant affirmation of its supremacy and power. Jesus loved to make the highest statements: "I and the Father are one." "All authority hath been given unto me in heaven and on earth." He made the first statements before the Resurrection, so we know that He was not fully conscious of its reality. But by the power of His word He brought about the realization.

Next in the process was that constant cleansing of the consciousness through denial, or fasting. He prayed much alone, and fasted. He was being tempted on every side, within and without, and was always overcoming. He daily put out of His mind all the ideas that bind men to the world. He recognized that the kingdom of the spiritual man is not of this world—that it is a world that transcends this and controls it; therefore He was not attached in any way to the things of sense. Personal self, the devil, told Him to turn stones into bread, but He did not yield to this temptation to use His God-given power for material gain. Personal sense took Him upon ambition's high place and showed Him what He might have in the fame of the world if He would worship personal sense, but He refused to lower His standard. He was using spiritual power and He was true to its character; He did not mix it with matter or with material ways.

When Jesus said, "The words that I have spoken unto you are spirit, and are life," He touched the inner Christ word which created all things, and we know that His words were vivified from that center with a life essence and moving power that will demonstrate the truth of His statement.

These words have rung through the souls of men and set them afire with God's Spirit throughout the ages. This is because they are spiritual words. Within them are the seeds of a divine life and they grow in the mind of all who give them place, just as a beautiful flower or a great tree grows from the seed germ planted in the ground.

Jesus recognized that the consciousness of man was submerged in the things of sense; that it could not perceive truth in the abstract, and that it must, under these conditions, be stirred into activity by some stimulating force dropped into it from without. Hence He sent forth His powerful words of Truth to the thirsty souls, and said to them, "Keep my word."

To keep His word is to revolve it in mind—to go over all its aspects; to believe it as a truth, to treasure it as a saving balm in time of need; and above all, to obey the law that it sets forth.

People in all ages have known about the saving power of words and have used them to the best of their understanding. Hebrews bound upon their foreheads and wrists parchments with words of Scripture written upon them. The Hindus, Japanese, Chinese, and the people of nearly all other known nations have their various ways of applying the sacred words to the modification of their ills, and the invocation of the invisible powers to aid them in both their material and spiritual needs.

Although these methods are faulty in that they use the letter of the word, instead of its spirit, they are useful to us as indicators of the universal belief in the power of the sacred word.

We know that words express ideas, and to get at their substantial part we must move into the realm of ideas. Ideas are in the mind and we must go there if we want to get the force of our words. The Hebrews' phylacteries and the lamas' prayer wheels are suggestive of the wordy prayers of the Christian; but their use is not keeping the sayings of Jesus Christ, nor reaping the inner substance of the mystical word. This can be done only by those who believe in the omnipresent Spirit of God and in faith keep in mind the words that express His goodness, wisdom, and power.

Jesus Christ more fully voiced this nearness of God to man than any of the prophets, and His words are correspondingly vivified with inner fire and life. He said that those who kept His sayings should even escape death, so potent was the life energy attached to them.

This is a startling promise, but when we understand that it was not the personal man, Jesus, making it, but the Father speaking through Him, we know that it was not an idle one; for He said, "The word which ye hear is not mine, but the Father's who sent me."

This is the reason why these words of Jesus endure, and why more and more they are attracting the attention of men.

Whoever takes these words into his mind should consecrate himself to the truth that they represent. That truth is not the doctrine of any church, nor the creed of any sect—not even Christianity. That truth is written in the inner sanctuary of every soul, and all know it without external formulas. It is the intuitive perception of what is right in the sight of God. It is the truth and justice which every man recognizes as the foundation of true living.

Whoever consecrates himself to follow this inner monitor and lives up to its promptings, regardless of social or commercial customs, consecrates himself to do God's will. He is fitted to take the words of Jesus and make them his own.

It is no idle experiment, this keeping in the mind the words of Jesus. It is a very momentous undertaking, and may be the most important task in the life of an individual. There must be sincerity and earnestness and right motive, and withal a determination to understand the spiritual import.

This requires attention, time, and patience in the application of the mind to solving the deeper meanings of the sayings that we are urged to keep.

People deal with sacred words in a way that is too superficial to bring results. They juggle with words. They toss them into the air with a heavenly tone or an oratorical ring and count it a compliance with divine requirements. This is but another form of the prayer wheel and the phylactery. It is the lip service that Jesus condemned because its object is to be "seen of men."

To keep the sayings of Jesus means much more than this. It has a significance peculiar to the inner life. Only after the inner life is awakened is the true sense of the spiritual word understood. But the sincere keeper of Jesus' sayings will, by his devotions, awaken the inner spirit, and the Lord will come to him and minister to his call, as lovingly as a father to a beloved son.

Jesus tells us that His words are Spirit, and then tells us to keep them. How can one keep a thing of which he knows nothing? How can one keep the words and sayings of Jesus unless he gets them into his consciousness and grasps them with his mind, his spirit?

Surely there is no other way to "keep" His sayings. Those who are doing so from any other standpoint are missing the mark. They may be honest, and they may be good, sincere people, living what the world calls pure Christian lives, but they will not get the fruits of Jesus' words unless they comply with His requirements.

Unless you perceive that there is something more in the doctrine of Jesus than keeping up a worldly moral standard as preparation for salvation after death, you will fall far short of being a real Christian.

Jesus did not deprecate moral living, but neither did He promise that it fulfilled the law of God. Very negative people are frequently trusty and moral. But that does not make them Christians after the Jesus Christ plan. His Christianity had a living God in it, a God that lived in Him and spoke through Him. It was a religion of fire and water—life as well as purity. Men are to be alive—not merely exist half dead for a few years and then go out with a splutter, like a tallow dip. Jesus Christ's men are to be electric lights that glow with a perpetual current from the one omnipresent Energy. The connection with that current is to be made through the mind by setting up sympathetic vibrations.

The mind moves upon ideas; ideas are made visible through words. Hence holding right words in the mind will set the mind going at a rate proportioned to the dynamic power of the idea back of those words. A word with a lazy idea back of it will not stimulate the mind. The word must represent swift, strong, spiritual ideas in order to infuse the white energy of God into the mind. This is the kind of word in which Jesus revelled. He delighted in making great and mighty claims for His God, Himself, His words, and for all men. "I and the Father are one." "All authority hath been given unto me in heaven and on earth." "The Father is greater than I." "Is it not written in your law, I said, Ye are gods?" "The works that I do shall he do also; and greater." These were some of the claims with which He stimulated His mind. And He produced the results—His words were fulfilled.

Many who for years have been students of the science of Christ and have a clear, intelligent perception of its truths are yet outside the kingdom of Spirit. They anxiously ask: "Why do I not realize the presence of Spirit?"

Have you kept the sayings of Jesus? Have you said to yourself in silence and aloud until the very ethers vibrated with its truth, "I and the Father are one"?

Have you opened the pores of your mind, by mentally repeating the one solvent of crystallized conditions, "I in them, and thou in me"?

This means mental discipline day after day and night after night, until the inertia of the mind is overcome and the way is opened for the descent of Spirit.

The personal consciousness is like a house with all the doors and windows barred. The doors and the windows of the mind are concrete ideas, and they swing open when the right word is

THE UNITY TREASURE CHEST

spoken to them. Jesus Christ voiced a whole volume of right words. If you will take up His sayings and make them yours, they will open all the doors of your mind, the light will come in, and you will in due time be able to step forth.

Another cannot do this for you, although you sometimes think it would be nice if some master of spiritual ideas would suddenly help you to his understanding.

But this is a childish dream of the moment. You want to be yourself, and you can be yourself only by living your own life and finding its issues at the Fountainhead. If it were possible for one to reveal Truth to another, we should find heaven cornered by cunning manipulators of mind and its glories stored up in warehouses awaiting a higher market.

Let us be thankful that God is no respecter of persons, that Truth cannot be revealed by one mortal to another. God is a special, personal Father to every one of His children, and from no other source can they get Truth.

Jesus Christ, who has clearly revealed the Father in His consciousness, may tell all men how it came about. He may point the way. He may say, "I am the way, and the truth, and the life," but there is always a condition attached to its realization: One must believe, keep His sayings, and follow Him. Summed up, it means that by adopting His methods one will find the same place in the Father that He found.

"If a man love me, he will keep my word: and my Father will love him, and we will come unto him, and make our abode with him."

CHARLES FILLMORE

VITALIZING POWER IN MAN

IT IS WRITTEN: "The prayer of faith shall save him that is sick." The prayer of faith is a prayer based on a firm conviction that there is a healing power in Spirit. This conviction is the foundation of our healing system. God is Mind, or Spirit. He is omnipresent, omniscient, omnipotent, and all-love. We make our appeal to the all-powerful, all-willing God, and the response never fails.

Jesus Christ said: "God is Spirit: and they that worship him must worship in spirit and truth." This means that we must exercise our spiritual faculties in the worship and the prayer that lead to spiritual healing.

Spirit is that inner man which we do not see with the outer sight, but which we know exists. To get in touch with Spirit, we stop the activity of the outer man; then there is a great awakening of power within us. Let us be still and come into the consciousness of this power, which is health to us. "It is the spirit that giveth life." Lay hold of Spirit with the central thought: *I am quickened by Spirit.*

Jesus Christ came proclaiming: "I am the way, and the truth, and the life." Again and again He made the proclamation that He came as the representative of a new life-current for the whole human family. "I came that they may have life, and may have *it* abundantly." "I am the bread of life . . . which cometh down out of heaven, that a man may eat thereof, and not die." He raised people who had let go of the life idea, and brought them

into such a consciousness of omnipresent life that they came out
of the tomb.

This life consciousness that Jesus Christ quickens is as greatly
needed in our day as it was in the time when He first worked
in the souls of men. If you go to a medical doctor and ask him
the cause of your ills, he will tell you that most of them come
from lack of vitality: that means lack of life. We all need vitalizing. The question is: How shall we get life? What is the source
of life? Those who teach of material remedies point us to various
things as the source—food, air, water, and so forth. Some claim
that drugs are the source; but people are fast losing faith in drugs,
and are reaching out to electricity and similar means of gaining
more abundant life. They are thus getting a little closer to the
healing system of Jesus Christ, but they yet lack the all-important
truth that God is life and that they who worship Him must worship Him in the life consciousness; that is, in Spirit. When we
worship God in His way, we are vitalized all at once; there is no
other way to get real, permanent life. We cannot get life from
the outer man, nor from anything external; we must touch the
inner current.

This was illustrated once in our Silent Unity room. Two electric fans that had been stored away for the winter were brought
out and placed ready for use. Someone turned the buttons on
the fans, but no movement followed. All kinds of means were
used in an effort to start them, but they would not go, and we
said: "The fans are out of order." Then it was suggested that
possibly the current was not turned on, and this proved to be the
case. One of our number touched the button in the wall that
connects the fans with the electric current, and instantly the fans
began buzzing merrily. We almost imagined that they were
laughing at us for not seeing sooner why they did not move.

Immediately it occurred to us that all who write to us for
help need this one thing—connection with the universal life current. This little incident came, not by chance, but as a clear
illustration from Spirit of the way in which man attempts to get
the life that keeps him going. He tries in external ways, and
applies all kinds of remedies to set into activity the organs of
the body, but he fails in the one thing needful: he does not make
connection with the great life current. All agree that we live by

power from God, power from an invisible life source, but there is great ignorance as to how we can connect with the current.

The life source is spiritual energy. It is deeper and finer than electricity or human magnetism. It is composed of ideas, and man can turn on its current by making mental connection with it.

When Jesus came teaching the gospel of Spirit, people did not understand Him. They did not know that universal Spirit is Principle and that we demonstrate it or fail to demonstrate it according to the character of our thinking. It has taken the race two thousand years to find that we turn the life current on by thoughts and words. We can have fullness of life by realizing that we live in a sea of abundant, omnipresent, eternal life, and by refusing to allow any thought to come in that stops the consciousness of the universal life flow. We live and move and have our being in life—mind life. You can think of your life as mental, and every faculty will begin to buzz with new life. Your life will never wane if you keep in the consciousness of it as Mind, or Spirit, but it will increase and express in fullness in your body. If you go on and on with the life idea in your consciousness, your body will never be run down, but will become more and more alive with spiritual life, until it shows forth the glory of Christ.

We must think life, talk life, and see ourselves filled with the fullness of life. When we are not manifesting life as we desire, it is because our thoughts and our conversation are not in accord with the life idea. Every time that we think life, speak life, rejoice in life, we are setting free, and bringing into expression in ourselves more and more of the life idea. Here is the place of abundant life, and we can fill both mind and body, both our surroundings and our affairs, with glad, free, buoyant life, by exercising faith in it. "According to your faith be it done unto you."

In this way we enter into the same consciousness of abundant, enduring, unfailing, eternal life that Jesus had, and we can readily understand His proclamation that those who believe in the indwelling Christ life will never die. If we are wise, we shall cultivate faith in, and understanding of, omnipresent life.

When we believe in limited life, the belief makes a starved condition of soul and body. This is illustrated in the parable of the prodigal son. Out in a far country, away from the center of life, the consciousness of life grows less and less, and there is "famine" in that country, because there is no conscious connection with the Source of life. Let us make connection with the Source. Let us turn on the current. Let us go in mind to the spiritual place that can be described only as I AM, "I am life," "I am Spirit," "I am one with universal life." This prayer of faith saves the sick. When we touch I AM, it changes the whole course of our thought and life.

The first step, then, in the realization of life and health, is to know that God is life, abundant, omnipresent, eternal; and the second step is to make connection with God life by declaring our oneness with it. You are the offspring of God—of life. In life you live, move, and have your being. "As the Father hath life in himself, even so gave he to the Son also to have life in himself." If you would have life from within, you must know yourself as the offspring, the son, of God. Your life source is from within. As a limited, personal man, you have no life of your own. "He that believeth on the Son [is conscious of himself as the son] hath eternal life; but he that obeyeth not the Son [is not conscious of himself as the son of God] shall not see life."

"Now on the last day, the great *day* of the feast, Jesus stood and cried, saying, If any man thirst, let him come unto me and drink. He that believeth on me, as the scripture hath said, from within him shall flow rivers of living water." "The water that I shall give him shall become in him a well of water springing up unto eternal life."

Within man's body we find the center where life is generated. This center is the fountain from which shall spring rivers of living water. In men of a material mind, this fountain does not give forth the pure, life-giving stream, because it is dammed up by material thoughts about life. But when one is quickened by Spirit through faith in the indwelling Lord, the Source of life, the waters of life are set free and purified, and become the river "the streams whereof make glad the city of God." The "city of God" is man's spiritual consciousness.

The prophet Zechariah saw this fountain of cleansing life, and he said: "In that day there shall be a fountain opened . . . for sin and for uncleanness." This is the fountain of purifying, healing

Christ life, quickened in man for his complete transformation and redemption. The work of this cleansing stream is the real healing. Anything less is temporary.

"He that will, let him take the water of life freely."

CLINTON E. BERNARD

TRUTH OR PSYCHOLOGY?

THE METHOD we teach is not inconsistent with psychology; it only goes farther than psychology. Psychology is based on mind; Truth is based on Mind—which means God, the universal principle of causation that includes all principles. However, true Christianity is not incompatible with any of the sciences, for it too is a science.

Charles Fillmore states that the new Christianity includes an understanding of psychology but does not stop with an analysis of mind. It "goes on to the highest phase of mind's possibilities, unity with Spirit." Furthermore he says: "Religion becomes practical and effective in everyday life when it incorporates psychology as part of its litany. Without religion psychology is weak in its fundamentals, and without psychology religion fails to give proper attention to the outlet of its ideals. The fact is that religion, comprehended in its fullness, includes psychology. Jesus was a profound psychologist."

It is good Christianity and good Truth to assume that before a man is a mental being he is a spiritual being; that, being spiritual, he is essentially good (no matter if he has no inkling of the fact and appears to be utterly gross), and will respond as such toward those who have sincere faith in his goodness.

Psychology, treating of man as a mental and physical being, must consider him in the light of his limitations as well as in the light of his abilities. Truth, treating of man as primarily a spiritual being, sets no limitations on him—indeed, considers him

[82]

illimitable. Psychology may say to him, "You cannot do this, because you are a human being." Truth says to him, "Because you are a spiritual being, you can do anything good."

Again, it should be emphasized that psychology and Truth are compatible. Truth is a whole and psychology is one of its parts.

3. Your Prayers Have Power

"Set aside a time every day, a definite time,
and pray whether you believe or not. . . .
If you will persistently affirm Truth, even
though you do not believe it at first, you will find
that your prayers have power. Faith
is like a mustard seed and it will grow.
Pray, pray, and keep praying; affirm, and yet
affirm once more. Your persistent prayers
will succeed."

—*Charles Fillmore*

PRAYER IS A HOMECOMING

THERE IS a place to which you can turn for rest and release from fear and care. It is a holy place. Stillness fills it. The peace of God is in it. There your mind becomes like a little child's, lovely and true and pure. There your thought is stayed on the things that are good and just and merciful. When you enter there, the world outside and all your troubles drop away and you rise at last, body stilled, mind stilled, refreshed and restored.

This place is not far away and difficult of access. It is right where you are now. It is right where you are whenever you shut the doors of the senses, still the importuning of little thoughts, and go along with God. It is the place of the silence.

It is not hard to enter the place of the silence. If it seems hard to you, perhaps you have been making it hard. No one can fight his way through to God. Weeping and pleading are futile. You must let go and let God.

Some persons link the silence with occultism and look for fantastic psychic experiences from it. The purpose of the silence, however, is not to have visions or to see colored lights. Such phantasia serve only to distract the individual from his true purpose, which is communion with God.

On the other hand the silence is not a state of daydreaming or sleep. If you feel sleepy, do not try to pray unless you first waken yourself by saying, "*Awake, thou sleepest.*" The silence demands such wakefulness as is required at no other time. It is your appointment with God.

In practicing the silence you should always try to be relaxed in body and receptive in mind.

"Underneath are the everlasting arms." Say this quietly. Feel the presence of God freeing you from every thought of tension. Let your whole body, every nerve, every muscle, every cell, relax and let go. Wherever you feel any tension, relax and let go. If you feel tense across your forehead, say, *"Relax and let go."* If your eyes feel strained, say, *"Relax and let go."* If you are tense in any part of your body, say, *"Relax and let go,"* until from the top of your head to the soles of your feet you are perfectly relaxed. This concludes the first step in the drill.

"Be still, and know that I am God." Say this silently. Repeat it over and over until the words take on new meaning, a living meaning, and you feel the stillness deep down inside, with your whole mind, your whole being.

This is the second step in the practice of the silence, and it is perhaps the most important of all. Only in stillness can you unify yourself with God, only when thoughts and feelings are quieted and the doors of the senses are shut. Not through our human powers and understanding do we attain our good, but by letting go of doubts, of limiting personal claims, and turning to God.

"Be still, and know that I am God." Know it. Know it now. You are comfortable, relaxed, still. You are in the presence of God.

Turn your attention now to the top of your head and say, silently or aloud as you wish, *"I am the light of the world."*

In the practice of the silence you will find it wise to use affirmations, for they will help you direct and control your thoughts. But there is a surer speech than that of syllables, a higher communion than that of words. God hears your inmost thoughts. Your faith and love speak for you. Your faith and love unify you with Him, make your mind His mind, your body His body, your spirit His Spirit, your life His life, your will His will.

You do not have to cajole or coerce God; His love has already encompassed the fulfillment of your needs. It is only you that your prayers have to change. Use affirmations to direct your thoughts, to make them clear, sharp, pointed; then be still and listen. It is God's voice that you wish to hear.

"I am the light of the world." Declare this. Then be still until you actually feel the light of Spirit through you and over you, feel yourself immersed as in a sea of light, your whole being illumined, awake, exalted, the light of the world.

Now center your attention just above the eyes, and declare, *"I am divine intelligence."*

Emerson said, "The only real prosperity that I can have is a rush of ideas." Divine Mind is a reservoir of ideas, good ideas, yours to draw upon, yours to use. No sluggishness, physical or mental, no doubt or fear can remain in you, for you have opened your mind to the inspiration of God. You are alive, awake, alert, joyous, and enthusiastic. You are divine intelligence.

Now center your attention at the eyes and say, *"I see with the eyes of Spirit."*

Your eyes are the watchful servants of a mind that sees only the perfection of Spirit. All sense of tension or fatigue is dropping away from your eyes before the inflow of divine energy. They are strong, clear-seeing eyes. Your spiritual vision, too, is renewed. You see the Truth more clearly. You see with the eyes of Spirit.

Centering your attention at the throat, affirm, *"All power is given unto me in mind and body."*

The power of God is working through you to free you from every negative influence. Nothing can hold you in bondage. You are the overcomer, a son of God. All power is yours to control your thoughts, to vitalize your body, to gain success, to bless others. Unleash your spiritual forces. All power is given unto you in mind and body.

Now fix your thought at the back of your neck and say, *"I am unfettered and unbound."*

You are free with the freedom of Spirit. No false condition has any power over you. You are the Christ, a son of the living God. Poised in the consciousness of your Christ mastery you are unfettered and unbound.

Now directing your attention toward your back, declare, *"I am strong in the Lord and in the power of His might."*

Your yoke is easy and your burden is light. The strength of

the Lord is pouring through your spinal column, strengthening
nerve and bone. No longer bowed by burdens, your own, your
family's or the world's, your back is straight and sturdy. Free,
poised, lighthearted, you face life confidently, strong in the Lord
and in the power of His might.

Turn your thought toward your heart and declare, *"I am the
perfect expression of divine love."*

Love transforms. Love transfigures. Love fills the heart with
harmony. Love fills the mind with kind, helpful thoughts. Love
fills the lips with words of praise and cheer. Love fills life, fills
it to overflowing with happiness and peace. Whatever the need
or problem, divine love is the answer; and you are the perfect
expression of divine love.

Now fix your attention at the pit of the stomach and say, *"I
am satisfied with divine substance."*

The substance of God erases fatigue from your body, renews
tissues, replenishes energy. It stabilizes your mind. It prospers
your affairs. Every longing of your soul, every need of your life,
is fulfilled. You are satisfied with divine substance.

When you have gained a full realization of substance, focus
your attention at the navel and realize, *"Divine order is established in my mind and body."*

The law is unchanging, absolute. Now you are in harmony
with that law. It governs and guides you. It is active in your
mind, harmonizing your thoughts. It is active in your body, adjusting its functions. It is active in your affairs, establishing peace,
success, and joy. Divine order is established in your mind and
body.

Now center your thoughts at the lower part of the abdomen
and say, *"I am alive forevermore in Christ Jesus."*

You have entered the secret place of life. Life charges your
mind, flows through your veins, permeates your tissues, every
nerve, every muscle, every cell. Your eyes shine, your skin glows,
your faculties are sharpened, your whole body radiates health.
You are one with life, the Christ life, ever renewing life. You are
alive forevermore in Christ Jesus.

Finally centering your thought in your feet and legs, affirm, *"I
walk in paths of righteousness and peace."*

The strength and swiftness of God enter into your feet and legs so that your way is made easy. The light of His intelligence shines around you so that your way is made plain. His Spirit goes before you so that your way is made successful. God's way for you is joyous, a way of safety and security. You walk in paths of righteousness and peace.

If you have faithfully followed all the steps of this drill in the silence you are now fully aware of your oneness with God. From the top of your head to the soles of your feet you feel His life tingling. Your mind is charged with His power. Your heart is lifted up by His love. Your whole being is filled with a new sense of peace and satisfaction. You can affirm in the knowledge that it is true, "I am the Christ, a son of the living God."

Now out of the stillness comes the "still small voice," not a human voice speaking in your native tongue, but the voice of God, which speaks as an inner knowing, a strong conviction, and carries to the listening heart the assurance that all is well.

"Ask, and it shall be given you; seek, and ye shall find; knock, and it shall be opened unto you." You have asked, and the Father's good is freely proffered. You have sought, and the way to perfection is revealed. You have knocked, and the doors of the kingdom are open. Fulfillment is yours. The power to bless others is yours. Receive and rejoice!

Truly "silence is the element in which great things fashion themselves together."

There are many kinds of silence.

There is the drowsy silence of the noonday fields. There is the restless silence of the sleeping city. There is the silence of the grief too deep for tears and of the joy too full for laughter. There is the understanding silence that falls between new lovers and old friends. The movement of the heavens, the growth of living things, is silent. There is the silence of human thought.

But deeper is the silence of the place of peace within you. Deeper is the silence where you commune with God. In the silence is strength for the tired body. In the silence is light for the joyless mind. In the silence is love for the lonely spirit. In the silence is peace for the troubled heart. There workaday worries fade away. There the whole being becomes a place of prayer, a holy temple set upon a hill. There God becomes a living presence. There you become His son. And you . . .

... shall have some peace there, for peace comes dropping slow,
Dropping from the veils of the morning to where the cricket sings;
There midnight's all a glimmer, and noon a purple glow,
And evening full of the linnet's wings.

EMMET FOX

THE GOLDEN KEY

(Author's Note: *I have compressed this message into four pages. Had it been possible I would have reduced it to four lines. It is not intended to be an instructional treatise, but a practical recipe for getting out of trouble. Study and research are well in their own time and place, but no amount of either will get you out of a concrete difficulty. Nothing but practical work in your own consciousness will do that. The mistake made by many people, when things go wrong, is to skim through book after book, without getting anywhere.*

Read The Golden Key *several times. DO exactly what it says, and if you are persistent enough you will overcome any difficulty.*)

SCIENTIFIC prayer will enable you, sooner or later, to get yourself, or anyone else, out of any difficulty on the face of the earth. It is the Golden Key to harmony and happiness.

To those who have no acquaintance with the mightiest power in existence, this may appear to be a rash claim, but it needs only a fair trial to prove that, without a shadow of doubt, it is a just one. You need take no one's word for it, and you should not. Simply try it for yourself, and see.

God is omnipotent, and man is His image and likeness, and has dominion over all things. This is the inspired teaching, and it is intended to be taken literally, at its face value. Man means every man, and so the ability to draw on this power is not the

THE UNITY TREASURE CHEST

special prerogative of the mystic or the saint, as is so often supposed, or even of the highly trained practitioner. Whoever you are, wherever you may be, the Golden Key to harmony is in your hand now. This is because in scientific prayer it is God who works, and not you, and so your particular limitations or weaknesses are of no account in the process. You are only the channel through which the divine action takes place, and your treatment will really be just the getting of yourself out of the way. Beginners often get startling results at the first time of trying, for all that is absolutely essential is to have an open mind, and sufficient faith to try the experiment. Apart from that, you may hold any views on religion, or none.

As for the actual method of working, like all fundamental things, it is simplicity itself. All that you have to do is this: *Stop thinking about the difficulty, whatever it is, and think about God instead.* This is the complete rule, and if only you will do this, the trouble, whatever it is, will presently disappear. It makes no difference what kind of trouble it is. It may be a big thing or a little thing; it may concern health, finance, a lawsuit, a quarrel, an accident, or anything else conceivable; but whatever it is, just stop thinking about it, and think of God instead—that is all you have to do.

The thing could not be simpler, could it? God Himself could scarcely have made it simpler, and yet it never fails to work when given a fair trial.

Do not try to form a picture of God, which is, of course, impossible. Work by rehearsing anything or everything that you know about God. God is Wisdom, Truth, inconceivable Love. God is present everywhere; has infinite power; knows everything; and so on. It matters not how well you may think you understand these things; go over them repeatedly.

But you must stop thinking of the trouble, whatever it is. The rule is to think about God, and if you are thinking about your difficulty you are not thinking about God. To be continually glancing over your shoulder, as it were, in order to see how matters are progressing, is fatal, because that is thinking of the trouble, and you must think of God, and of nothing else. Your object is to drive the thought of the difficulty right out of your consciousness, for a few moments at least, substituting for it the thought of God. This is the crux of the whole thing. If you can become so absorbed in this consideration of the spiritual world that you really forget for a while all about the trouble concerning which you began to pray, you will presently find that you are safely and comfortably out of your difficulty—that your demonstration is made.

In order to "Golden Key" a troublesome person or a difficult situation, think, "Now I am going to 'Golden Key' John, or Mary, or that threatened danger"; then proceed to drive all thought of John, or Mary, or the danger right out of your mind, replacing it by the thought of God.

By working in this way about a person, you are not seeking to influence his conduct in any way, except that you prevent him from injuring or annoying you, and you do him nothing but good. Thereafter he is certain to be in some degree a better, wiser, and more spiritual person, just because you have "Golden Keyed" him. A pending lawsuit or other difficulty would probably fade out harmlessly without coming to a crisis, justice being done to all parties concerned.

If you find that you can do this very quickly, you may repeat the operation several times a day with intervals between. Be sure, however, each time you have done it, that you drop all thought of the matter until the next time. This is important.

We have said that the Golden Key is simple, and so it is, but, of course, it is not always *easy* to turn. If you are very frightened or worried it may be difficult, at first, to get your thoughts away from material things. But by constantly repeating some statement of absolute Truth that appeals to you, such as *There is no power but God*, or *I am the child of God, filled and surrounded by the perfect peace of God*, or *God is love*, or *God is guiding me now*, or, perhaps best and simplest of all, just *God is with me*—however mechanical or dead it may seem at first—you will soon find that the treatment has begun to "take," and that your mind is clearing. Do not struggle violently; be quiet but insistent. Each time that you find your attention wandering, just switch it straight back to God.

Do not try to think out in advance what the solution of your difficulty will probably turn out to be. This is technically called "outlining," and will only delay the demonstration. Leave the question of ways and means strictly to God. You want to get out of your difficulty—that is sufficient. You do your half, and God will never fail to do His.

"Whosoever shall call upon the name of the Lord shall be saved."

CHARLES FILLMORE

THE ATOMIC PRAYER

"THE MAJORITY of people have crude or distorted ideas about the character and the location of Spirit. They think that Spirit plays no part in mundane affairs and can be known by a person only after his death.

"But Jesus said, 'God is Spirit'; He also said, 'The kingdom of God is within you.' Science tells us that there is a universal life that animates and sustains all the forms and shapes of the universe. Science has broken into the atom and revealed it to be charged with tremendous energy that may be released and be made to give the inhabitants of the earth powers beyond expression, when its law of expression is discovered.

"Jesus evidently knew about this hidden energy in matter and used His knowledge to perform so-called miracles.

"Our modern scientists say that a single drop of water contains enough latent energy to blow up a ten-story building. This energy, existence of which has been discovered by modern scientists, is the same kind of spiritual energy that was known to Elijah, Elisha, and Jesus, and used by them to perform miracles.

"By the power of his thought Elijah penetrated the atoms of hydrogen and oxygen and precipitated an abundance of rain. By the same law he increased the widow's oil and meal. This was not a miracle—that is, it was not a divine intervention supplanting natural law—but the exploitation of a law not ordinarily understood. Jesus used the same dynamic power of thought to break the bonds of the atoms composing the few loaves and fishes of a little lad's lunch—and five thousand people were fed.

[97]

"Science is discovering the miracle-working dynamics of religion, but science has not yet comprehended the dynamic directive power of man's thought. All so-called miracle workers claim that they do not of themselves produce the marvelous results; that they are only the instruments of a superior entity. It is written in I Kings, 'The jar of meal wasted not, neither did the cruse of oil fail, according to the word of Jehovah, which he spake by Elijah.' Jesus called Jehovah Father. He said, 'The works that I do in my Father's name, these bear witness of me.'

"Jesus did not claim to have the exclusive supernatural power that is usually credited to Him. He had explored the ether energy, which He called the 'kingdom of heaven'; His understanding was beyond that of the average man, but He knew that other men could do what He did if they would only try. He encouraged His followers to take Him as a center of faith and use the power of thought and word. 'He that believeth on me, the works that I do shall he do also; and greater *works* than these shall he do.'

"The great modern revival of divine healing and mental healing is due to the application of the same law that Jesus used. He demanded faith on the part of those whom He healed, and with that faith as the point of mental and spiritual contact He released the latent energy in the atomic structure of His patients and they were restored to life and health.

"Have faith in the power of your mind to penetrate and release the energy that is pent up in the atoms of your body, and you will be astounded at the response. Paralyzed functions anywhere in the body can be restored to action by one's speaking to the spiritual intelligence and life within them. Jesus raised His dead body in this way and Paul says that we can raise our body in the same manner if we have the same spiritual contact.

"What have thought concentration and discovery of the dynamic character of the atom to do with prayer? They have everything to do with prayer, because prayer is the opening of communication between the mind of man and the mind of God. Prayer is the exercise of faith in the presence and power of the unseen God. Supplication, faith, meditation, silence, concentration, are mental attitudes that enter into and form part of prayer. When one understands the spiritual character of God and adjusts

himself mentally to the omnipresent God-Mind, he has begun to
pray aright.

"Audible prayers are often answered but the most potent are
silently uttered in the secret recesses of the soul. Jesus warned
against wordy prayers—prayer uttered to be heard of men. He
told His disciples not to be like these housetop prayers. 'When
thou prayest, enter into thine inner chamber, and having shut thy
door, pray to thy Father who is in secret, and thy Father who
seeth in secret shall recompense thee.'

"The times are ripe for great changes in our estimate of the
place and the character of God. The seven-day creation of the
universe (including man) as described in Genesis is a symbolic
story of the work of the higher realms of mind under divine law.
It is the privilege of everyone to use his mental abilities in the
superrealms, and thereby carry out the prayer formula of Jesus:
'Seek ye first his kingdom, and his righteousness; and all these
things shall be added unto you.' "

The foregoing extract is from our "Health and Prosperity" column in *Unity* for May, 1927. These comments are peculiarly applicable to the present and also to a subject that has been agitat-
ing the public mind for some time, the atomic bomb.

Of all the comments on or discussions of the indescribable
power of the invisible forces released by the atomic bomb none
that we have seen mentioned its spiritual or mental character. All
commentators have written about it as a force external to man
to be controlled by mechanical means, with no hint that it is the
primal life that animates and interrelates man's mind and body.

The next great achievement of science will be the understanding of the mental and spiritual abilities latent in man through
which to develop and release these tremendous electrons, protons, and neutrons secreted in the trillions of cells in the physical
organism. Here is involved the secret, as Paul says, "hid for ages
and generations . . . which is Christ [superman] in you, the hope
of glory." It is through release of these hidden life forces in his
organism that man is to achieve immortal life, and in no other
way. When we finally understand the facts of life and rid our
mind of the delusion that we shall find immortal life after we die,
then we shall seek more diligently to awaken the spiritual man
within us and strengthen and build up the spiritual domain of our

being until, like Jesus, we shall be able to control the atomic energy in our body and perform so-called miracles.

The fact is that all life is based upon the interaction between the various electrical units of the universe. Science tells us about these activities in terms of matter and no one understands them, because they are spiritual entities and their realities can only be understood and used wisely by the spiritually developed man. Electricians do not know what electricity is, although they use it constantly. A reporter once asked an officer of the General Electric Company to give him a concise definition of electricity. His answer was "Electricity is faith." A long explanation followed in which the analogy between faith and electricity was shown. The Christian uses faith and gets marvelous results, the electrician uses electricity and also gets marvelous results, and neither of them knows the real nature of the agent he uses so freely.

The man who called electricity faith doubtless thought that he was making a striking comparison when in fact he was telling a truth, that faith is the neutron of the mind and it is the match that starts the fire in the electrons and protons of innate Spirit forces. Faith has its degrees of voltage; the faith of the child and the faith of the most powerful spiritual adept are far apart in their intensity and results. When the trillions of cells in one's body are roused to expectancy by spiritual hope, a positive spiritual contact results and marvelous transformations take place. When Jesus asked His patients, "Believe ye that I am able to do this?" He was making such a contact. Also when He told those to whom He ministered, "Thy faith hath made thee whole," He used the same law. When He turned water into wine and fed five thousand by multiplying a few loaves and fishes, He performed in a masterly and beneficial way what our scientists made possible in a destructive way by releasing through the atomic bomb the pent-up forces of Spirit.

Scientists have invented a machine that records the force of thought. Every thought expressed by the mind radiates an energy as it passes through the brain cells, and this machine measures the force of these radiations. Sir James Jeans, the eminent British scientist, gives a prophecy of this in one of his books. He says in substance that it may be that the gods determining our fate are our own minds working on our brain cells and through them on the world about us. This will eventually be found to be true, and the discovery of the law of release of the electronic vitality wrapped up in matter will be the greatest revelation of all time. When we awake to the fact that every breath we draw is releasing this all-potent electronic energy and it is shaping our life for good or ill, according to our faith, then we shall begin to search for the law that will guide us aright in the use of power.

People the world over are amazed and terrified when they read of the destruction wrought on the cities and people of Japan by two atomic bombs. But do we realize that millions of people are killed every year by atomic force? Doctors tell us that it is the toxin generated in our own body that kills us. What produces this destructive force? It must be our own mind, and the remedy must also be in a change in that mind. Paul expressed this when he said, "Be ye transformed by the renewing of your mind."

All persons who have dismissed the idea of miracle in the marvelous works of Jesus and His followers, have looked forward to a time when the law they used would be explained, but nearly all expected it to come through spiritual means. But now science has opened up a kingdom having all the possibilities of the kingdom of heaven taught by Jesus. However Jesus said this kingdom is within us and would be exercised constructively through our mind under divine law. The latest discovery of science shows that through the development of the atom a power will be cast right into our midst that will in its physical aspect make the earth equal to our wildest dreams of heaven. Broadcasting stations sending out on the ether light, heat, power, will be established the world over, and every householder will have receiving sets which he can turn on or off at will. The cost will be negligible. Even the climate of the whole planet will be transformed, destructive forces no longer possible, and peace reign forever. Labor as we now have it will disappear, production will become so easy that a man will in a week raise enough food to last him a year. Everybody will produce so abundantly that he will beg people to take his goods without money and without price. Money will automatically disappear and a loving interchange of commodities follow. Lighter-than-air forms of building material will be discovered and our dwellings will float in the air and be transported from place to place like airplanes. Everybody will have everything he wants, and no one will work for wages. Art, science, religion, music, and the finer things of life will be the occupation of all the people and those who do not expand their minds to enjoy the finer things of life will be out of step with the times.

Our men of science have found the key that unlocks the door to the physical realm in the kingdom of the heavens, but the spiritual domains are yet to be found and their doors unlocked.

There must be a change of mind by the people of the earth before the tremendous uplift to be wrought by atomic energy can become beneficial and permanent. Greed and selfishness will find a way to exploit it to boost their ambition unless they are taught the truth. We should therefore redouble our efforts to show man that the power that rules the world is within him. "Greater is he that is in you than he that is in the world."

IN HIS NAME

DID IT EVER occur to you that you are almost daily taking God's name in vain? Unless you are very watchful, very careful, you are doing so.

When God called Moses to lead the Children of Israel out of Egypt, "Moses said unto God, Behold, when I come unto the children of Israel, and shall say unto them, The God of your fathers hath sent me unto you; and they shall say to me, What is his name? What shall I say unto them?

"And God said unto Moses, I AM THAT I AM: and he said, Thus shalt thou say unto the children of Israel, I AM hath sent me unto you.

". . . this is my name for ever, and this is my memorial unto all generations."

I AM, then, is God's name. Every time you say, "I AM sick," "I AM weak," "I AM discouraged," are you not speaking God's name in vain, falsely?

I AM cannot be sick; I AM cannot be weary, or faint, or powerless; for I AM is All-Life, All-Power, All-Good.

"I AM," spoken with a downward tendency, is always false, always "in vain." A commandment says, "Thou shalt not take the name of Jehovah thy God in vain; for Jehovah will not hold him guiltless that taketh his name in vain." And Jesus said, "By thy words thou shalt be justified, and by thy words thou shalt be condemned."

If you speak the "I AM" falsely, you will get the result of false speaking. If you say, "I am sick," you will get sickness; if you say, "I am poor," you will get poverty; for the law is, "Whatsoever a man soweth, that shall he also reap." "I AM" spoken upward, toward the good, the true, is sure to outpicture in visible good, in success, in happiness.

Does all this sound foolish to you? Do you doubt that such power goes with the speaking of that name? If so, just go alone, close your eyes, and in the depth of your own soul say over and over the words, "I AM." Soon you will find your whole being filled with a sense of power which you never had before—power to overcome, power to accomplish, power to do all things.

I am, because Thou art. I am what Thou art. I am one with Thee. O Thou infinite I AM! I am good. I am holy. I am well. I am, because Thou art.

"The name of Jehovah is a strong tower: the righteous runneth into it, and is safe." They who think rightly about the power of the I AM, spoken upward, simply have to run into it, as into a strong tower or fortress, and they are safe.

Did you ever go into a meeting where the drift of all the "testimonials" given was the I AM spoken upward—"I am happy to be here," "I am glad I am a Christian," "I am hoping and trusting in God," and so forth? Attend such a gathering, and almost before you know it, you will find yourself lifted entirely above all your troubles and anxieties. You leave such a meeting with a feeling of joy and lightness, and a consciousness that you have the power to overcome all the home troubles and worries; you go, singing and confident, toward the very fire which, an hour before, seemed about to consume you.

Dear friends, you who at times feel almost discouraged, you who are being continually "sandpapered" by the petty worries and anxieties of life, just try for one week always saying the I AM upward, toward the good, and see what the result will be. Instead of saying, "I am afraid it will rain," say, "I hope it will not rain"; instead of "I am sorry," say, "I would have been glad had it been so and so"; instead of saying, "I am weak and cannot accomplish," say, "I AM, because Thou art; I can accomplish, because I AM." You will be astonished at the result.

The Christ, speaking through Jesus, said to the Jews who were boasting of being descendants of Abraham: "Verily, verily, I say unto you, Before Abraham was born, I am." And Paul, writing to Timothy, said: "Let every one that nameth the name of the Lord depart from unrighteousness." Let everyone who speaks the I AM keep it separated from false speaking. Let it be spoken always upward.

Jesus also said, "Whatsoever ye shall ask in my name"—that is, in the name of I AM—"That will I do." Whenever you desire—not supplicate, but desire, speaking the "I AM" upward—He will give what you ask. Every time you say, "I am happy," you ask in His name for happiness. Every time you say, "I am unhappy," you ask in His name for unhappiness. "Hitherto," He said to the disciples, "have ye asked nothing in my name: ask, and ye shall receive, that your joy may be made full." Is not this just the trouble? Hitherto what have we been asking in His name? Have we been asking for health or for sickness, for happiness or for unhappiness, for riches or for poverty, by the manner of our speaking the I AM?

Have we spoken it upward, toward the good, or downward toward the not good? That which we have been receiving will tell the story. Jesus said that if they asked rightly in His name, their joy would be full. Is your joy full? If not, then give heed to your asking.

The disciples healed "in the name of Jesus Christ." In the name of Jesus Christ is the name of the I AM.

Suppose that a messenger is sent out from the Executive Mansion at Washington to do certain things in the name of the President of the United States. These three little words, "In his name," invest the messenger with the full power of the President, so far as the performing of that service is concerned.

"Whatsoever ye do in word or in deed, do all in the name of the Lord Jesus, giving thanks to God the Father," said Paul, in writing to the Colossians. Whatever we do heartily and sincerely in the name of Christ or the I AM, carries with it the power of the I AM to accomplish—a power from a higher source as the presidential messenger receives his power from a higher source. All power is given to Christ. Doing all things "in His name" puts aside our mortal personality and lets the Christ do the work. When Moses, with a sense of his personal insufficiency for so great a work, shrank from it, saying, "Oh Lord, I am not eloquent . . .

for I am slow of speech, and of a slow tongue . . . Jehovah said unto him, Who hath made man's mouth? . . . is it not I Jehovah? Now therefore go, and I will be with thy mouth, and teach thee what thou shalt say."

In Edward Everett Hale's story "In His Name," a story in a setting of seven hundred years ago, it is no fairy tale that invests the words "In His Name" with such magic power. This little password carried safely, through the most dangerous places, all who went on errands of good. Locked doors were readily opened at the sound of the words. Soldier, sentry, officer of the guard, all gave way respectfully and instantly before it. Men were willing to leave their homes at a moment's notice and plunge into the greatest hardships "for the love of Christ" and "in His name."

Ministering today in His name, I say to you, troubled one, anxious one, weary one: Be strong! Be of good courage! Be hopeful! The world—the mortal—is overcome already. The Christ, the I AM, speaking through Jesus, has spoken, saying: "I have overcome the world."

"To him that overcometh [that is, to him who recognizes that already the world is overcome by the I AM, that there is nothing in all the universe but the I AM] will I give of the hidden manna, and I will give him a white stone, and upon the stone a new name written, which no one knoweth, but he that receiveth it."

"He that overcometh, I will make him a pillar in the temple of my God, and he shall go out thence no more; and I will write upon him the name of my God," even the name I AM.

GEORGIANA TREE WEST

PRAY WITHOUT CEASING

MANY PUZZLING questions arise in the mind of the earnest Truth student who has outgrown the limited conception of God as a sort of superman and is coming into the broader understanding of God as Spirit, the creative principle of the universe. One of the most troublesome of these questions is: "If God is Principle, how can we pray to Him, and how can Principle know anything of our needs?"

These trusting hearts found much comfort in praying to a personal God to whom they could pour out their troubles and difficulties and of whom they could beg aid much as they would of a loved and trusted earthly adviser. Many such individuals suffer a distinct sense of loss when their intelligence, guided by the Spirit of truth within themselves, is forced to accept a broader and truer conception of God. A better understanding of the true nature of prayer as revealed by Jesus Christ will clear up this seeming problem.

First, what is prayer? Webster defines prayer as "an expressed petition," and the Standard Dictionary definition of the verb pray makes prayer a form of devout address. The Truth student uses this last definition, for "devout address" means devoting the entire attention to one idea. What is prayer but turning the attention toward God? A good workable definition of prayer is this: Prayer is man's means of making conscious contact with God. Since man lives and moves and has his being in God, he is naturally in contact with God every moment of his existence, but he

[107]

is not always conscious of the spiritual presence. Only when he is conscious or aware does he feel the beneficent influence in his daily living. Prayer may be called the gateway to God, a gateway opened in consciousness through which the invisible power of Spirit is delivered into visibility.

Some of us are laboring under the idea that to pray we must use what Webster calls "an expressed petition." We go into lengthy discussions and explanations of our difficulties in our prayers. We fail to realize that, as Unity so frequently stresses, God needs no information. We are the ones that need information; we need to be informed of God's presence in our life. Through prayer we receive our assurance of this presence. To receive this assurance we must free our mind of our difficulties and be still and know that God's will for us is good will. With all the faith of a little child we must thank the heavenly Father that His good will is now done in our life and cheerfully and expectantly look for the manifesting of that good will.

An illustration will help you get this idea more clearly. Suppose you are out in a storm; the rain is pouring down, and you are cold and drenched to the skin. What do you want? You want a dry haven of refuge. You see a light in the distance. You stumble and drag yourself in its direction. You finally arrive and find a house, warm, brightly lighted, and perhaps a glowing fire in the grate. Naturally you are glad and quickly divest yourself of your wet, uncomfortable outer garments. You are grateful because you have come into that which you desired. Now would it be intelligent for you to keep your wet clothes on and insist on explaining how cold it was outside, how dreadfully you had suffered, going into endless details about the difficulties you had been through and refusing to put on the warm dry garments offered you? Would that be even sensible? Yet that is too often the very thing we do when we seek God in prayer.

We are buffeted by the storms of life, drenched by the bitter tears of grief that we see all around us. What are we seeking? We are seeking a haven from discord—heaven, harmony. We seek it in prayer but keep right on letting our troubles run through our mind. This is not praying. We are in the position of the one who was seeking haven in the storm: just as long as we keep on telling God of our troubles we are not partaking of His good will for us.

It is true that "your Father knoweth what things ye have need of." He knows our need of more life, of more love, of more wisdom, of more power, and of greater abundance of good. He knows our needs just as mother earth knows the need of all plant life that depends upon her for sustenance. The roots reach out to gather what they need for the growth of the plant. All that they need is right there for them and the supply immediately begins to fulfill their demand.

Likewise God knows our needs through the omnipresence of His all-loving, all-wise mind. Our prayers are the means by which we reach out to receive more of God's good for this plant of earthly existence. In God-Mind there is an immediate knowing when we reach out for more of life, of love, of wisdom, of plenty. There is an immediate response because our Father knoweth the need. The order and harmony of the whole universe comes right into action for the fulfillment of our need; we have only to make our desire known through prayer, believing. It is this prayer of faith that lays hold of God's good, just as the root lays hold of the sustenance in the earth, and delivers it into our life. The idea that God knows our needs does not imply that He has listed our sins, our unkindnesses, our prevarications, one by one, and recorded our every ache and pain. It does not mean that God has to be informed of every little discord and inharmony in our life. It does mean that God knows the need of health and harmony for us here and now and provides life and wisdom and love to the extent that we call for it to fulfill our need. As we turn with faith, believing, to that great sender of good there is an instant response, for it is our desire that is the need that God knows. When we turn to God for the fulfillment of these desires or needs, we are praying.

To follow Jesus Christ's instructions concerning prayer we must earnestly endeavor to break up the old habit of merely telling our troubles to God; we must learn to ask, believing that we receive. To do this we must loose and let go of all mental images of difficulty, lack, and limitation. We must remember that we are praying for one purpose only, to open our desires unto God, and He who opens His hand and satisfies "the desire of every living thing" will fulfill our need according to our faith.

Many people labor under the mistake of believing that the only

time we need to pray is when we are in trouble. This is most unreasonable when you stop to think about it, just as unreasonable
as thinking that the only time to study a foreign language is when
you find yourself placed under the necessity of using it. Plainly
this is absurd; it is the daily attention that you give to anything
that makes it instantly available in your time of need. It is as true
of prayer as of anything else.

Undoubtedly Paul was expressing this same idea when he
said, "Pray without ceasing." This instruction has been quite a
puzzle to many literal-minded people. They wonder if the only
people who really are fulfilling the law concerning prayer are
those who withdraw from the world and spend their entire life in
contemplation of things spiritual. Jesus did not teach that this is
the only way to pray without ceasing; the way given in the New
Testament is the way of putting God first in everything. That is
praying without ceasing.

How can we put God first in our life and so pray without
ceasing? Like everything else worth while it takes patient endeavor. The way to the goal may seem long and difficult, but we
must remember that "the journey of a thousand miles begins with
one step." Let us take the first step by consecrating ourselves to
God in our first waking moments. Let us, asking absolutely nothing, turn our mind to the one omnipresent spiritual presence and
rejoice in our at-one-ment with our Father-Mother. Let the
prayer be *"Of myself, I am nothing; but with Thee I am all life,
love, wisdom, and power, and this day I go forth expressing Thee
in every thought, word, and action. I can do this because Thou
hast given me of Thy Spirit. I am filled with praise and thanksgiving."* To start the day in this fashion is the first step in praying
without ceasing.

The human side of us will find many excuses for not doing
this. We are so busy in the morning. We cannot think clearly
until we have had our cup of coffee. This is the type of excuse
that the human side always presents when the sense consciousness wants pampering and has no desire to make the effort to
seek conscious union with the Most High. If your thoughts tempt
you away from forming this habit of giving your first waking moments to acknowledging the presence of God, talk strongly to

yourself. Discipline your thoughts and your feelings; say to your busy mind, *"Be still that I may know God."*

Having consecrated ourselves to God in our waking moments, we should take the second step, that of setting aside a period every day at a definite time to ask, believing we receive, whatsoever we need, and to send forth the prayer of understanding for those whom we desire to help. There is great value in having such a period of prayer at an appointed time. It teaches us stability and dependability.

The third step toward our goal of praying without ceasing is to keep our thoughts, words, and acts in accord with that which we have established in silent prayer. We must endeavor throughout the day to think, speak, and act from our God consciousness, weeding out destructive thoughts by substituting for them constructive thoughts. If we faithfully follow the first and second steps we shall find it easier to do this. With conscious endeavor we will find ourselves automatically turning to God even when making biscuits or cutting out a dress or tackling a difficult customer. The trouble with most of us today is that we think we live most of our life outside of Spirit. We have not the consciousness that we live in Spirit every minute of the day, because we are not consecrating our simplest thoughts, words, and actions to God. No matter how simple the task, we should pause an instant, knowing: *"Thy will is my will, dear Father-God; Thy wisdom, strength, and power works in me to accomplish perfectly this task of the moment."* In this way we make of ourselves perfect instruments of God's activity. We shall be astounded at the ease with which we complete tiresome and difficult tasks. Emerson says, "We lie in the lap of immense intelligence which makes us receivers of its truth and organs of its activity." The more conscious we are of this—the more aware we are of the power of God working within us—the more truly we are praying without ceasing and the more rhythmic and harmonious our life becomes.

It is not difficult to understand why we do not pray without ceasing, for ever since we were babies we have been taught to go forward without taking God into immediate consideration. Once we form the habit of acknowledging His presence in every undertaking, no matter how trivial it seems, we have started an automatic process of right thinking and as we go through the day we find ourselves knowing: *"God works with me"* or *"God sees through my eyes"* or *"God speaks words of love through me to everyone I meet."* This may take time and practice, but if we are truly in earnest and are sincere in our endeavor, we shall make good progress.

Having endeavored to pray without ceasing throughout the day, we consecrate ourselves to God at night as we relax for sleep. All mistakes of the day sink into oblivion, and with a heart rejoicing in the day's overcoming let the prayer be *"I am protected and controlled by divine love and infinite wisdom, and all is well."* And so to sleep.

We have definite work to do if we are going to learn to pray without ceasing. The thoughts we think, the things we say, and the acts we perform indicate how much of conscious contact we are making with our Creator, the spiritual source of our being. Only through such contact do we gain power to bring the invisible Christ Spirit indwelling into the realm of visible good.

CHARLES FILLMORE

FAITH PRECIPITATIONS

WHEN ASKED what electricity is, a scientist replied that
he had often thought of it as an adjunct to faith, judging from the
way it acts.

This linking of faith and electricity seems at first glance fantastic, but when we observe what takes place when certain sub-
stances in solution and an electric current are brought in conjunction, there seems to be a confirmation of the Scripture passage:
"Now faith is assurance of *things* hoped for."

Just as the electric current precipitates certain metals in solution in acid, so faith stirs into action the electrons of man's
brain; and acting concurrently with the spiritual ethers, these
electrons hasten nature and produce quickly what ordinarily requires months of seedtime and harvest.

In the time of Elisha, the widow so distressed with debt that
she had even mortgaged to slavery her two children appealed to
the prophet, who said, "What hast thou in the house?" She said,
"Thy handmaid hath not anything in the house, save a pot of
oil." He told her to borrow all the empty vessels her neighbors
had and then to go into the house and shut the door, and to pour
the oil in the pot into all those vessels; which she did until they
were all full. She then paid her debts and had plenty left.

Jesus fed four thousand persons at one time and five thousand at another by the same means. He also "precipitated" the
elements of wholeness many times and healed the multitude. He
required cooperation in faith on the part of those He healed in
order thus to complete the healing circuit.

Speedy answers to prayer have always been experienced and always will be when the right relations are established between the mind of the one who prays and the spiritual realm, which is like an electrical field. The power to perform what seems to be miracles has been relegated to some God-selected one; but now we are inquiring into the law, since God is no respecter of persons, and we find that the fulfillment of the law rests with man or a group of men, when they quicken by faith the spiritual forces latent within them.

The reason why some prayers are not answered is lack of proper adjustment of the mind of the one who prays to the omnipresent creative spiritual life.

Jesus was the most successful demonstrator of prayer of whom we have any record, and He urged persistence in prayer. If at first you don't succeed, try, try again. Like Lincoln, Jesus loved to tell stories to illustrate His point, and He emphasized the value of persistence in prayer. He told of a woman who demanded justice of a certain judge and importuned him until in sheer desperation he granted her request.

Every Christian healer has had experiences where persistent prayer saved his patient. If he had merely said one prayer, as if giving a prescription for the Lord to fill, he would have fallen far short of demonstrating the law. Elijah prayed persistently until the little cloud appeared or, as we should say, he had a "realization"; then the manifestation followed.

The Bible is treasured as the word of God because it records so many of these apparent miracles; but the fact is that all over this land enough demonstrations of the supermind are taking place every day to fill many books of the size of the Bible. Some of them are recorded and people read about them, but these are few compared with the many that are happening. All of which goes to prove that there is a restorative law that, if taken advantage of, will heal the world of all its ills.

Many of the old-school faith healers object to the scientific explanation of the healing process. They have believed in a personal God and that all superworld forces are set in motion by His personal intervention. However it is much more satisfying to logical minds to know that God is the law and that the Spirit that we thought of as a projection of Him is in fact He Himself in His

YOUR PRAYERS HAVE POWER   [115]

own spiritual identity. This is the teaching of Jesus, and our men of science are proving it to be true. An understanding of this all-accessible Truth is making seers, prophets, and mighty men of God out of pygmies. On every hand men of mediocre ability are becoming world leaders through exploiting the supermind qualities that they have merely glimpsed as existing within them.

These ephemeral Caesars have gained an inkling of the disciplined mind's dominion and are using it to control the negative mass thought, and through the hypnotic force of words they evolve chaos and dark night the world over.

When men accept and understand Jesus' teaching about the mastery of the spiritual man, all the evils that arise from these upstart saviors will disappear. But now in the night of mind's eclipse

> We petty men
> Walk under his huge legs, and peep about
> To find ourselves dishonorable graves.

Then the question arises, If this supermind ability is in every man, why is it not more widely understood and used?

There are several answers to this pertinent question, the most plausible being the lack of human initiative. Men prefer to let others do their thinking for them. This is especially true in religious matters. The race thought has been so saturated with the belief that spiritual revelation must come through some authorized channel that the man without an ecclesiastical degree is timid about expressing an opinion about God or man's spiritual nature.

Jesus broke this hypnotic spell when without ecclesiastical authority He claimed to be the Son of God.

We should remember that Jesus included as sons of God all those who, as He said, are "my sheep," that is, follow Him. He quoted Psalm 82, in which it is written,

"I said, Ye are gods,
And all of you sons of the Most High."

The church elders and the people cried, "Crucify him!" Jesus taught great truths, which were grasped by but a few open-minded followers, and they formed a new church. After doing mighty works for hundreds of years, they in turn built an ecclesiastical hierarchy from which the common people were excluded. The Church Fathers gathered and selected certain religious manuscripts and compiled the Bible, which they proclaimed to be the very word of God, to be read and interpreted by those only having the authority of the Church.

Here again we see positive thought submitting to negative thought, thereby keeping the world in darkness for ages.

As Luther started the Protestant Reformation so we are now at the beginning of another reformation, in which the freedom and power of man spiritually will not only be taught but demonstrated.

The supermind demonstrations that mark this modern religious reformation seem so at variance with nature that they are still looked upon as miracles, notwithstanding the fact that logic and science shout from the housetops the universality of law.

Those who study the spiritual import of Jesus' teaching have revealed to them a mental technique for which no adequate language has yet been invented.

The Jews demanded of Jesus that He tell them plainly, and His reply was that His works would testify that He was the Son of God and that He and the Father were one. We who have experienced Spirit baptism freely testify to the dynamic thrill that ripples through the nerves for days and months and is often repeated in silent meditation for years after the first outpour. Thus revelation, observation, and actual experience prove that man develops spirituality according to the divine pattern called in Genesis the image and likeness of God.

The natural man in the physical world is merely the beginning formation of the man planned by creative Mind. When the natural man finishes his unfoldment he enters the next stage, that of the Christ man illustrated by Jesus. In our schools the student is expected to get his education in a certain number of years. So in the divine school we are limited to the period that is spoken of as "the end of the age," * the age of the Christ man just now beginning. Jesus was the first man or "fruit" of the earth's first age, that of the natural man. He opened the way for all those who aspire to the attainment of immortality.

To the present time the followers of Jesus have been told by

* Scriptural reference quoted from the Emphatic Diaglott.

spiritual leaders that He taught the immortality of the soul only. But now it is revealed that He immortalized His body and said, "Follow me." It was man's sins that brought death to his body, and his redemption must include the healing of the body. When the mind or soul is healed of its sins the body will respond. "Your body is a temple of the Holy Spirit which is in you, which ye have from God."

So we find as we study and apply the doctrine of Jesus that our body must be included. Faith in the omnipresent pure substance precipitates the substance in the body and we are transformed.

Proofs may be found in profusion that the divine law of body restoration is in action in a large way right here in our midst. The literature of Unity teems with testimonials of persons who have been healed and are grateful to God for renewed health, strength, prosperity, and happiness. Thus it is not necessary to strengthen your faith by reading about the work of God in ages past; you can personally consult your neighbor, who can doubtless tell you of marvels fully as great as any recorded in the Bible.

The majority of cases that come to us belong to the class of the discouraged woman told of in Luke 8:43, who "spent all her living upon physicians, and could not be healed." Doctors have pronounced them incurable, and as a last resort they turn to God. The hardest part of the work in their healing is to get out of their mind the verdict of the doctor that their case is incurable. We have discovered that there are no incurables. "With God all things are possible." Any experienced metaphysical healer will tell you that he has been the instrument through which all the popular diseases have been healed.

Some of the stories told by patients are beyond human credence; for example, the restoration of the eyes of a man from which they had been removed, and the growth of the nose of a woman who had lost it by disease. These are very rare but well authenticated in metaphysical circles. I am not prepared to give the names of these cases, but I can testify to my own healing of tuberculosis of the hip. When a boy of ten I was taken with what was at first diagnosed as rheumatism but developed into a very serious case of hip disease. I was in bed over a year, and from that time an invalid in constant pain for twenty-five years, or until I began the application of the divine law. Two very large tubercular abscesses developed at the head of the hip bone, which the doctors said would finally drain away my life. But I managed to get about on crutches, with a four-inch cork-and-steel extension on the right leg. The hip bone was out of the socket and stiff. The leg shriveled and ceased to grow. The whole right side became involved; my right ear was deaf and my right eye weak. From hip to knee the flesh was a glassy adhesion with but little sensation.

When I began applying the spiritual treatment there was for a long time slight response in the leg, but I felt better, and I found that I began to hear with the right ear. Then gradually I noticed that I had more feeling in the leg. Then as the years went by the ossified joint began to get limber, and the shrunken flesh filled out until the right leg was almost equal to the other. Then I discarded the cork-and-steel extension and wore an ordinary shoe with a double heel about an inch in height. Now the leg is almost as large as the other, the muscles are restored, and although the hip bone is not yet in the socket, I am certain that it soon will be and that I shall be made perfectly whole.

I am giving minute details of my healing because it would be considered a medical impossibility and a miracle from a religious standpoint. However I have watched the restoration year after year as I applied the power of thought, and I know it is under divine law. So I am satisfied that here is proof of a law that the mind builds the body and can restore it.

CONSTANCE J. FOSTER

NOTHING DOUBTING

I AM CONVINCED that every prayer we make is answered.
But sometimes we do not fully realize what we are really praying
for. On our knees or in the secret quiet of our closet we ask God
for abundance or love or health. When weeks pass and we still
get only lack, continued loneliness and misunderstanding, or
more illness, we cry out that God has not heard us. He has. He
has not only heard us, but He has given us exactly what we asked
for. The difficulty lies not in the answer, but in the fact that we
asked amiss.

There is an old saying that goes: "Beware your wish, for you
will most assuredly have it." We might say the same thing of our
prayers, for wishing is a form of prayer. We do not sufficiently
understand the spiritual law governing prayer and its answer.
We think of a wish or a prayer as something that is very unlikely
to be granted unless we are exceptionally lucky.

Actually our wishes and prayers bring the most inescapable
results in the world. They are coming true constantly in our life
and our affairs. If you want to know what you have been praying
for, just take a good look at the situation in which you find yourself as of this moment. It is the answer to your real prayer. If you
do not like what you have received, you can stop blaming God
for not hearing you and get busy changing your prayer. You can
stop asking amiss.

God hears you all the time, you see, not just when you take
time out to talk to Him. My friend Justine wonders why the

larger home she has been praying for does not materialize. She does not realize that ten minutes spent in asking God for it does not cancel the seven or eight hours a day she spends thinking, "Oh, dear, housing shortage—no place to be had—high rentals— what shall we do?"

Repeating affirmations, whether about housing, health, or harmony, no matter how sincerely, will not wipe out the effect of the fears, worries, and doubts that crop up the rest of the time. For you cannot throw a switch that cuts God off from you and your thoughts. Many people seem to think that they can put through a direct call to Him when they choose and hang up the receiver the rest of the time. They are not aware that in Him we live and move and have our being and that no thought of ours is hidden from Him.

The answer we get is a perfect replica of our dominant thought pattern, for this indeed is our true prayer, and make no mistake—God hears it. The law is just and invariable, as undeviating as the law of gravity in the physical universe. Apples do not fall "up" from trees. God does not answer the part-time thinking that we call prayer. He gives us back, by the inexorable law of His being, the outpicturing of our own most sustained trend of thought. "As he [man] thinketh within himself, so is he."

That is why it is so important that we keep our thoughts centered on the thing or condition or situation that we want rather than on what we do not want. We should be like the farmer who prayed for rain and then carried an umbrella to church. We should be like Jesus, who thanked the Father for hearing Him and answering His prayer even before He had made it. We should pray and then act as if we had already received what we prayed for, because we should truly believe the promise, "Ask, and it shall be given you."

"What in the world are you doing?" a mother asked her little daughter when she came in from the barn all covered with straw.

"Getting the feed ready for the pony I prayed for," she answered!

Needless to say, the little girl got her pony.

The making and keeping of the most vivid possible mental pictures of what you long to see come true in your life is an element of prayer that does not seem to be sufficiently realized. The imagination is a very important part of man's mental equipment. Long before he could reason, weigh, and consider, he was capable of dreaming up visions. Everything that has ever been objectified, from the first wheel to a beautifully designed modern automobile, was first a mental image in someone's head. Nothing from a suspension bridge to a best-selling novel was ever created without imagination, the catching of the glint of a dream. Later the ideas of inventors reach the blueprint stage and finally become material things that we can hear, see, touch, taste, and smell.

What has all this to do with prayer? Everything. The more steadfastly we hold to the desires of our heart the surer and swifter will be their outpicturing in our affairs. Every good thing that we can ever ask or desire already exists as a reality in Spirit, but to bring it into manifestation we must have steadfast faith that what we perceive spiritually can be brought forth into physical manifestation. Prayer is the force that enables us to keep our faith steadfast.

I am convinced from my own experience that when prayers are instantly answered, it is always due to the vividness with which the pray-er is able to see himself enjoying the blessing prayed for. If it is so real that he can smell, see, and taste it, believe and accept it, and give thanks for it, the answer follows immediately. We foolishly call such an answer a miracle. Actually it is simply the natural consequence of the operation of a higher spiritual law with which we are not generally acquainted as yet.

Let me recount just one such miracle in my own life, which happened when I was able to shake off all doubts and fears and build a mental picture of perfection that was more real than the false one of appearances. Do you remember that Jesus said, "Judge not according to appearance, but judge righteous judgment"?

My small son, exploring the kitchen cabinet, had discovered a box of whole cloves and promptly popped one into his mouth. At once he began to sputter and choke on it, turning red in the face and gasping for breath. I swung him upside down, expecting that he would cough up the foreign object, but nothing happened except that he managed to get his breath again. The emergency passed, and I did not give it another thought, assuming that he must have swallowed the clove. Since it had rough, sharp edges I gave him a piece of bread to eat and some mashed potatoes for his supper.

A day or two later he developed a brassy little cough that was quite troublesome, and I began to notice a distinct odor of cloves about his breath. I took him to the doctor who said that an X ray would not show up a nonmetallic object but that the child had probably inhaled the clove into his bronchial tubes or lungs. The condition grew worse, and the two-year-old's sleep was considerably disturbed by the constant hacking. He began to look pale and rundown, and his appetite became steadily poorer.

Finally the doctor said that arrangements must be made to take the baby to a hospital in Philadelphia, where the bronchoscope could be used to remove the clove. It would be a grueling experience for my little boy, and I dreaded to have him subjected to the pain and fright.

I had been praying all along but without success. It is very hard to pray with faith, nothing doubting, when one is so concerned about a loved one and the immediate false appearance is so close that it warps perspective and assumes the proportions of the real.

But the night before the date set for our trip from North Carolina to Pennsylvania and the hospital ordeal, I sat down quietly in the room next to my little boy's and prayed for his complete deliverance and healing. I don't think I used any words at all; our Father knows what we have need of. I just put myself in a state of communion with the Spirit of perfection and all-good. Then I began to visualize my small son as I had seen him on so many occasions, happily digging in the garden. I could literally see the flashing blue of his overalls, the glint of the sun on his yellow curls, the laughing little face. I could smell the earth and the flowers. I could hear his chuckle when he found a fat earthworm.

It was this perfect child I claimed as the Father's true and only manifestation of love and harmony. Suddenly a feeling of deep peace washed over me, and all anxious concern for the morrow slipped away. I felt relaxed and at rest. I yawned, actually felt sleepy and ready for bed for the first time in days.

I was just slipping into bed when the sound of violent cough-

ing came from my child's room. Instead of being tight and rasp-
ing this cough was violently explosive and spasmodic. I hurried
to the child at once, turning on the light in the room. When I
picked him up from the crib, there on the small pillow lay a black
object that turned out to be the almost unrecognizable clove,
now soft and swollen from long contact with moist tissues. The
answer to my prayer had come in exactly the time it took me to
brush my teeth and wash my face for the night—a matter of five
or ten minutes at most.

Coincidence? No. A miracle? The answer again is no. The answer to prayer? Yes, an instantaneous answer. Why? I believe
that what enabled the answer to be manifested immediately was
the vividness of the picture I was able to make of the true perfection for which I was praying and the fact that I was able to enter
into it so completely that for the fraction of a second it was indeed real.

When we do not get the answer we expect and desire it is
only because we pray amiss. Without realizing it, we have
through a belief in something false made our dominant prayer a
negative one, and so we receive what we have asked for—more
confusion and negation.

Remember you cannot throw a switch that cuts God off. He
hears you all the time, and He gives you what you ask for most
consistently. If you do not like it, change the trend of your
thought. "Be ye transformed," as Paul says, "by the renewing of
your mind."

I can assure you that if your realization of perfection is vivid
enough, nothing doubting, your faith will be rewarded instantly.

HILDA GREEN

GOD OWNS EVERYTHING

I HAD AN experience some time ago while in Florida nursing, and I feel led to tell the simple story so that others may grasp the lesson I learned and come to realize God in a deeper sense, as I did. It is the story of Carolyn, her faith, and a bunch of bananas.

I was in Carolyn's home for ten days caring for her mother and new baby sister. My patient had many little books and papers with the name Unity on them. She tried to explain the teachings to me, but I was annoyed rather than pleased. Carolyn, the eight-year-old child, however gave me a concrete example of "All things whatsoever the Father hath are mine." I had forgotten that God has planted in the child heart the ability to have confidence in Him that the adult usually loses along the path of the years. Therein lies my story.

On Saturday afternoon I was putting away the groceries that had been sent from the town four miles away, and Carolyn was helping.

She asked, "Did you get any bananas? I love them."

"No," I replied, "but I'll get some for you Tuesday when I order again."

"I really want them today though," she said with a smile.

I followed her into the bedroom and found her on her knees, offering what I considered a very unorthodox prayer.

"Dear Jesus, I know You have lots of bananas and I know You are willing for Mother and nurse and me to have some; so please send us a half dozen today. Thank You. Amen."

Well, I was so shocked I stood as though turned to stone. Then at supper Carolyn said, "Nurse, how long does today last?"

"Till bedtime for you, dear," I replied.

"No, I mean tomorrow doesn't start till in the night, does it?"

"Oh, I see what you mean. Today lasts until twelve o'clock," I explained.

"I hope God sends my bananas by bedtime."

"But, dear, it has started raining and the roads are bad now," I said. "You won't be too disappointed if you don't get them." I was trying to prepare her, for I was sure she would not receive the fruit that day.

"You must not know God as I do. He won't disappoint me. He never does," she avowed.

At bedtime she made a request of me. "Nurse, will you wake me when my bananas come?"

I assured her that I would, and she dropped off to sleep at once. At a quarter to eleven she roused up and said sleepily, "Have they come?"

"No, not yet. Go back to sleep."

"But it is still today if they aren't here," she insisted.

"Yes," I said, "today has another hour and fifteen minutes." I was amazed that no misgiving had entered her mind. My heart ached for her, because my judgment told me that she would be sorely disturbed at God's not answering her prayer.

Some time later I was still wide awake, troubled, when I heard a car stop outside. I arose, threw my coat around me, and with a flashlight went to answer the door.

There stood my patient's pastor and his wife. He said, "I know it seems foolish to disturb you by coming out here at this hour of the night, but after my wife and I were in bed and asleep, I awoke worried, with a feeling that something was wrong here. We dressed again and came to inquire."

"No, nothing is wrong," I told them.

"In that case," his wife replied, "we will not even come in. Oh, by the way, I bought some nice bananas at the market tonight, and brought some to you."

I turned and looked at the clock. It lacked seven minutes to midnight! "Yes, there was something wrong," I said suddenly, "a child's prayer had to be answered. You came to bring bananas, not because they were needed but because of Carolyn's absolute confidence in God."

Then I told them the story as I have told it here, and tears were in all our eyes as we considered a little child's progress into a new vital faith life. The pastor and his wife went in with me to waken Carolyn. She accepted the fruit without evidencing surprise, but she did say in a natural way, "Thank you, Jesus," before she filled her mouth with the fruit.

Later as we talked it over she said to me solemnly, "Nurse, when you want anything ask God for it. He owns everything and He will give it to you."

Through the months this experience that was given me that night has been a bright and shining light that has led me ever into a deeper and sweeter trust in God.

I WILL PRAY FOR YOU

A LARGE number of the letters that come to Silent Unity include requests for prayers for others. Often the one requesting prayers says: "Help me to pray for my dear one. Tell me how to pray for him, how to help him."

The following meditations will be helpful to you if you are praying for someone else. They will help you to lift up your thoughts about the one for whom you pray; they will help you to realize the Truth about him.

When you pray for another you give him the greatest gift you have to give; and the wonderful thing about praying for someone else is that you cannot pray for another without feeling the blessing and the good effect of your prayers for him in your own heart, mind, and life.

I pray for your healing

You are created in the image and likeness of God. His life and health flow through every part of your being. His vital energy is in every cell. His order blesses every function of your body. His breath is the breath of your life.

Whenever I think about you, I see you as whole and perfect. I give thanks that appearances are not the Truth in God's sight. I give thanks that all things are possible with God. I give thanks that you are a spiritual being, that your life is "hid with Christ in God," that in Him you live and move and have your being.

[127]

As I pray for you in faith and in Truth, I feel a great surge of healing life through my own being. I know that this life in which we live is omnipresent. I know that you are healed. Praise God!

I pray for your prosperity

Whatever your need, God is the source. I affirm your oneness with God. I know that your supply is now at hand. I see you accepting your good. I see your affairs blessed to overflowing with all the good that God has for you.

There is supply for you; there is work for you; there is a right place for you to live. As I pray for you, as I send you my loving thoughts, I see you as God sees you—prosperous, blessed, successful in all that you undertake.

In praying for your prosperity, I know that my own affairs are enriched and blessed. For the prosperity of God is for all. His prospering Spirit is in all. I know that you are prospered in every needed way now. Praise God!

I pray for your happiness

I pray for you to be blessed in whatever way will mean happiness to you. I cannot know the desires of your heart, but I do know that happiness and joy are God's will for you. So I now affirm that God is coming forth into your life as pure joy, as radiant happiness. I give thanks that the events of your life are shaping themselves into ways that are for your good and blessing.

I give thanks that the love of God is within your heart, and I know that this love is mighty to attract your own to you. I see you expressing the love of God; I see you radiant with the love of God. I see you happy, free, glorious.

In praying for your happiness, I, too, am filled with a happy spirit. I know that the happiness of God is omnipresent. I know that you are blessed with true happiness now. Praise God!

I pray for you to be comforted

There is within your heart a Holy Comforter that lifts you out of sadness and sorrow and fills you with new light and understanding. I see you filled with the peace that passes understanding. I see you lifted up in spirit; I see you strengthened in purpose and fortified in your will to go forward in life. I see you quickened in faith and renewed in mind and body.

I send you my love. I send you my prayers. I affirm the oneness, the unity of all life. I see you infolded in the eternal life of God. I see you comforted and sustained in the knowledge that there is no death, that life is truly without beginning or end in God.

As I pray for your peace, I feel a great peace infolding me. I am at peace. I know that you are at peace. Praise God!

I pray for your freedom

You have a Spirit in you that is unfettered and unbound. This Spirit in you knows no limitations, is not bound by fear, by feelings of unworthiness, by bondage to habit. I see you now as free. I see you as the perfect child of God.

All the longings of your soul find perfect fulfillment in God, the Spirit indwelling in you. The past no longer haunts you. Your failings no longer pursue you. You are free! The self of you that God created is your true self, your real self. It stands undefeated, undismayed.

As I affirm your perfect freedom in Christ, I feel a glorious sense of freedom. I know that the freedom of Spirit is omnipresent. I know that you are free. Praise God!

I pray for your guidance

The spirit of God is like a compass in your heart. I know that His Spirit continually points out the right direction to you. My prayer for you is that you may be receptive continually to the divine guidance that comes to you from within.

In any decision God is with you, your light to show you the way. In any need He is at hand, your strength, your wisdom, your ability to act unhesitatingly, to move in the direction of your highest good.

As I pray for you, I give thanks that all things are working together for your good, and I give thanks that there is a Spirit in you that is revealing to you, step by step, the way that is rewarding for you.

As I pray for your guidance, my own feeling of being divinely guided is quickened. I know that I, too, am shown the way through the power of the indwelling Spirit. I know that the wisdom of Spirit is omnipresent.

I know that your way is made clear to you. Praise God!

THE PRAYER OF FAITH

God is my help in every need;
God does my every hunger feed;
God walks beside me, guides my way
Through every moment of the day.

I now am wise, I now am true,
Patient, kind, and loving, too.
All things I am, can do, and be,
Through Christ, the Truth that is in me.

God is my health, I can't be sick;
God is my strength, unfailing, quick;
God is my all, I know no fear,
Since God and love and Truth are here.

PRAYER FOR WORLD LEADERS

Through the Christ Mind, you are unified in thought, purpose, and understanding for the good of all humanity.

PRAYER FOR PEACE

In the name of the Lord Jesus Christ, we pray for and decree a permanent peace, uniting all the nations of the earth in a league of justice and righteousness, in which the life, liberty, and love of God shall be paramount.

LOWELL FILLMORE

THE ANSWER

When for a purpose
I had prayed and prayed and prayed
Until my words seemed worn and bare
    With arduous use,
And I had knocked and asked and knocked and asked again,
And all my fervor and persistence brought no hope,
I paused to give my weary brain a rest
And ceased my anxious human cry.
    In that still moment,
After self had tried and failed,
There came a glorious vision of God's power,
And, lo, my prayer was answered in that hour.

ELLA SYFERS SCHENCK

MORNING PRAYER

Lord, in the quiet of this morning hour
I come to Thee for peace, for wisdom, power
To view the world today through love-filled eyes;
Be patient, understanding, gentle, wise;
To see beyond what seems to be, and know
Thy children as Thou knowest them; and so
Naught but the good in anyone behold;
Make deaf my ears to slander that is told;
Silence my tongue to aught that is unkind;
Let only thoughts that bless dwell in my mind.
Let me so kindly be, so full of cheer,
That all I meet may feel Thy presence near.
O clothe me in Thy beauty, this I pray,
Let me reveal Thee, Lord, through all the day.

4. God Is the Health of His People

"God is the health of His people. God is infinite life. Let us hold to the Spirit of God, demonstrating itself in life everywhere. . . . The Spirit of Truth is in the midst of you. It is in you, and you will never have peace of mind, you will never have success in any way, you will never have health of body, you will never have anything satisfactory until you demonstrate its presence and its power in your life."

—*Charles Fillmore*

MYRTLE FILLMORE

HOW I FOUND HEALTH

I HAVE MADE what seems to me a discovery. I was fearfully sick; I had all the ills of mind and body that I could bear. Medicine and doctors ceased to give me relief, and I was in despair, when I found practical Christianity. I took it up and I was healed. I did most of the healing myself, because I wanted the understanding for future use. This is how I made what I call my discovery:

I was thinking about life. Life is everywhere—in worm and in man. "Then why does not the life in the worm make a body like man's?" I asked. Then I thought, "The worm has not as much sense as man." Ah! intelligence, as well as life, is needed to make a body. Here is the key to my discovery. Life has to be guided by intelligence in making all forms. The same law works in my own body. Life is simply a form of energy, and has to be guided and directed in man's body by his intelligence. How do we communicate intelligence? By thinking and talking, of course. Then it flashed upon me that I might talk to the life in every part of my body and have it do just what I wanted. I began to teach my body and got marvelous results.

I told the life in my liver that it was not torpid or inert, but full of vigor and energy. I told the life in my stomach that it was not weak or inefficient, but energetic, strong, and intelligent. I told the life in my abdomen that it was no longer infested with ignorant ideas of disease, put there by myself and by doctors, but that it was all athrill with the sweet, pure, wholesome energy of

God. I told my limbs that they were active and strong. I told my eyes that they did not see of themselves but that they expressed the sight of Spirit, and that they were drawing on an unlimited source. I told them that they were young eyes, clear, bright eyes, because the light of God shone right through them. I told my heart that the pure love of Jesus Christ flowed in and out through its beatings and that all the world felt its joyous pulsation.

I went to all the life centers in my body and spoke words of Truth to them—words of strength and power. I asked their forgiveness for the foolish, ignorant course that I had pursued in the past, when I had condemned them and called them weak, inefficient, and diseased. I did not become discouraged at their being slow to wake up, but kept right on, both silently and aloud, declaring the words of Truth, until the organs responded. And neither did I forget to tell them that they were free, unlimited Spirit. I told them that they were no longer in bondage to the carnal mind; that they were not corruptible flesh, but centers of life and energy omnipresent.

Then I asked the Father to forgive me for taking His life into my organism and there using it so meanly. I promised Him that I would never, never again retard the free flow of that life through my mind and my body by any false word or thought; that I would always bless it and encourage it with true thoughts and words in its wise work of building up my body temple; that I would use all diligence and wisdom in telling it just what I wanted it to do.

I also saw that I was using the life of the Father in thinking thoughts and speaking words, and I became very watchful as to what I thought and said.

I did not let any worried or anxious thoughts into my mind, and I stopped speaking gossipy, frivolous, petulant, angry words. I let a little prayer go up every hour that Jesus Christ would be with me and help me to think and speak only kind, loving, true words; and I am sure that He is with me, because I am so peaceful and happy now.

I want everybody to know about this beautiful, true law, and to use it. It is not a new discovery, but, when you use it and get the fruits of health and harmony it will seem new to you, and you will feel that it is your own discovery.

CHARLES FILLMORE

A SURE REMEDY

HERE IS a mental treatment that is guaranteed to cure every ill that flesh is heir to: Sit for half an hour every night and mentally forgive everyone against whom you have any ill will or antipathy. If you fear or if you are prejudiced against even an animal, mentally ask forgiveness of it and send it thoughts of love. If you have accused anyone of injustice, if you have discussed anyone unkindly, if you have criticized or gossiped about anyone, withdraw your words by asking him, in the silence, to forgive you. If you have had a falling out with friends or relatives, if you are at law or engaged in contention with anyone, do everything in your power to end the separation. See all things and all persons as they really are—pure Spirit—and send them your strongest thoughts of love. Do not go to bed any night feeling that you have an enemy in the world.

Be careful not to think a thought or to say a word that will offend. Be patient, loving, and kind, under all circumstances. You can do this if you are faithful to the silent hour, because there you will be helped to overcome the selfishness of the carnal sense.

There is an immutable law lying back of this healing method. God is love, and love is manifest as life. God is thus manifest in and through all His creations. If we do aught to cut off the love of any person we are cutting off the love of God; hence, we are cutting off the life that flows through all. When we, by withdrawal from our fellows, in any way cut the cords of love that bind us together as men and women, we at the same time sever

[141]

the arteries and veins through which the universal life flows. We then find ourselves mere bundles of strained nerves, trembling and shaking with fear and weakness, and finally dying for the lack of God's love. But omnipresent Spirit ever seeks to flow into us and to stimulate us in every faculty. We must, however, by our words and acts acknowledge this all-powerful Presence as the moving factor in our lives, because each of us has inherent free will, which welcomes or rejects all, even God not being excepted.

Self-condemnation is also a great error, leading to dire results. If you have accused yourself of ignorance, foolishness, fear, sickness, anxiety, poverty, anger, jealousy, stinginess, ambition, weakness, or if you are melancholy and indulge in the "blues," ask forgiveness, for each, of the loving Father in whose image and likeness you spiritually have perfect life. Say often to this omnipresence:

I do now sacrifice these human limitations unto Thee, O Father! I am obedient unto the law of my being, and I know that in Thee I am brave, true, energetic, wise, pure, perfect, strong, rich, and courageous. Thou art my almighty Resource, and I do trust Thee utterly.

ONE IS YOUR HEALER

REMEMBER that there are usually three possible methods of dealing with every question. Two of these are extremes, while the third is a method falling midway between them.

"What shall be my attitude toward doctors and material remedies since I am depending upon God for my health?" This is a question that often puzzles the Truth student. Every person has his choice of three answers.

Some have taken the extreme view that doctors are directly opposed to divine methods, and that they and all their devices should be shunned. Others are inclined to go to the opposite extreme and consider physicians as all-wise and almost superhuman in their ability to cure every ailment. These people run to the doctors for every little ache and pain. Neither of these viewpoints seems wise or satisfactory. The attitude of the Truth student toward the medical profession should be quite different from either of these.

A Truth student should realize that divine healing employs quite a different system from that used by all schools of medicine, each having its special methods. Medical science employs drugs, serums, lights, instruments, appliances. Divine healing employs right thinking and faith in God. The Christian metaphysician depends upon God directly for healing, while the physician depends upon God indirectly. Each school has its own method. There should be no hard feeling between schools, but a patient who is receptive toward spiritual healing should strengthen his faith in the healing power of God by depending upon Him.

There should be no condemnation in the mind of the Truth student for doctors or their methods, nor should he have any criticism for any student who calls on a doctor for help, nor for himself if he should ever feel it necessary to call upon a doctor.

But one who wishes divine healing should fix his faith so firmly on God as the one source of health that he does not waver. He should not divide his attention between the two methods. When a person realizes clearly that his life comes from God he will depend upon God and will feel that it is not necessary to depend upon any other means of healing.

Faith is such a powerful force in man that when he accepts God as the healing agent, so-called miracles will result. Jesus Christ, the great healer, promised that our prayers would be answered according to our faith. While a Truth student should have the most kindly feeling toward doctors at all times, he should not divide his faith between God and them.

We give thanks that there are so many efficient and able physicians, surgeons, and nurses, because the world needs them. Those who are not yet strong enough to trust God must have other help.

I am sure all doctors admit that they do not accomplish the healing but that the invisible forces of nature do the work. The doctor's work is to help make conditions favorable for these forces to do their best. That a person under a doctor's care can receive help through prayer is proved true every day. Often the hand of a surgeon is guided by prayer; but if we who know Truth continue to depend upon material means for our healing, how are we ever going to develop our faith and cultivate the healing power within us? If we would strengthen our faith we must begin to depend upon it and use the power of Spirit within us. The possibilities of spiritual healing are greater than those of any other method, because with God all things are possible.

If a mother did not let her little child try to walk because she feared it would be too difficult for the poor little thing to manage its feet, so far as she is concerned the child would never learn to walk. If we continually protect our faith from actual use by substituting material remedies for it, how shall we ever make it strong enough to serve us?

Since God life is manifest in every living thing and the effects of God wisdom may be seen on every hand directing the wonders of nature, the seasons, and the courses of the stars, there is no reason why we should not have implicit faith in God, who made us, to keep us in repair.

A man who has faith can endure much greater hardships than one who has no faith. A certain newspaper story tells of a group of men who were lost in the jungle. One had no faith and he died. The others had faith. They came through and got back to civilization. The person who has faith finds it easy to keep his head during great catastrophes. Faith is one of the powers by which man is able to co-operate with God.

According to the measure of our faith divine healing power becomes active in us. One who divides his faith between material remedies and God, doubting God's ability to heal, cannot expect to receive the good results that a unified and awakened faith would produce.

Fear and doubt are both enemies of health. We must be fearless even to the extent that the diagnosis (or the treatment prescribed) by a physician or surgeon does not frighten us. We must cultivate such an abiding faith that even the thought of a hospital cannot alarm us or shake our faith in God as the supreme healer working within to restore the body to perfection and wholeness. Thus our faith, kept free from doubt, confusion, or panic, works with the power of God to bring about the perfect healing either for ourself or for others.

We must not fear the doctor or accept his pronouncements as final when they are discouraging. We must realize that there is One who is greater than any material remedy, of whom we say, "Closer is He than breathing, and nearer than hands and feet," and with whom all things are possible. This invisible, all-powerful One accomplished marvelous healings through Jesus Christ two thousand years ago. Jesus testified that it was the Father within Him that did the work. In the Lord's Prayer, Jesus referred to Him as "our Father." Since He is our Father, He is in every one of us, ready to heal and bless us if we will but call upon Him.

Thousands of people are healed every year through the power of prayer. Thousands of unsolicited testimonials pour in to Unity every year praising God for healings that have been received through this divine power. This being so, we know that the heal-

ing power of God is a fact. When we ask for healing, God is ready
to heal, but we must make our mental condition right for Him to
reach us. Remember how perfect faith healed the woman who
merely touched the hem of Jesus' garment.

Worry, greed, anger, grief, and all emotional upsets prevent
the divine power from doing its perfect work in us. We must
learn to be peaceful, poised, and obedient to the Spirit within.
We must be patient and relaxed. We must have faith.

Healing played an important part in Jesus' ministry, and His
disciples also did healing. Doubtless the members of the early
Church depended upon God for their healings. As the years went
by the original healing faith seems to have been ignored, until
healing came to be thought of as pertaining to the soul and not to
the body. To excuse lack of faith some Christians have said that
Christ merely did the healing to prove that He was the Son of
God. But according to Matthew, Jesus said, "Heal the sick," and
in Luke we find this: "I send you forth . . . [to] heal the sick."
Jesus Christ and His healing ministry remain the same yesterday,
today, and forever.

There are wonderful healings taking place today. They are often referred to as miracles. But they are not miracles in the true
sense, because they are done according to law, but law that is
higher than the known laws of nature.

True healing belongs to God. All other methods are but patch-
work compared with His true healing power. When a skillful surgeon sets a bone, he can do no more. He must wait for the life
forces in the body to knit the parts of the bone together. If these
bodily forces do not function properly, then there is little he can
do to make the bone whole.

When a man cuts his finger he takes for granted that the cut
will grow together and heal, and so it does. The healing life in
the body is at work all the time, and it heals when it is not too
much inhibited by fear and other emotions. It is continually repairing many frazzled and ragged fringes that we never know
about. This service of nature is the working out of the perfect
idea of God's life in us, and by consciously co-operating with it
through harmonious thinking we may keep open the way for
God's perfect healing power to work in us in full measure.

Bless the doctors. Bless the hospitals. Bless the remedies, and co-operate in prayer with those whose faith is not strong enough to depend entirely upon God. But we urge every Truth student to strengthen his faith, to cultivate the true healing power within himself and thus be saved body and soul by the Christ indwelling in him; not merely saved after death but saved from error and sickness, saved in perfect health and eternal life, here and now.

CLARA PALMER

IT PAYS TO PRAY FOR HEALING

Do NOT BEWAIL conditions. Pray about them. Turn the light of Truth upon them. Turn the light of love and understanding upon them, and you will help to solve the conditions and eliminate disease and suffering.

Many years ago I was in a physical condition worse by far than death. Among the many friends who felt that my passing would be an act of divine mercy and the only way out for me, one with divine understanding began to promote the idea that instead of praying for my release through death it would be better to pray for my healing.

In those days Christian healing was not as freely accepted as it is today. It was because of love that this group of friends wanted to see me released; the condition was so hopeless, and the future loomed just a prolongation of suffering and helplessness. It is love, love ignorant of the divine power within the body to heal it, that makes many a person stand by the bedside of one near and dear witnessing the suffering that he is unable to relieve and praying, "Father, release this dear one quickly that his sufferings may cease."

In fact in the old days I had witnessed cases where passing on seemed the only way out for the patient, a blessed release. But since the time when that one single friend stood out for my recovery, insisting that it would pay to pray definitely for my healing, I have never accepted the idea that anything except wholeness, such wholeness as God alone can bestow, is the remedy for sickness.

[148]

It pays to pray for healing. No matter what the condition, verdict, or hopeless appearance, it pays to pray for healing. It pays to keep right on praying! Just review your school days in thought for a moment. In your class some children learned their arithmetic rapidly and could solve the problems almost instantly. Others were not so adept at problems, but they grasped grammar, geography, spelling, or drawing very quickly. The teaching was not given up because a child did not lay hold of a certain subject readily. Even so in healing we do not give up praying and praising God for wholeness because a soul does not immediately respond to the principle of new life and health.

Never say die! God is a God of life, a living God who has His being in you, in the one for whom you pray. Right there is a good foundation on which to base your prayer for healing, on which to base your faith. The healing Christ, the God of healing, is not apart from the one for whom you pray; He is not a mystical figure in a far-off heaven or a person who walked among men two thousand years ago. God, the God of eternal wholeness, the source of all life, Christ, the perfect expression of God life and wholeness is in you, in this loved one for whom you would pray.

Instead of slipping into the hopelessness of helpless negation stand on your consciousness of life in Christ, stand on your faith in God as a God of life, a God of the living, and hold your loved one in a thought such as this:

God is a God of life and wholeness. You have your being in Him, He has His being in you. In His life, by His life, through His life, because of His life, you now live. Wholly, completely, eternally you live. You are healed and fully restored by the quickening of God's life in you.

If the affirmative form of prayer is new to you and you are a bit cautious about using it, frame the words to meet your comprehension, but do not for an instant lower the standard of life, health, and wholeness in your thoughts or in your faith, in your conversation, ministrations, expectations, attitude. You see, prayer runs further than the mere speaking of words. Prayer extends into the activities that follow it, and if you would pray as Jesus prayed and get the results that Jesus got, you must do as He did and let the realization of the answered prayer become manifest through you in all that you think, say, and do. Such prayer is bound to quicken you and to quicken others for whom you pray, with whom you associate, of whom you think, with a stronger, clearer realization of health and wholeness.

Health is not a thing apart from God. Health is the first fruits of the consciousness quickened in His life. When you pray for health you are merely asking for the life of God to find perfect expression in you, through you, and in the one for whom you pray. You are never praying against God's will when you pray for healing, for a God who is life cannot will sickness and death, a God who is love cannot will suffering and destruction, a God who is faith cannot will uncertainty, doubt, and confusion. God uses man's extremity when through ignorance, fear, unrest, greed, and untruth it has come about as the level from which He lifts man up to the state of righteousness and wholeness again; but error is not, nor can it ever be, the outworking of the divine principle of life that in all Truth God is.

It pays to pray for healing! This day everything seems to be echoing this statement. As I write a train going east can be heard passing under the bridge about a half mile away. It has carried my thoughts away to the East, to the most courageous little girl I ever knew, who conquered a hopeless case of osteomyelitis through her tenacious faith in the healing life of God within her body, within the diseased bone. Today the child, a woman grown, rejoices in the freedom of a perfect body. To her it means something not to be a cripple. That child knew she could be healed because she knew me and knew how I had been healed.

From East Coast to West Coast my mind leaps to another girl of high-school age who has emerged from a frame and cast because she knew of the healing of the girl in the East. When told that she could not walk again she replied, "What God has done for that girl, God will do for me," and it has been done. East, west, north, south, it would have made no difference in which direction that train was moving, I should have known that there were people in the localities through which it passed who had been healed through prayer and faith in God.

It pays to pray for healing! No case is so grave or of such long standing, no physical inharmony is so slight, that it does not pay to pray for the healing of it. The healing power of God adapts itself just as thoroughly to our minute needs as to our critical ones, and it works just as efficiently in the gravest complications as it does in cases of the slightest need for healing.

Wherever there is any need for healing and whatever its degree, cause, or appearance, it pays to pray about it and to pray instantly. A need for healing is an opportunity to experience an exquisite quickening of God life. You cannot pray for healing either for yourself or another without releasing a clean, sweet current of pure, upbuilding God life in your consciousness. You cannot experience a healing without its influence benefiting not just one person but many.

It pays to pray for healing, and the dividends accruing from it can be traced back to the days when God healed the Children of Israel. They mount in number from the ministry of Jesus Christ to the present time. How many cripples, think you, have stood upright on their feet and walked since Peter took one by the hand and said, "In the name of Jesus Christ of Nazareth, walk." What was done through prayer and faith for one cripple can be done for all. The healing power of the Almighty is not withheld. In each and every person it is the life-renewing, health-sustaining power of God given to each one to use.

How many eyes have been opened, how many have been benefited, how many pairs of glasses have been discarded, how many times has vision been corrected since Jesus Christ opened the eyes of the blind? One healing begets another. The healings that took place in the days of Jesus Christ startled the world. Have they ever ceased? No, they are more numerous today than ever before. Next year, next century, they will be more numerous still, for the healing principle set in motion through prayer and faith is the principle of divine life. It is God expressing Himself as wholeness through the minds and bodies of the people.

Your faith will never grow through non-use. Use your faith. Glorify God with your healing prayers. Even though the Truth you have learned seems but an infinitesimal gleam at the moment, put it to work. Pray for the healing of the people. Pray for the healing of the nations. Many will be quickened, many will be healed, many will call you blessed because of the unifying, restorative life of Spirit that you shared through your healing prayers and faith and word.

You are a lamp of God, and when you let His light of wholeness shine through you, you help to fill the world with the power and the glory of His healing presence. You help to open the eyes of the blind so that they may see with clear vision, you help to straighten and free the cripple, you help to heal the wounds of heart, mind, and body, you help to lift the race up into the consciousness of health, unity, and wholeness.

It pays to pray for healing, and there are thousands who long to be healed! Will you unite with me each day in a prayer for healing for all who need it? Nationality, religious creed, color, social condition—none of these things are a barrier to the healing love of God. The greater the number who pray for healing the larger the multitudes who will be healed, for prayer is educational. You cannot pray heartily for wholeness without gaining knowledge, for the light of divine wholeness will pour into your mind and heart. The knowledge of God as life, the knowledge of Jesus Christ as the divine healer and helper of the race will quicken you, and you will see and understand many healing points that had been incomprehensible to you before. You will move toward the goal of all-inclusive love, life, and eternal wholeness with the throngs who are today following the Christ, the throngs who have been healed, who are being healed, who will be healed by the love and understanding and power of Almighty God.

The power within you that causes you to pray warrants the answer to your prayer. It pays to pray for healing!

H. B. JEFFERY

A TRANSCENDENT TREATMENT

"As Moses lifted up the serpent in the wilderness,
even so must the Son of man be lifted up."

Beloved of God—greeting!
In my integrity within me, where I know and see as God,
 I know and see you, O beloved, to be free, wise, and immortal!
I see you unfettered and unbound, triumphant! glorious! splendid!
I see you unweighted by human thought of limitation,
 unweighted by matter!
I see you unbound, undiseased, buoyant!
I see you strong! mighty! forceful! powerful! divine!
I see your eye lit with fire from on high!
I see your tongue tipped with celestial instructions!
I behold you bright! joyous!
I see you victorious! undaunted!
I see you spotless! beautiful!
I see you deathless, abiding!
I see you flawless! fearless! transcending yourself
 and all your affairs—independent!
I see you smiling! sound! sane! strong!
I see you to be the strong son of God, brother
 of Jesus Christ and joint heir of the Father to
 the kingdom!
I see you alive with God and upheld by His free
 Spirit forever!
All the world sees you as I see you, now and
 evermore.

R. H. GRENVILLE

GOD IS WITH YOU

God is with you where you are,
    In the busy thoroughfare,
In the watches of the night
    You are in His loving care.

Oh, what peace of mind is yours
    When this truth is understood:
There is nothing anywhere
    To divide you from your good!

In the heavens, on the earth,
    Close beside you or afar,
All is well with you, beloved;
    God is with you where you are.

5. Plenty Everywhere

"In your mind see plenty everywhere. Yes, it is hard sometimes to overcome the thought that there is not enough, for it is an insidious thought that has been in consciousness for a long time. But it can be done. It has been done and is being done by others. The prosperity law is not a theory but a demonstrated fact, as thousands can testify. Now is the time to open your mind and to see plenty."

—*Charles Fillmore*

JOHN DAVIS

A FORMULA FOR PROSPERITY

VARIOUS SCHEMES have been worked out for getting rich quick. Most of them fail, but there is one formula that has never yet failed to enrich the person who used it. It is as certain in its operation as the law of gravitation because it is based upon principles that are as sure and unfailing as any physical law. It is God's own prosperity plan and it has proved itself in actual practice many times.

Take the case of Kenneth S. Keyes as an example. Keyes decided to go to Florida to get in on the boom. The boom burst just about the time he arrived in Miami and he found himself in bad shape financially. But after a while he happened upon this prosperity formula. The first year he used it his income increased 60 per cent. The next year his income jumped up 100 per cent. It has increased until now the Keyes Company is the largest real estate company in the State of Florida and in 1945 grossed over thirteen million dollars.

Mr. Keyes taught the formula to one of his salesmen who found himself in debt. Within one year the salesman had paid off his indebtedness and had a sizable bank account. He became so successful that he went into business for himself and was soon making more than fifteen thousand dollars a year.

Or consider the case of R. G. LeTourneau. About twenty-five years ago, in early middle age, he found himself heavily in debt. He had a family to support and only a grammar school education. His case looked hopeless. But he too discovered this formula and

put it to work. Today he is head of the company that is the world's
largest maker of earth-moving machinery and does well over forty
million dollars worth of business annually. He has established
schools for underprivileged children. He has founded the world's
largest charitable organization, the LeTourneau Foundation. He
owns three airplanes and travels an average of twenty thousand
miles a month.

John D. Rockefeller started using this formula when he was
earning less than five dollars a week. William Colgate happened
to learn of it when he left home penniless to go out into the world
and seek his fortune. He founded one of the largest soap businesses
in the world. Heinz pickles are known all over the world but it is
not generally known that Heinz used this formula to build his
success. Kraft cheese is a household word today. Mr. Kraft also
learned about the formula in his early business career. The list of
successful men who have used it would be too long to print here.

One of the most amazing things about the formula is that more
people do not use it. For it is no closely guarded secret. You yourself have heard of it many times. But perhaps it seemed too simple.
Perhaps you could see no reason why it should work. Perhaps you
have never analyzed the principles that make the formula work.
The purpose of this article is not to introduce you to some new
secret but to induce you to try an old one.

The formula is simple. It consists in taking God into partnership and agreeing to give this Partner ten per cent of the proceeds
of your business. Ten per cent isn't much to give a partner in
business, especially a partner who is all-wise and all-powerful.

The divine principles under which this formula operates are
not unusual or mysterious but can be observed functioning
throughout nature. They are: (1) There is one basic substance
whose source is God. This one substance manifests itself in various
forms such as energy, health, prosperity, sustenance, etc. Money
is only a symbol of one of the forms of this one substance. (2) This
basic substance, regardless of the form it may take, must *flow
through* some channel or be provided with an outlet as well as an
inlet. (3) Before this substance can be available a channel must
be prepared for it. (4) There is a basic unity underlying all, which
inseparably unites the good of the individual with the good of the
whole.

In considering the "flow through," think for a moment of a large water wheel with millions of tons of water backed up behind it. The inlet is open. But the outlet is closed so that the water cannot flow. As long as this condition exists the wheel can realize no power. Or, consider what happens when you turn on an electric switch. The electricity is there in the wire all the time, but when the switch is off you have stopped it from flowing. When you throw the switch you open the circuit so the electrical power can flow through. Before our lungs can be filled with air they must first be emptied, and to realize the power of the divine substance we must open our outlet gate and allow it to flow through us.

Christ understood this law when He instructed us to "Give, and it shall be given unto you" and stated, "It is more blessed to give than to receive." The influx of divine ideas, which is the basis of all prosperity, obeys this law. Shortly after LeTourneau started tithing he received an idea, apparently out of the thin air, concerning a new type of road machine. This idea started him on his road to fortune, and since that time he has continued to receive the kind of ideas he needed when he needed them. One of his engineers told me, "We don't know where he gets all those ideas of his, but most of them are not only good but entirely new and revolutionary."

Before we can receive divine substance we must prepare a receptacle for it.

The receptacle for divine substance, in whatever form, is always a need for that substance which has been created in accordance with its legitimate use. Consider, for example, how this works out in the case of the polar bear, whose white coat is provided automatically simply because he needs it.

Tithing creates this legitimate need for more prosperity; the prosperity flows to us automatically. Spending money recklessly or foolishly will not have this same result. This does not create a legitimate need; rather it is apt to leave us needy. Just as we would not give a child ten dollars to spend on lollipops, God will not increase our supply merely because we spend our money foolishly on ourselves. Legitimate use is a condition which Christ stressed. Using a portion of our income to further the spiritual evolution of man or to help our brother in some other way is righteousness.

There is no sin in being rich. To be rich is sinful only when we fail to use our riches properly. Until it is used, wealth does no one any good, not even the man who owns it. In Jesus Christ's parable of the talents, the servants who used their talents were rewarded with more; but the servant who buried his talent in the ground had even that one talent taken from him.

There is a basic unity which makes the good of the individual the good of the whole.

There is one great inclusive whole in which all individuals are parts, just as the individual cells of the human body join together to make one man. Jesus used the phrase, "Thou art made whole," in curing disease. The same principles that are used in healing the body work in healing lack of prosperity. Since we are all but "members" of the one body, as St. Paul expressed it, we cannot help others without helping ourselves. When the hand pulls a thorn from the foot the hand is also helping itself, for it is helping the body upon which both the hand and the foot are dependent for their existence. Jesus Christ illustrated this unity by the statement: "I am the true vine . . . ye are the branches." And when each man ceases to regard himself as a separate, individual entity, entirely apart from mankind, and comes to see himself as but one of the "branches" or members which make up the body of humanity, he cannot fail to see that whatever he does to help others helps himself and whatever he does to hurt others inevitably hurts himself.

When we tithe we are helping other members of the great body of mankind of which we are also a part. This being true, it is literally impossible for us not to realize beneficial results.

This formula worked for Henry P. Crowell of Quaker Oats, M. W. Baldwin, the railway equipment manufacturer, A. A. Hyde, the man who made Mentholatum, and many other successful men. In a few years after he began tithing Mr. Keyes found that the tenth he gave to God was more than his entire income had ever been before. William Colgate's business prospered so much from tithing that soon he was giving more than a tenth. He kept increasing the amount until finally he was giving half his income and still he prospered. At last he gave his entire income.

This formula is waiting for you to use it. A good agent or broker would charge you much more than ten per cent to obtain additional business for you. He could never give you the "breaks," "hunches," new ideas, and all sorts of good things that your unseen partner can bring you. God Himself has guaranteed the formula: "Prove me now herewith, saith Jehovah of hosts, if I will not open you the windows of heaven, and pour you out a blessing, that there shall not be room enough *to receive it*."

LOWELL FILLMORE

BLESS YOUR MONEY

MANIFEST THINGS may be thought of as symbols that
represent intangible things. One manifest thing may serve as a
symbol of a number of different mental and spiritual conditions.
For instance, water used in baptism may be thought of as representing a mental cleansing process. To the engineer, water may
represent power; to the soul athirst, it may represent refreshment
and inspiration.

The fact that one material substance may represent so many
different conditions should not be confusing. We are not perplexed
when a certain word in our language represents many meanings.
For example, the word *cleave* has opposite meanings: "to part or
divide by force," and "to adhere closely." The word *draft* has many
meanings; such as "act of drawing a load," "act of selecting soldiers," "the quantity drawn in at one time in drinking," "a sketch,"
"an order for payment of money," "a current of air moving through
an enclosed place," "the depth of water necessary to float a vessel,"
the thing "drawn directly from a barrel." All these meanings and
a number of others may be expressed by the one word *draft*. We
are not puzzled when the word appears in a sentence, because the
context makes its meaning clear. As a word may represent many
different things, so the physical thing known as water may symbolize different mental or spiritual characteristics.

A rock may represent faith, solidity, a burden, or even danger,
according to the idea one has in mind. Jesus spoke of Peter as the

rock upon which He would build His church. We think of Peter as representing faith. We sometimes speak of "standing on a rock" when we feel that we are well established in understanding. Again, when we think someone is heading for disaster we say he is going "on the rocks."

There should be no confusion because of the varied symbolism of which one object is capable. Money may represent several mental and spiritual qualities. It may symbolize God's bounty. It may merely mean poor reward for hard work, or it may represent a good time that we are to enjoy. Money may even represent poverty when we believe it is hard to get. Money represents a wide range of ideas, from those of the man who thinks it is the most worthwhile thing in life down to the one who believes it is the root of all evil. He who wishes to be on friendly terms with money, yet not dominated by it, should think of it as a symbol of God's abundant, inexhaustible substance. Whether the amount of money a person has in his possession be large or small, it may represent God's inexhaustible abundance if he desires to have it perform that office for him. He may consider it a messenger from God assuring him of God's loving care and His ability to supply all our needs. He may acknowledge this messenger and accept the promise contained in the message that each coin brings, by blessing all money that comes to him.

Even though money may seem to come to us as the result of hard work, we should see back of it the spiritual source of all good. Try to think of every cent you get as coming straight from God's loving hand. If we look beyond the employer to our loving Father-God and thank Him for this manifestation of His supply, and then bless it, thinking of it as more than a hard-earned salary, we can magnify its usefulness. In doing this we magnify our ability to receive more of the good that God has prepared for us; we bring ourselves into a closer understanding and contact with the great invisible storehouse. When we bless His little messengers we bless Him who sends them.

Blessing money in the name of God stamps that money with a new spiritual value. A dollar to which spiritual value has been imparted is capable of bringing us much greater good than it could bring us if it were a mere material dollar. "It is the spirit that giveth life." When spiritual blessings are placed on material objects, such objects are surrounded with spiritual, quickening energy. Money of itself can do nothing. It has value only because the mind of man has set a value on it. By blessing it we still further enhance its value. Why not treat our money in a large way by letting it represent God's values in addition to man's values! One may not feel like blessing a mere penny when one receives it, yet a penny is just as much a symbol of God's substance as is a hundred-dollar bill.

Do not forget that in blessing our substance we are dealing with ideas and not with material objects. We can place as high a spiritual value upon ideas as we choose. We can see our money as representing supreme value since it comes from God. If we can do this, we shall find that the money coming to us will do many things for us that we did not dream it could do.

It is a good idea to set aside one tenth of one's money income for the Lord's work, especially blessing it. However, the blessing will do much good whether you tithe or not. Also it is helpful to bless all money spent. The blessing does not need to be spoken audibly, just a silent blessing will do. Let it go with the payment of a bill, a purchase, a gift, whatever the money may be used for. Send each coin on its way as a messenger of God's abundance to others and the channels for the circulation of substance through your affairs will be widened. Like an electric current, your good flows in a circuit. You receive freely from God, and you must give freely. What you spend should go freely with a blessing and not grudgingly. You complete the circuit by giving in the same spirit of thankfulness in which you receive. This free attitude opens the way for a larger current of giving and receiving to come into your life. "I will bless thee . . . and be thou a blessing."

The power of blessing is a mystery. We do not know how it works, but we know that it does work. A wholehearted blessing not only helps our affairs, but it fills us with an inner light that seems to satisfy our soul and make us happy. In blessing we are blessed.

You will never be sorry for having pronounced a blessing upon anybody or anything. Bless even what seems to be not good, and by the mysterious power that blessing brings it will be made to bring good to you, in addition to affording you the wonderful opportunity of experiencing the joy that comes from blessing. Bless the good and it will increase. Bless what seems to be evil, and something good will come out of it to justify your blessing.

CHARLES FILLMORE

GOD WILL PAY YOUR DEBTS

"Forgive us our debts, as we also have forgiven our
debtors." In these words Jesus expressed an infallible law of mind,
the law that one idea must be dissolved before another can take
its place. If you have in your mind any thought that someone has
wronged you, you cannot let in the cleansing power of Spirit and
the richness of spiritual substance until you have cast out the idea
of the wrong, have forgiven it fully. You may be wondering why
you have failed to get spiritual illumination or to find the consciousness of spiritual substance. Perhaps the reason is here: a lack of
room for the true thoughts because other thoughts fill your mind.
If you are not receiving the spiritual understanding you feel you
should have, you should search your mind carefully for unforgiving
thoughts. "Thoughts are things" and occupy space in the mind
realm. They have substance and form and may easily be taken as
permanent by one not endowed with spiritual discernment. They
bring forth fruit according to the seed ideas planted in the mind,
but they are not enduring unless founded in Spirit. Thoughts are
alive and are endowed by the thinker with a secondary thinking
power; that is, the thought entity that the I AM forms assumes an
ego and begins to think on its own account. Thoughts also think
but only with the power you give to them.

Tell me what kind of thoughts you are holding about yourself
and your neighbors and I can tell you just what you may expect
in the way of health, finances, and harmony in your home. Are
you suspicious of your neighbors? You cannot love and trust in

[166]

God if you hate and distrust men. The two ideas love and hate, or trust and mistrust, simply cannot both be present in your mind at one time, and when you are entertaining one, you may be sure the other is absent. Trust other people and use the power that you accumulate from that act to trust God. There is magic in it: it works wonders; love and trust are dynamic, vital powers. Are you accusing men of being thieves, and do you fear that they are going to take away from you something that is your own? With such a thought generating fear and even terror in your mind and filling your consciousness with darkness, where is there room for the Father's light of protection? Rather build walls of love and substance around yourself. Send out swift, invisible messengers of love and trust for your protection. They are better guards than policemen or detectives.

Do not judge others as regards their guilt or innocence. Consider yourself and how you stand in the sight of the Father for having thoughts about another's guilt. Begin your reform with yourself. That means much to one who enjoys an understanding of mind and its laws, though it may mean little to the ordinary individual. He who knows himself superficially, just his external personality, thinks he has reformed when he has conformed to the moral and governmental laws. He may even be filled with his own self-righteousness and daily lift up his voice to praise God that he is not as other men are, that he has forgiven men their transgressions. He looks upon all men who do not conform to his ideas of morality and religion as being sinners and transgressors and thanks God for his own insight and keenness. But he is not at peace. Something seems lacking. God does not talk to him "face to face," because the mind, where God and man meet, is darkened by the murky thought that other men are sinners. Our first work in any demonstration is to contact God, therefore we must forgive all men their transgressions. Through this forgiveness we cleanse our mind so that the Father can forgive us our own transgressions.

Our forgiving "all men" includes ourselves. You must also forgive yourself. Let the finger of denial erase every sin or "falling short" that you have charged up against yourself. Pay your debt by saying to that part of yourself which you think has fallen short: *"Thou art made whole: sin no more, lest a worse thing befall thee."* Then "loose him, and let him go." Treat sin as a mental transgression, instead of considering it as a moral defection. Deny in thought all tendency to the error way and hold yourself firmly to the Christ Spirit, which is your divine self. Part company forever with "accusing conscience." Those who have resolved to sin no more have nothing in common with guilt.

"Shall I be in debt as long as I hold debts against others?" We find this to be the law of mind: a thought of debt will produce debt. So long as you believe in debt you will go into debt and accumulate the burdens that follow that thought. Whoever has not forgiven all men their debts is likely to fall into debt himself. Does this mean that you should give receipted bills to all those who owe you? No. That would not be erasing the idea of debt from your mind. First deny in mind that any man or woman owes you anything. If necessary, go over your list of names separately and sincerely forgive the idea of debt which you have been attaching to each person named. More bills may be collected in this way than in any other, for many of these people will pay what they owe when you send them this forgiving thought.

Debt is a contradiction of the universal equilibrium, and there is no such thing as lack of equilibrium in all the universe. Therefore in Spirit and in Truth there is no debt. However, men hold on to an idea of debt, and this idea is responsible for a great deal of sorrow and hardship. The true disciple realizes his supply in the consciousness of omnipresent, universally possessed abundance. Spirit substance is impartial and owned in common, and no idea of debt can enter into it.

Debts exist in the mind and in the mind is the proper place to begin liquidating them. These thought entities must be abolished in mind before their outer manifestations will pass away and stay away. The world can never be free from the bondage of financial obligations until men erase from their minds the thoughts of "mine and thine" which generate debts and interest. Analyze the idea of debt and you will see that it involves an idea of lack. Debt is a thought of lack with absence at both ends; the creditor thinks he lacks what is owed him and the debtor thinks he lacks what is necessary to pay it, else he would discharge the obligation rather than continue it. There is error at both ends of the proposition and nothing in the middle. This being true, it should be easy to dissolve the whole idea that anyone owes us or that we owe anyone anything. We should fill our mind with thoughts of all-sufficiency, and where there is no lack there can be no debts. Thus we find that the way to pay our debts is by filling our mind with the substance of ideas that are the direct opposite of the debts.

Thoughts of abundance will more quickly and surely bring what is yours to you than any thoughts you can hold about debtors discharging their obligations to you. See substance everywhere and affirm it, not only for yourself but for everyone else. Especially affirm abundance for those whom you have held in the thought of owing you. Thus you will help them pay their debts more easily than if you merely erased their names from your books of accounts receivable. Help pay the other fellow's debts by forgiving him his debts and declaring for him the abundance that is his already in spirit. The thought of abundance will also bring its fruits into your own life. Let the law of plenty work itself out in you and in your affairs. This is the way the Father forgives your debts: not by canceling them on His books but by erasing them from His mind. He remembers them no more against you when you deny their reality. The Father is the everywhere present Spirit in which all that appears has its origin. God's love sees you always well, happy, and abundantly provided for; but God's wisdom demands that order and right relation exist in your mind before it may become manifest in your affairs as abundance. His love would give you your every desire, but His wisdom ordains that you forgive your debtors before your debts are forgiven.

To remedy any state of limited finances or ill-health that has been brought about by worry one must begin by eliminating the worry that is the original cause. One must free one's mind from the burden of debt before the debt can be paid. Many people have found that the statement "*I owe no man anything but love*" has helped them greatly to counteract this thought of debt. As they used the words their mind was opened to an inflow of divine love and they faithfully co-operated with the divine law of forgiveness in thought, word, and deed. They built up such a strong consciousness of the healing and enriching power of God's love that they could live and work peacefully and profitably with their associates. Thus renewed constantly in health, in faith, and in integrity, they were able to meet every obligation that came to them.

The statement "*I owe no man anything but love*" does not mean that we can disclaim owing our creditors money or try to evade the payment of obligations we have incurred. The thing denied is the burdensome thought of debt or of lack. The work of paying debts is an inner work having nothing to do with the debts already owed but with the wrong ideas that produced them. When one holds to the right ideas, burdensome debts will not be contracted. Debts are produced by thoughts of lack, impatient desire, and covetousness. When these thoughts are overcome, debts are overcome, forgiven, and paid in full, and we are free from them for all time.

Your thoughts should at all times be worthy of your highest self, your fellow man, and God. The thoughts that most frequently work ill to you and your associates are thoughts of criticism and condemnation. Free your mind of them by holding the thought: *"There is now no condemnation in Christ Jesus."* Fill your mind with thoughts of divine love, justice, peace, and forgiveness. This will pay your debts of love, which are the only debts you really owe. Then see how quickly and easily and naturally all your outer debts will be paid and all inharmonies of mind, body, and affairs smoothed out at the same time. Nothing will so quickly enrich your mind and free it from every thought of lack as the realization of divine love. Divine love will quickly and perfectly free you from the burden of debt and heal you of your physical infirmities, often caused by depression, worry, and financial fear. Love will bring your own to you, adjust all misunderstandings, and make your life and affairs healthy, happy, harmonious, and free, as they should be. Love indeed is the "fulfilment of the law."

The way is now open for you to pay your debts. Surrender them to God along with all your doubts and fears. Follow the light that is flooding into your mind. God's power, love, and wisdom are here, for His kingdom is within you. Give Him full dominion in your life and affairs. Give Him your business, your family affairs, your finances, and let Him pay your debts. He is even now doing it, for it is His righteous desire to free you from every burden, and He is leading you out of the burden of debt, whether of owing or being owed. Meet every insidious thought, such as "I can't," "I don't know how," "I can't see the way," with the declaration: "Jehovah is my shepherd; I shall not want." You "shall not want" the wisdom, the courage to do, or the substance to do with when you have once fully realized the scope of the vast truth that Almightiness is leading you into "green pastures . . . beside still waters."

In the kingdom of Truth and reality, ideas are the coin of the realm. You can use the new ideas that divine wisdom is now quickening in your mind and start this very moment to pay your debts. Begin by thanking God for your freedom from the debt-burden thought. This is an important step in breaking the shackles of debt. The funds to pay all your bills may not suddenly appear in a lump sum; but as you watch and work and pray, holding yourself in the consciousness of God's leadership and His abundance, you will notice your funds beginning to grow "here a little, there a little," and increasing more and more rapidly as your faith increases and your anxious thoughts are stilled. For with the increase will come added good judgment and wisdom in the management of your affairs. Debt is soon vanquished when wisdom and good judgment are in control.

Do not yield to the temptation of "easy-payment plans." Any payment that drains your pay envelope before you receive it is not an easy payment. Do not allow false pride to tempt you to put on a thousand-dollar front on a hundred-dollar salary. There may be times when you are tempted to miss paying a bill in order to indulge a desire for some thing. This easily leads one into the habit of putting off paying, which fastens the incubus of debt on people before they realize it. It is the innocent-appearing forerunner of the debt habit and debt thought that may rob you of peace, contentment, freedom, integrity, and prosperity for years to come. The Divine Mind within you is much stronger than this desire mind of the body. Turn to it in a time like this, and affirm: *"Jehovah is my shepherd; I shall not want"* this thing until it comes to me in divine order.

Bless your creditors with the thought of abundance as you begin to accumulate the wherewithal to pay off your obligations. Keep the faith they had in you by including them in your prayer for increase. Begin to free yourself at once by doing all that is possible with the means you have, and as you proceed in this spirit the way will open for you to do more; for through the avenues of Spirit more means will come to you and every obligation will be met.

If you are a creditor, be careful of the kind of thoughts you hold over your debtor. Avoid the thought that he is unwilling to pay you or that he is unable to pay you. One thought holds him in dishonesty and the other holds him subject to lack, and either of them tends to close the door to the possibility of his paying you soon. Think well and speak well of all those who owe you. If you talk about them to others avoid calling them names that you would not apply to yourself. Cultivate a genuine feeling of love for them and respect their integrity in spite of all appearances. Declare abundant supply for them and thus help them to prosper. Pray and work for their good as well as for your own, for yours is inseparable from theirs. You owe your debtor quite as much as he owes you and yours is a debt of love. Pay your debt to him and he will pay his to you. This rule of action never fails.

Far-seeing Christians look forward to an early resumption of the economic system inaugurated by the early followers of Jesus Christ. They had all things in common and no man lacked anything. But before we can have a truly Christian community founded upon a spiritual basis we must be educated into a right way of thinking about finances. If we should all get together and divide all our possessions, it would be but a short time until those who have the prevailing financial ideas would manipulate our finances, and plethora on one hand and lack on the other would again be established.

The world cannot be free from the bondage of debt and interest until men start to work in their minds to erase those ideas from consciousness. If the United States forgave the nations of Europe all their debts and wiped the books clear, the law would not necessarily be fulfilled; for there would probably remain an idea that they still owed us and that we had made a sacrifice in canceling the obligations. We should not feel very friendly about it and would not truly forgive them, and in that case the error thought would be carried on. We must first forgive the error thought that they owe us money and that we would be losing money by canceling the debts. The man who is forced to forgive a debt does not forgive it.

Above all we should fill our mind with the consciousness of that divine abundance which is so manifest everywhere in the world today. There is as much substance as there ever was, but its free flow has been interfered with through selfishness. We must rid our mind of the idea of selfish acquisitiveness that is so dominant in the race thought, and in that way do our part in the great work of freeing the world from avarice. It is the duty of every Christian metaphysician to help in the solution of this problem by affirming that the universal Spirit of supply is now becoming manifest as a distributing energy the world over; that all stored-up, hoarded, vicious thoughts are being dissolved; that all people have things in common; that no one anywhere lacks anything; and that the divine law of distribution of infinite supply, demonstrated by Jesus Christ, is now being made manifest throughout the world. "The earth is the Lord's, and the fulness thereof."

There is a legitimate commerce that is carried on by means of what is called credit. Credit is a convenience to be used by those who appreciate its value and are careful not to abuse it, for to do so would be to ruin it. However, many persons are not equipped to use the credit system to advantage and are likely to abuse it. In the first place, few individuals are familiar with the intricacies of sound credit systems and often assume obligations without being certain of their ability to meet them, especially should some unforeseen complication arise. Frequently an individual loses all that he invests and finds himself involved in a burden of debt in addition. Such things are not in divine order and are largely responsible for retarding prosperity.

No one should assume an obligation unless he is prepared to meet it promptly and willingly when it comes due. One who knows God as his unfailing resource can be assured of his supply when it is needed. Then why should he plunge into debt when he is confident of his daily supply without debt? There are no creditors or debtors in God's kingdom. If you are in that kingdom, you need no longer be burdened with the thought of debt either as debtor or creditor. Under divine law there is no reaching out for things that are beyond one's present means. There is an ever-increasing richness of consciousness coming from the certain knowledge that God is infinite and unfailing supply. Outer things conform to the inner pattern, and riches are attracted to the one who lives close to the unselfish heart of God. His environment is made beautiful by the glory of the Presence and there is satisfying and lasting prosperity in his affairs.

There is but one way to be free from debt. That is the desire to be free, followed by the realization that debt has no legitimate place in God's kingdom and that you are determined to erase it entirely from your mind. As you work toward your freedom you will find it helpful to have daily periods for meditation and prayer. Do not concentrate on debts or spoil your prayers by constantly thinking of debts. Think of that which you want to demonstrate, not that from which you seek freedom. When you pray, thank the Father for His care and guidance, for His provision and plenty, for His love and wisdom, for His infinite abundance and your privilege to enjoy it.

Here are a few prosperity prayers that may help establish you in the truth of plenty and erase the error thought of debt. They are offered as suggestions for forming your own prayers but may be used as given with excellent results.

I am no longer anxious about finances; Thou art my all-sufficiency in all things.

The Spirit of honesty, promptness, efficiency, and order is now expressed in me and in all that I do.

I am free from all limitations of mortal thought about quantities and values. The superabundance of riches of the Christ Mind are now mine, and I am prospered in all my ways.

MYRTLE FILLMORE

PROSPERITY IN THE HOME

THERE NEED BE no poor homes. Every home can be prosperous. You can prove this by getting busy along the right lines. Every visible item of wealth in the world today can be traced to its invisible source. Food comes from grains. Grain is planted in the earth; but who sees or knows the secret quickening that touches the seed and makes it to bear a hundredfold? No one. That is all carried out in the invisible source of things; but the result of an unseen force acting upon the grain is food for the multitude.

The physical substance which we call the earth is the visible form of the spiritual substance that pervades all things. The grain is put into the earth; the quickening thought that runs through the spiritual universe causes the life germ to start and to take hold of the physical substance that nourishes it.

The word is the seed. The word is dropped into the spiritual substance. It germinates. It grows. It brings forth after its kind. "Do men gather grapes of thorns, or figs of thistles?"

You who farm, and you who garden, choose the seed for next year's planting from the finest specimens of this year's crop. You reject every defective seed that you detect. If you think that your own harvest does not give you the right seed for the coming planting, you send abroad for the best to be had. In this way you make sure of the nature of your coming crop.

If you want prosperity in your home, you will have to exercise the same intelligent discrimination in your word seed that the farmer uses in selecting his seed.

When you talk and talk "hard times," you are sowing "hard times" seed. By the sure law of growth and yield, what kind of harvest will you reap? If a farmer sowed thistle seed, and then complained that his field did not yield him wheat, you would say: "The foolish man! If he wanted wheat, why didn't he sow wheat?"

You can begin now to bring prosperity into your home. The first thing for you to do is to discard the words that have in them the idea of poverty, and then select carefully the words that hold the idea of plenty. Never make an assertion, no matter how true it may look on the surface, that you do not want continued or reproduced in your home. Do not say that money is scarce; the very statement of such a thought will send money fleeing from your fingers. Never say that times are hard with you; these words will tighten your purse strings until Omnipotence will be powerless to loosen them to slip in even a dime.

Begin right now to talk plenty, think plenty, give thanks for plenty.

The spiritual substance out of which visible wealth comes is never depleted. It is right with you all the time. It will respond to your faith in it. It will yield according to your demands upon it. It is never affected by your ignorant talk about hard times, but you are affected because your ideas govern your demonstration. The unfailing resource is always willing to give. It has no choice in the matter; it must give, for that is its nature. Pour your living words of faith into substance, and you will be prospered, though all the banks in the world shut their doors. Turn the energy of your thought upon "plenty" ideas, and you will have plenty, no matter what people about you are saying.

Another thing: you are not to take your prosperity as a matter of fact. You are to be as deeply grateful for every demonstration as you would be for some unexpected treasure poured into your lap. You are to expect prosperity because you are keeping the law, and you are to give thanks for every blessing that you gain. This will keep your heart fresh. Thanksgiving for good may be likened to the rain that falls upon the ready soil, refreshing vegetation and increasing the productiveness of the soil. When Jesus Christ had only a little supply from which to feed a multitude, He gave thanks for what He had, and that little grew into such an abundance that all were satisfied, and much was left over.

Blessing has not lost its power since the times when Jesus Christ used it. Try it and prove its efficacy. The same power of multiplication is within it. Praise and thanksgiving have within them the quickening spiritual power that produces growth and increase.

Never condemn anything in your home. If you want new articles of furniture or clothing to take the place of those which may be at the point of giving out, do not talk about what you have as being old or shabby. Watch your ideas; see yourself clothed as befits a child of the King, and your house furnished as pleases your ideals. Use the patience, the wisdom, and the assiduity that the farmer employs in his planting and cultivating, and your crop will be as sure as his.

The truths that are here spoken are vitalized and energized by the living Spirit. Your mind and heart are now open and receptive to the ideas that will inspire you with the understanding of the potency of your own thought and word. You are prospered. Your home has become a magnet, drawing to it all good from the unfailing, inexhaustible reservoir of supply. Your increase comes through your righteousness.

"The blessing of Jehovah, it maketh rich;
And he addeth no sorrow therewith."

MARCUS BACH

THE LORD'S SIDE OF
THE LEDGER

FOLLOWING my talk at a Rotary Club meeting, one of the
members called me aside.

"I happen to be the town banker," he said, "and since you are
interested in religion, I have a question. Did you have a chance to
get acquainted with the man who introduced you this noon?"

"Just casually," I replied. "He wanted to know something about
me and my work."

"But did you find out anything about *him?*"

"No, I didn't. Why?"

"Well, sir," said the banker, "that fellow came to town six years
ago. He dropped in at the bank and asked to borrow seven
thousand dollars. Said he planned to start a trucking business. He
scraped up enough security to satisfy me that he wasn't too bad
a risk, and I let him have the money. When I made out the deposit
slip for the seven thousand, he said: 'Just a minute. I'd like to put
seven hundred of that into a special account. That's the Lord's
money.' I guess you know how I felt. I thought I was up against
a crackpot for sure."

He chuckled as he said this, but there was no doubt that the
incident and his misgivings were still fresh in his mind. Glancing
around almost ruefully to make sure he was not being overheard,
he continued:

"That fellow put that seven hundred dollars into an account
and used it for charity, giving the money little by little to religious

causes and the like. And little by little he kept depositing in that account, too. Now, I know there are people who tithe and all that, but here's my question: Do you find many people who take this thing that seriously?"

"Let me ask you," I suggested, "how has our friend been doing businesswise in the past six years?"

"Amazingly well," the banker acknowledged in a puzzled voice. "He has built up a fleet of eight trucks. Guess it's eight, maybe nine. And all the time he keeps giving away more and more money. I've heard about big men and big concerns doing things like that. I do my own bit in this matter of giving. Every good citizen does, but this 'ten percenting' on a loan strikes me as kind of reckless! Is this something general, would you say?"

It was a good question—so good, in fact, that with the banker's permission I dropped around to the trucker's office. The "reckless tither" was a different man from the one I had met at Rotary. At the meeting he had been casual and reflective. In the center of his small but efficient headquarters, he was alert and decisive.

He explained his "ten percenting" by saying: "It's simply part of my program. It started when I realized I didn't have a single Christian principle to which I subscribed unquestioningly. Everything I believed was held conditionally, subject to the situation and open to change. Going to church, belief in certain doctrines, even the good old Golden Rule was always flexible enough to adjust to circumstances. One day when things were at low ebb, I decided to get down to cases. I guess I'm the kind of person who has to do something with religion that he can keep on a record. I couldn't put love or sentiment in a book, but tithing was something I could keep track of, something I could see and handle and test myself with. That's about all there is to it. It's just part of my program."

He had no other explanation. No revival, no special sermon, no outside persuasion had brought him to this new, controlling factor in his life. He had never heard of Teresa of Avila who said: "Teresa and this money are nothing. But Teresa and this money and God are everything." No one had told him about the fabulous Borda who, when asked about his unusual generosity, explained, "God gives to Borda and Borda gives to God." It was an inner compunction that challenged this Midwestern trucking executive to put into practice the Christian concept of stewardship in a way that he could "see and handle." That was why he had tithed on the loan from the bank. It was his first big step into a new adventure.

I got to wondering if it might be this desire for a concrete, workable demonstration of God's law that persuaded other businessmen to keep a "Lord's side" of the ledger.

In southern Iowa I met a car dealer who is regarded as the town's "number 1" citizen. Generous and civic-minded, he has built his life around the belief that giving is the only justification for getting.

"It started seventeen years ago," he told me. "Ever since then I have had a special account in the bank. I have a stated time when I close my fiscal year with the Lord. And immediately I open it again. It's not my money; it's His."

He had always had the resources for giving, but not the will. He was led into his present activity when he learned that other persons with less resources than his had the will and were doing more than he was in their handling of God's promises. He opened the Lord's side of the ledger and learned that wealth becomes integrated in life only as it relates to a spiritual philosophy. Did he find that tithing paid off in good breaks? He said he was more concerned with the ideal than with the odds of the possibilities!

This man's stewardship, which had been kept hidden for years but which in a town of three thousand was bound to be found out, served as an inspiration to others. I met a storekeeper who testified that his life was changed because of the example set by the car dealer.

"He had lots of money," he said. "I had nothing. But if God's law works with dollars it will work with pennies, too. I used to drink a lot. I quit because it dawned on me that I was a fool to spend my money that way. I wish I could get across to everyone the wonderful thing that happens to a man when he changes from his own will to God's will. God's will for me was that I should be a better man. The greatest forward step in my life was when I took the money I would ordinarily have spent for drink and put it into a special fund for the Lord. You can say it's just one of those things. You can call it a game. I know it works."

From the appearance of his store, from his enthusiasm, from the respect in which his fellow men held him, it was apparent that if it was a game it was a good one, and it did work.

My research has convinced me that every successful man has a plan for his life. By "successful" I mean one who has come to a sense of self-unfoldment, who has reached or is aspiring to his highest ideal, and who lives in a consciousness of the presence of God. The plan invariably includes an honest partnership with the Lord.

"Yes, Mr. Banker, this is something pretty general, as many in your profession already know."

For the practice of tithing is growing. It knows no denominational lines. It has no selfish motives. It does not vaunt itself. Asking no material reward, it receives such a reward just the same as a bonus for stewardship. Seeking no honor, it gathers respect to itself. Beginning with money, it expands itself into other fields: the use of time, the daily task, the improvement of character.

Being something that can be "seen and handled" it develops into an over-belief with which a man is ready to set out on other spiritual ventures. Requiring great faith, it strengthens the belief that setbacks and bad breaks are provisional and never final. Tested and proved, it is the absolute guarantee of a divine order moving in and through the seeming disorder and dissolution of the world. It is a practice that ties one's religious convictions together.

The only way to test it is to try it. And the only way to try it is to begin.

HOW TO FIND EMPLOYMENT

THE FIRST STEP in seeking employment is to know that God has a place of service for you. He knows you, understands your need, and appreciates your ability. He works in your mind and life as the living principle of Truth that opens new ways before you and inspires you with new ideas that make your success assured.

For all who are seeking work there is a living message in the parable that Jesus told when He likened the kingdom of heaven to the householder who went out early in the morning to hire laborers for his vineyard. Again at the third, sixth, and eleventh hours of the day he did likewise, and he questioned the persons standing in the market place: "Why stand ye here all the day idle? They say unto him, Because no man hath hired us. He saith unto them, Go ye also into the vineyard."

Even as work was supplied to every idle person in the market place, so work is supplied today to all who apply to Jesus Christ, the Master Workman. Idleness has no part nor place in the kingdom of God. Turn therefore to Him with your whole heart, and your days of idleness will be ended. There is always something to do. Whether the service at hand is remunerative or not, do it to the glory of God; your activity, your joy in working, your enthusiastic service will open the way to profitable work and permanent prosperity.

"Why stand ye here all the day idle?" "Because no man hath hired us." Evidently the needs confronting the unemployed in the market place of which Jesus spoke were much the same as those which confront many persons of the present day. The infinite voice of love and wisdom that directed them into the vineyard to work is the same voice that today speaks through the heart and consciousness of those who are inwardly quiet before Christ and receptive to Him. It likewise directs them to the place of service that God has prepared for them and instructs them in the fulfillment of their duties.

Affirm: *"The Spirit of the Lord goes before me and makes easy and successful my way."*

God has a place for you. Remember this, especially if appearances say that work is scarce. There is a perfect place for anyone who has a loving, earnest desire to serve. Anyone who during his search for employment bears in his heart and mind not only his own need for work and supply, but also the needs of others, and who seeks in some way to help others, is sure to find work that is adapted to his peculiar ability, that he will enjoy, that will be adequately recompensed, and that will lead to success.

Put your problem squarely up to God. Talk things over with Him as you would with an understanding friend or prospective employer. God is more than your employer, He is the omnipotent Spirit of prosperity and success, the all-conquering Spirit that never has failed and never can fail. If you feel that you are specially qualified for a certain position or that some particular job is perfectly adapted to you, talk with God about it; but do not hold to it or think of it as the only suitable place that you might fill, because by so doing you may raise a barrier between you and some other occupation that would prove most satisfactory.

Hold fast to Truth and apply it to every thought, job, and service. Truth cleanses your mind of every thought of doubt, injustice, fear, or failure. It revivifies you in spirit and erases every negative claim of old age. Never give up. Be willing to try new paths if need be, willing to learn, willing to co-operate with others. The world is changing, working conditions have changed, and there are greater opportunities now than ever before for those who are spiritually equipped to put Truth to the test and prove its wonder-working power in office, business, home, institution, factory, mill, forest, on the farm, in any place or form of service.

Before you go farther in your search for work, get still, and revalue the assets that you have to offer your new employer.

You are a child of God. He has withheld nothing of Himself from you; therefore you have courage and confidence of the sort that straightens your shoulders and lifts your chin. You have a knowledge of Truth, which shines from your eyes in a straightforward look of honesty and trustworthiness. You have understanding love, which makes itself felt as good will and as ability to co-operate with other workers. You have the knowledge that the Spirit of the Lord goes before you to make easy and successful your way, and you smilingly, fearlessly, gladly meet the one whom you would serve, and he in turn feels the fine spirit that you manifest.

Measure yourself; raise your standard; work with God. By so doing you enter upon the pathway of peace and true success. We rejoice when we think of all the good qualities that you give forth. We know that you put love, loyalty, wisdom, good judgment, and joy into all that you do. Equally well we know that as you improve and enrich your life with these qualities, you receive again in abundance the reward of the Father.

"The Spirit of the Lord goes before you and makes easy and successful your way."

GOD BLESS THIS BUSINESS

WE ARE IN business to serve others; we know that as we serve we succeed. We recognize the truth that our ability to serve is our reason for being in business. We strive to widen and improve our capacity to serve.

God is the silent, senior partner in this business. We acknowledge His wisdom and His power. We do all that we can to conduct this business along lines He approves.

The guiding principles behind every decision we make, every transaction, every plan for the future, are the principles of love and service taught by Jesus Christ.

In consciously using Christian principles, we accept God's guidance and claim His promise to prosper those who serve Him.

This business is dedicated to honest service in the name of Jesus Christ. We are about our Father's business.

PURSE BLESSING

DIVINE LOVE blesses this purse and keeps it abundantly filled. It is open both to give and to receive in perfect proportion and divine order.

The substance in this purse is blessed for its true use. The owner expresses wisdom, love, and good judgment in handling this money.

All through whose hands this money passes are enriched and blessed with wisdom, love, and good judgment.

6. Living the Life

"Here, in the silence, we shall know the presence
of God, and see clearly just how we are
to go about living the life that He is giving us
so we may bring forth the order, beauty, and freedom
that He has planned and that are now awaiting
our understanding use. . . . When you know
that living, as God has planned it, here and now,
is beautiful and that you can know just what
God's plans are for you, you will be really
interested in living, won't you?"

—Myrtle Fillmore

EMMET FOX

LIFE IS CONSCIOUSNESS

THE TRUTH movement, as we call it, is the most important
thing in the world today. The Truth movement, which centers
in the belief in the omnipresence and availability of God, is the
most important thing in the world, because it is the only thing
that can save the world. Nothing else can. Everything else has
been tried.

People have tried building up might and power, and have
used it to wreck themselves. Man has built up intellectual power;
and especially since four centuries ago, since the Renaissance,
education has been intellectual. People are surprised when you
tell them that there is any other kind of education.

Those of us who have had the advantages of a higher education know that so-called intellectual study gives very, very little
help in the practical business of living. This Truth movement
comes along, takes hold of people and changes them. It restores
health if that has been lost, restores estate if that has been lost,
restores self-respect if that has been lost. It puts people on their
feet, and shows them that there is something in life worth living for.

Among the various sections of the present-day Truth movement, Unity is probably the most important. Your work is practical. It has the character and equality of Jesus Christ, because it is
kindly and friendly. You do not put fear into people. When they
come, you tell them that God is the only power; you tell them to
relax, and become quiet, and turn to that power; and that is the
highest message that you can teach.

I think it is well for us to remind ourselves what it is that we really believe and have. The answer is that we really have the key to life. We do not just approach life from a particular angle as other schools of healing do, but we have the key to life; and that key is the knowledge that *life is a state of consciousness.*

The explanation of all your problems, the explanation of your difficulties, and the explanation of your triumphs in life boil down to this: *Life is a state of consciousness.* That is the beginning and the end. That is the final step in metaphysics. All the other steps but lead up to that.

Isaac Pennington, the Quaker, said, "All truth is a shadow, but the last truth." And the last truth is that life is consciousness. You are and you have and you do in accordance with your consciousness. That is the beginning and the end. There are other ways of looking at life that are superficially correct, but ultimately the truth is that your life is a state of consciousness. Your so-called physical body is the embodiment of a part of your consciousness. Your home is the embodiment of another part of your consciousness. The kind of work you are doing—whether you are in work that you love, or whether you are doing drudgery that you hate—is the expression of your consciousness at that point. The kind of people you meet, the people you attract into your life, are the expression of your consciousness about your fellow men.

If you came to see me and told me that you couldn't get along with people, I should tell you to get a card about the size of a post card, and write this on it, *"Like attracts like,"* and then put it inside your closet—not where other members of your family will see it, because that would sometimes be embarrassing. When you are grumbling and finding fault they could point their finger at it, and that would be very embarrassing; so put your card inside the closet.

People come to me and say, "If you only knew the kind of family I have, if you only knew the kind of people I have to be with and work with!" I say, "The law of Being says, 'Like attracts like.' "

The ultimate explanation of all things is that life is a state of consciousness.

Take this table. You say this is solid wood, and that is true as far as it goes. But the next step, going deeper, is that we find it is really made up of molecules with great distances, relatively, between them. So it is not solid at all. It is made up of molecules, and that is true as far as it goes. But these again are made up of atoms, and these of electrons and protons, and so on. We hear talk of vibrations, of rays, of all these things, and they are good descriptions as far as they go; but in the ultimate, beyond all these things, we come back to a state of consciousness.

Before you change your state of consciousness nothing else can change.

All trouble, all disappointment, all depression, all limitation is a state of consciousness that must be changed. People are trying to change outer conditions but leaving their consciousness unchanged, and it cannot be done.

The only fundamental way to change things is to change your consciousness because you always must and always will get the conditions that belong to your consciousness. You cannot cheat nature. You can drag to you, through will power, certain things that do not belong to you, but you can only keep them for a short time. The moment you take your hands off they fly away. That was the real cause of the financial collapse of 1929. Then Wall Street made its famous nose dive. The prosperity that had been built up was not true prosperity. People had been gambling on the stock market and elsewhere and had attracted or dragged to themselves prosperity that they were not entitled to by right of consciousness, and of course they could not keep it.

The same thing applies to health. You can compel a certain part of the body to picture health for a short time, but if you do not have the consciousness of health you cannot keep it. You "heal" a person of rheumatism and he has sciatica, you "heal" him of that and he has trouble with his sight, you "heal" his sight and his right lung weakens, and so on. These are not healings. They are temporary curcs, because they are attempts to put into the body something that doesn't belong there by right of consciousness.

When you want to solve your problems you can see at once that the only scientific way is to start in to change your consciousness. Likewise you must change the consciousness of a patient if you want to heal him. Nothing can come to you securely, nothing can stay with you permanently, except what you are entitled to by your consciousness.

Emerson said, "No man and no institution was ever ridden down or talked down by anything but itself." People may slander you, but nobody can hurt you except yourself. Nobody can wreck a church or a center or a movement or a country except itself.

A woman said, "I started a center and everything went beautifully until some horrible person spoiled everything." I replied, "You are the horrible person who spoiled your center, because if you started a center and it didn't go, then you did not have a right consciousness for that work. You should have changed your consciousness until you did have a good center, and then nobody else could spoil it for you."

Your body, your home, your city, your country, the universe, are pictures of consciousness. Your private life outpictures your own consciousness. The national life is the outpicturing of the national consciousness. So you see how foolish it is to try to change the outer picture without changing the inner consciousness.

People come to see me and say, "I am broke. I need a thousand dollars. I need the money." Or, "I have had a quarrel with somebody," which usually means that they expect the other person to bend to their will and come crawling on his knees for forgiveness. They say, "Put these things right." I say, "Change your consciousness. I do not treat for money. I do not patch up quarrels like that. But I do help you to change your consciousness." Some of them smile and say, "Oh, no, my consciousness is really quite good. Other people are to blame—my mother or my sister." I answer, "No; the real trouble is in your consciousness; and all the time you are trying to work on outer things and leaving your consciousness unchanged no permanent good can come to you."

The movies came to the big cities first, and finally arrived in a remote mining camp in the Rockies. The picture was announced and the tent was put up. The residents had never been to a movie before. The tent was packed with cowboys and miners, and at a given moment during the showing of a blood-curdling melodrama the villain began to choke the heroine. An old cowboy in the front row pulled out his gun and fired six shots into the villain. Everybody laughed, because in those days a gunshot didn't mean much. There were only a few bullet holes in the wall, and of course the picture went on as scheduled.

Why do we laugh at the cowboy? You all laughed, you know. What should he have done? Instead of firing at the screen, he should have turned around and fired into the projector. That would have stopped the picture.

Too often you try to change outer things instead of changing the inner. Then you are firing at the screen instead of the projector. So nothing happens. But when you start to change your consciousness you are firing at the projector, and then things happen. If you don't like the picture on the screen, change the reel. If you didn't like the picture you were seeing, and would like to see some other, you wouldn't get a cloth and try to rub it off as if from a blackboard. You would take out that reel and put in the reel you wanted.

The scientific way to approach life, if you do not like the picture you are getting, is to change the reel.

How do we change the reel? By rising in consciousness. *The only real healers are practical ones.* I have met a few theoretical so-called healers. I have met people who told me just how healing should be done. They understood the theory. They knew how it should be done but couldn't do it. They were purely theoretical.

The way to meet a problem is to raise your consciousness. If you do this, the problem disappears. In the Bible a valley always stands for trouble, sin, limitation; and the mount for uplifted thought, and prayer for understanding. We must go up the mount; raise our consciousness.

Most people who have a problem concentrate on that problem. They take it to bed with them and stay awake all night thinking it over. Let go of the problem. Rise above it in consciousness. How can you do this? Go up quickly, in a flash if you can; but you can't always do it that way. You will find that by reading the Bible, or some available spiritual book, or a Unity publication, or by repeating some favorite inspirational hymn, your consciousness is rising. If a diver goes down to the bottom of the sea he wears lead shoes, but if he wants to come up to the surface of the water quickly he kicks off the lead shoes. Then he rises rapidly. When we rise in consciousness we kick off our lead shoes, and then we begin to be healed, or the patient begins to be healed; but it is the consciousness that you have to heal.

There is no other way. The great key to consciousness lies in the "Word," which Unity has been teaching for more than fifty years. "In the beginning was the Word, and the Word was with God, and the Word was God. . . . All things were made through him and without him was not anything made that hath been made."

The first chapter of John is a reflection of the first chapter of Genesis; both deal with creation: "God said." John explains the Logos. The Greek word *Logos* means the great creative Word. The great creative word is I AM. It is the secret of life. We are given it in Deuteronomy, and Jesus identified Himself with it. Jesus was a great reader of the Psalms and Isaiah and Deuteronomy. The key to life is not somewhere outside of life. You can't go up to it. No great seer or saint will go up and bring it down for you. It is not thousands of miles across the sea. It is very nigh unto you. It is with you all the time. I AM is the great secret. I AM is the famous Lost Word.

All through history mankind has felt intuitively that there is a way out, if only it can find it. All the old fairy tales tell the story again and again. Aladdin had a wonderful lamp. He rubbed it and received the things he wanted. The lamp was the creative word. You know about Cinderella. She was in the kitchen, miserable and unhappy like so many others, and then something happened. A pumpkin turned into a carriage, and a pair of white rats turned into white horses, and so on. But there must have been a change in Cinderella's consciousness first.

Always men and women have felt intuitively that there is a way out; that it is not necessary to be angry and mean and resentful and bitter; that it is not necessary to grow old and die; that it is not necessary that man should fight and grab for prosperity and food. What is life worth if living is to be a constant struggle for necessities? Men and women have always known intuitively that there is a way out if only they can find it. They have always known that God means all life to be noble and creative and joyous. And this is true.

The way out lies in the spoken word. In the Bible the "word" means any definitely formulated thought—not just the drifting thought that floats through your mind. The word is creative, and the strongest and most creative word is "I am." Whenever you say "I am," you are calling upon the universe to do something for you and it will do it. Whenever you say "I am," you are drawing a check on the universe. It will be honored and cashed sooner or later and the proceeds will go to you. If you say, "I am tired, sick, poor, fed up, disappointed, getting old," then you are drawing checks for future trouble and limitation. When you say, "I am divine life," "I am divine Truth," "I am divine freedom," "I am substance," "I am eternal substance," you are drawing a check on the bank of heaven, *and surely that check will be honored with health and plenty for you.*

Remember you don't have to use the actual grammatical form "I am." Every time you associate yourself in thought with anything, or think of yourself as having anything, you are using a form of "I am." The verb "to have" is a part of the verb "to be." In the very ancient languages, there is no verb "to have." It is a modern improvement like the radio and the automobile. "I have" means "I am," because you always have what you are, and you always do what you are.

That is the significance of "I am," and today more people have come to know about it than ever before, and this is a wonderful thing. Unity has taught it. In the Truth movement in London we taught it. But few people realize what it means. Whatever you associate yourself with, that you are bringing into your consciousness. What is the first thing we do when we talk at all? We say, "I am this," "I am that." Perhaps my father was Mr. Jones. Therefore I am a Jones. The neighbors across the way are Robinsons. They are strangers to me, because I am a Jones. Immediately the baby picks up all the prejudices of old man Jones. Or we say, "I am a Frenchman," or "I am a German," or "I am an Englishman." The Frenchman gets a great many prejudices concerning the German and the Englishman, the German gets prejudices concerning the Frenchman and the Englishman, and the Englishman gets them concerning the Frenchman and the German. Why pick up any prejudices?

Then the child grows older, and of course his family is interested in politics. Again he sets up in his mind a whole army of prejudices. He belongs to a certain party because his father does.

He goes to a particular school or college and collects more preju-
dice. He should use the "I am" to say "I am for freedom." He
should use it to throw down the walls of resentment.

It is your "I am" whatever way you use it, and there is one
thing that nobody can do for you, and that is save your soul, because nobody can speak the "I am" for you. Nobody can say "I
am" for you or another; he would have to say "You are" or "He
is," and that would not be "I am."

In Revelation we read, "To him that overcometh . . . I will give
him a white stone, and upon the stone a new name written, which
no one knoweth but he that receiveth it." The white stone means
the ascension of the divine nature, because of its understanding.
The new name is the new character and the new life. You speak
for yourself and you save your own soul, and it is said to be secret
because only you can use it.

Teachers can write books for you, they can talk to you, but
they cannot save your soul, because they cannot think for you.
When anyone uses "I am" for you, it becomes "You are." It is *your*
"I am" that must save you, and nobody on earth can use it but
you. The "I am" is God in action. God is not a man. God is working through you. You are not separated from God. God does not
sit far up in the sky and send you a good idea. God is the I AM
giving you a new embodiment, a new creation. Whatever you
believe, that you create. You are the I AM. God knows Himself in
your consciousness, and that is knowing God. God is I AM THAT I
AM, but you are I AM.

I want to emphasize this point. You build your consciousness
with your "I am." Nobody else can do it for you, and you can't
cheat. Sometimes you can cheat in business, sometimes you can
cheat in gambling, but you cannot cheat with the "I am." Appearances count for nothing. Your consciousness is built with the "I
am." According to your "I am" so are your conditions. You are not
using the "I am" only when you think and speak affirmations.
Perhaps this has been a weakness in our movement, that we have
tended to overrate affirmations. We have to use them because
they are a memorandum of what we are to think. The class
thoughts in *Unity* magazine are a memorandum. But you are
using the "I am" in every action all day long. Every action that
you do all day long you are building into your own consciousness.

You will never build anything into your consciousness until you do it in practice. Meditating an hour in the morning before breakfast helps very little unless you carry the realization with you into your everyday living.

If you lie or cheat or are selfish, then that is what you are building into consciousness. We have dwelt much on thought (what we call words), but we haven't always insisted it is the practical conduct all day long that builds up consciousness. People tell me that they spend an hour every morning building up their consciousness, but often as soon as the hour is up they have forgotten it.

You build your consciousness by the things you do all day long. It is by such things that we are judged. God does not judge us. We judge ourselves by the consciousness we build, because life is a state of consciousness. Let us build true consciousness and hasten the day of freedom.

CLARA BERANGER

THOU SHALT NOT BE AFRAID

FOR YEARS I have been reading the Bible, loving its beauty, quoting many of its passages at appropriate times, believing its promises. Yet it was not until I began seriously to study its history and the history of its people that I could see it in its entirety as a story of the Spirit of God at work in the hearts and lives of men. However much the language of the different books may vary, however much the ideas and customs may have changed under different environments, the theme that runs through the whole book like a recurrent melody is that man is illumined and made divine by the touch of God.

Of the many passages in the Bible that have solaced man in times of trouble, and offered him protection in times of danger, one of the best known and most dearly loved is the 91st Psalm. In any emergency we need, as never before in our history, the comfort and sense of security that the beautiful words of this psalm offer. We need its reminder that, no matter what outward evil we "behold and see," we can and we shall be delivered if we hold fast to our faith in God, and practice His presence in our life.

The first verse tells us that "He that dwelleth in the secret place of the Most High shall abide under the shadow of the Almighty." * Literally translated from the original Hebrew, "secret place" means "covert," a hiding place provided by God as a protection from enemies. From Jesus we get an inner meaning. In

* All Scriptural references in this article are quoted from the Authorized or King James Version of the Bible.

the Sermon on the Mount He says: "When thou prayest, enter
into thy closet, and when thou hast shut thy door, pray to thy
Father which is in secret; and thy Father which seeth in secret
shall reward thee openly." By entering into the closet or our in-
nermost consciousness by closing the door to outward-pointed
thought, and through prayer establishing oneness with God, we
can be certain that God hears and answers. So the secret place is
our own superconsciousness, the point of contact between the
human mind and the Divine Mind.

If we make this secret place, this place of union with God,
our dwelling or "fixed abode," adds the Psalmist, we shall be
under the direct care and guidance of the God whose power is
"almighty."

I will say of the Lord, He is my refuge and my fortress: my
God; in him will I trust." Could any affirmation be stronger or
more faith-inspiring than this short, simple verse? It tells us that
God is a permanent stronghold, a safe shelter to which we can
trustfully go in time of danger. Today, when we seem threatened
by new fears and unfamiliar dangers, we can get help by thinking often of this powerful passage, by believing it with all our
heart, and by saying it over and over again until every word is
engraved upon our memory.

"Surely he shall deliver thee from the snare of the fowler, and
from the noisome pestilence." Even at the safe time when this
was written, it must have had both a literal and a figurative
meaning. Fowlers were men who hunted wild birds with traps
and snares; and "the noisome pestilence" was one of those infec-
tious, evil-smelling diseases which plagued and decimated the
populations of the time. Yet in a wider sense it must also have
meant then, as we can take it to mean now, that God protects
those who trust in Him from all danger, whether it be the traps
and treachery of an enemy or an epidemic of disease.

The next verse, clothed in beautiful imagery, carries the idea
of God's protection still further. "He shall cover thee with his
feathers, and under his wings shalt thou trust." Does not this give
a comforting mental picture of birds sheltering their young under
soft feathery wings, of mothers shielding their babies in strong,
loving arms? If we visualize the infinite care and devotion that
even the humblest of mothers is ready to give to a helpless infant,

we see that no other metaphor could so well have conveyed to us the idea of God's ever-present care for His children.

The end of the verse, "His truth shall be thy shield and buckler," means simply that knowledge and use of the truth about God is our safeguard, our defensive armor against all dangers.

"Thou shalt not be afraid for the terror by night; nor for the arrow that flieth by day;

"Nor for the pestilence that walketh in darkness; nor for the destruction that wasteth at noonday."

The things we see by the light of day never seem to assume the fearsome aspect of the visions that come to haunt us in the night. But if we hold fast to faith in God, says the Psalmist, nothing need frighten us, neither the terrors we conjure up at night nor the destruction we see by day. During these days when tales of destruction and wanton waste assault our eyes and ears from newspaper and radio, we need to remember and follow the simple commandment: "Thou shalt not be afraid."

"A thousand shall fall at thy side, and ten thousand at thy right hand; but it shall not come nigh thee.

"Only with thine eyes shalt thou behold and see the reward of the wicked.

"Because thou hast made the Lord, which is my refuge, even the Most High, thy habitation;

"There shall no evil befall thee, neither shall any plague come nigh thy dwelling."

It does not seem to me that the first two of these verses, numbers 7 and 8 of the Psalm, mean what they are often construed to mean: a promise of personal immunity from death when thousands are falling around us. Rather in conjunction with the next two verses they affirm that if we are accustomed to taking refuge in the Lord, to trusting regularly in His power and goodness, we need not be terrified by the sight of death, because we know that no matter what happens to the physical body, neither evil, nor disease, nor death itself can touch our immortal, God-given spirit. Through our inner power of discernment we can "behold and see" that wickedness carries within itself the seeds of its own punishment or "reward."

The two verses that follow give another exquisite expression of God's care for His children. I have used them many times, in many moods and circumstances, and they never fail to give me a feeling of calm and an assurance of safety:

"For he shall give his angels charge over thee, to keep thee in all thy ways.

"They shall bear thee up in their hands, lest thou dash thy foot against a stone."

To interpret this passage truly, we must start by defining the word "angel." Although the English usually implies a super-human being with diaphanous wings who floats airily about in the clouds, there is nothing in either the Hebrew or the Greek word from which "angel" is derived that means more than "messenger," without distinction between human and divine messenger. But the early Hebrews thought of God as surrounded by a retinue of heavenly creatures and of angels as God's agents who brought guidance and encouragement to those for whom He had a special message. In other words, angels were believed to be the intermediaries between God and man.

In the New Testament the supreme intermediary, the divine messenger who brought the truth of God to all His children, was Jesus. "And the word which ye hear is not mine, but the Father's which sent me. . . . But the Comforter, which is the Holy Ghost, whom the Father will send in my name, he shall teach you all things, and bring all things to your remembrance, whatsoever I have said unto you."

Considered in the light of the teachings of Jesus, every noble thought we hold in our consciousness, every spiritual intuition we trust, every idea of beauty, goodness, or truth that inspires us, every inner urge for light we feel is a messenger from God, an angel to aid us on our path to spiritual fulfillment.

Thus these two verses, so simply and beautifully worded, become both a promise and a challenge. They tell us that in all our ways, wherever they may lead us, we are protected by the thoughts that come to us directly from God; and we are safely lifted up above whatever hazard or "stone" may lie upon the path our feet must tread. But ours is the responsibility to keep our heart open to the messages that God sends, to keep our mind free from the destructive and unloving thoughts that clog the channel between human mind and divine mind, to put into daily practice the inspiration and guidance we receive.

Verse 13, "Thou shalt tread upon the lion and adder: the young lion and the dragon shalt thou trample under feet," is a clear statement of our power to overcome all kinds of danger, from overt brutality, as symbolized by the lion, the strongest of all beasts, to covert treachery, that strikes without warning, as symbolized by the adder and dragon. Not only have we power to meet and overcome all visible and invisible perils, says the Psalmist, but to crush them completely, to trample them under our feet.

The last three verses give what is perhaps the most definite assurance of help and salvation in the whole Bible:

"Because he hath set his love upon me, therefore will I deliver him: I will set him on high, because he hath known my name.

"He shall call upon me, and I will answer him: I will be with him in trouble; I will deliver him, and honour him.

"With long life will I satisfy him, and shew him my salvation."

To the man who centers his love upon God, who knows that the name of God is synonymous with all good, He promises release from burdens, liberation from evil. Furthermore, the God-loving man will be set above the trials and tribulations that beset the man who is unaware of God.

The two final verses suggest the inspiring word of Isaiah: "Thou wilt keep him in perfect peace, whose mind is stayed on thee"; for both the prophet and the Psalmist state that the man who trusts in God, who calls upon Him in prayer, is serene in faith that his prayer will be answered. He is not afraid in times of trouble, for he believes that God is ever present to help him, to free him from all difficulties, to preserve him from all evil, and to honor him with life, love, and wisdom for the rest of his days.

Even in troublous times we too can achieve blessed serenity by setting our love upon God, by trusting Him to deliver and keep us safe under all circumstances: "I will say of the Lord, He is my refuge and my fortress: my God; in him will I trust."

We can remain steady and unafraid, no matter what terror or destruction assails us by night or by day: "For he shall give his angels charge over thee, to keep thee in all thy ways."

We can be calm in the present, and hopeful for the future by holding fast to our faith in God's promises: "He shall call upon me, and I will answer him: I will be with him in trouble; I will deliver him, and honour him."

Let us know then from the depth of our heart that we can always find shelter under the protecting wings of God. Let our faith in Him be an ever-present armor against terror and destruction. Let us cast out every thought and impulse of fear by repeating to ourselves over and over and over again, "Thou shalt not be afraid."

JAMES DILLET FREEMAN

YOU ARE NOT ALONE

MOST OF US have friends or relatives who are very close and very dear to us. Yet there are times when we feel all alone. We have things to meet and we feel we have to meet them alone. But we do not have to meet anything alone. God is with us.

God is with you. You do not have to face your problems alone. You do not have to make your overcomings alone. There is One with you always who will help you in everything you have to meet.

This does not mean that you do not have to make any effort yourself. You have to make all the effort of which you are capable. But you do not have to depend on your own resources alone. You have access to God. If we felt that we had only human resources to depend on, we might feel discouraged indeed, for often when we have a struggle to make we do not seem to have much to struggle with. The qualities of heart and mind and body that we need do not seem to be there. But if we hold on, if we do not lose heart but persist in effort and prayer, we shall find that we have qualities we never guessed we had, God's qualities.

You may feel however that you have no awareness that God is with you. If that is so, you can develop it. How can you develop it? You can develop it through prayer. It may come immediately. It may come slowly. But if you consciously and persistently seek the presence of God, you will find that presence.

This seeking does not have to be laborious. Regular periods of prayer are helpful if you have the time and the desire for them; but best of all, throughout the day remind yourself that God is with you. Especially the first thing on waking and the last thing before falling asleep, remind yourself that God is with you. Whenever something comes up, whenever you feel that you need strength or freedom or wisdom or peace, remind yourself that God is with you, helping you.

In this way you will come to know that truly God *is* with you. You will come to feel His loving, living presence. This does not mean that something phenomenal will happen. God is Spirit. He is intelligence, love, life. And you will feel His presence as a quickening of your intelligence, love, and life. You will feel Him as a new sense of assurance and peace such as you never had before. You will feel Him as new vitality and strength.

Do not be discouraged if you do not see instant results. Have patience with yourself. Success is often the result of patient persistence through failure.

Many persons have to build a consciousness of the presence of God thought by thought as one builds a house brick by brick. It does not matter if you are not able to build the entire edifice in a day. "It is acceptable according as a man hath, not according as he hath not." The important thing is that you keep trying. "And ye shall seek me, and find me, when ye shall search for me with all your heart."

Know that God is with you right now, this minute, helping you right now to meet the present need. Put out of mind yesterday's regrets, tomorrow's fears. It is right now that God is with you and you have only one thing to meet, the present moment. God is with you as you meet it!

God is always willing to help us, but sometimes we do not let Him help us until we have exhausted all our resources. A man who does not know how to swim exhausts and frustrates himself in aimless struggles. If he would relax and float, he would discover that the water would support him, and with intelligent effort he could get to shore. Sometimes we struggle until we are nearly exhausted before we are willing to relax and let God support us. Then we make the astounding discovery that He does support and sustain us, and with a little intelligent effort we reach the shore!

And often success is nearer than it seems to be. Sometimes

where no visible results appear, a great work has been done in the invisible. "Fear not . . . for from the first day that thou didst set thy heart to understand . . . thy words were heard." The work of God is largely done in the invisible; it is a spiritual work done on heart and mind. But it is no less real because it is invisible.

So if you should come to the point where you feel like giving up, it is then you must hold on. Hold then steadfastly to the thought that God is with you and keep steadfastly on. For it is then, even in that moment, that the victory may appear.

For God is with you, your guaranty of victory. He does not forsake you. He loves you. He sustains you. He will help you up. He will help you on. He will help you to assurance in yourself. And with Him in your heart you yet will walk free and secure.

God is with you! That is the truth. Keep it before you. Think it, affirm it, repeat it until you have fixed it indelibly in your mind and heart, until you feel it in the inmost fiber of your being. You will feel it. Be sure of that. You will feel it so clearly that you will never doubt it again. Then nothing you have to meet will ever seem overpowering again, for you will know that with you is something infinitely more powerful, something braver than any fear, stronger than any weakness, firmer than any wavering, wiser than any doubt. You will know that in you is the divine capacity to meet every situation, the wisdom to know what should be done, the strength to do it. You will know that with you is God, and knowing, you will never be alone again.

God is with you.

M. J. READING

A BEAUTY TREATMENT

ARE YOU ENTIRELY satisfied with your personal appearance? Do you wish you had soft brown eyes like Mary Jones, or glistening white teeth like Walter Jackson, or shining golden hair like Lois Smith?

The urge to acquire a better personal appearance is constantly stirring within almost every person in the world. This urge, interpreted in the desire for the expression of greater beauty, has resulted in millions of dollars in profit for business concerns; it has furnished employment for many thousands of people, and it has produced changes in fashion when the temptation might have been strong to let things remain as they were.

If you are dissatisfied with your appearance, perhaps you are working from the wrong angle. Perhaps you are working on the wrong side of your face—the outside! You may be applying cold cream, rouge, and powder needlessly. Maybe the latest hairdress or, if you are a man, the most modern haircut, or the brightest necktie, or the most colorful coat is not all that is necessary. Perhaps all your face or personal appearances need is better backing. Not the backing of what some term "nerve," or courage, or faith, or confidence, but a backing of the heart. In fact, your heart is the only real backing your face has, and in spite of everything that you may do it shows right through. All the cosmetics and beauticians and clothes in the world cannot prevent that. If what is behind your face is ugly, be sure the world will see it no matter how hard you try to hide it.

So if you want to be beautiful, start working on what is back of your face. Give your heart a beauty treatment every day.

Here is a most excellent formula for beauty. If applied diligently, this beauty formula cannot help doing wonders for any face. It is not a formula that can be purchased at any cosmetics counter. Each person has to make it for himself. In fact, it will not work for you if anyone else makes it. That has been the trouble to a great extent with our search for more beauty. We have depended upon someone else to create it for us.

The materials or ingredients of this formula are not even for sale at any store. However the supply is unlimited and is free to all. It is as good for men as for women. You need have no fear of using too much or of using it too often. Here is the formula:

First. Take a lot of *love*. You cannot use too much. It is the softener. The treatment would be absolutely worthless without it.

Second. Add a lump of *kindness*. It is the lubricator. It prevents friction. Without it the going would indeed be rough and bumpy.

Third. Pour in a large measure of *good cheer*. It chases gloom out of dark corners and lights the way to happiness.

Fourth. Do not forget *compassion*. It is important but must be used with great discretion.

Fifth. Now put in a big gob of *sense of humor*. It is the spice of life and adds pep to insipid and uninteresting occasions.

Sixth. Use a great deal of *patience*. It promotes harmony and leads to success.

Seventh. Dump in a large portion of *faith in people*. It is great for increasing ambition and stimulating effort.

Eighth. Stir in plenty of *hope*. It stops the blues.

Ninth. Mix with all these an abundance of *courage*. It keeps you from turning yellow.

Tenth and last. Gather up the *smiles* you can find and sprinkle liberally over the other ingredients. Like the sauce to a dinner, they cover a multitude of mistakes and relieve dull monotony.

Now when all these are blended into a rosy cream, apply a generous amount of it to the heart every day. Do not wipe off the surplus. Leave it there to be absorbed. Massage well and follow at once with vigorous exercise for at least one hour. Love somebody! Do a kind act or speak a kind word! Be cheerful! Give somebody a lift! Look for the humor in everyday living! Be patient with others' shortcomings! (You have some of your own, you know.) Have faith in somebody! Hope for the best always! Face life with courage—and *smile!*

This treatment tends to take up the sagging skin, tone up the flabby muscles, and remove the ugly bulges, where greed, hate, envy, criticism, and nagging have left their marks.

Follow these directions faithfully for thirty days, and you will not only feel better, but you will be able to see a difference in the face that looks back at you from the mirror.

Continue the treatment for six months and your friends will remark, "How much better you are looking!" And when it has become a habit, keep it up. In a year you will notice that the number of your friends has grown.

Keep it up indefinitely, and you will have a heart beautiful enough to admit you to the charmed circle of the world's greatest people. Kings and courtiers alike, the high and the lowly everywhere, will pay you tribute. They will never even see the wrinkles in your face, if there are any; and it is very doubtful that there will be any, because all there will be is the light that will be shining from within!

To impress it on your memory, I am going to list once more the ingredients of this marvelous beautifying formula:

Love, kindness, good cheer, compassion, sense of humor, patience, faith in people, hope, courage, and last but certainly not least, smiles! You will probably have your own way of mixing these ingredients and *your* way will probably be as good for you as any that can be suggested. Perhaps you have some friends that you would like to initiate into this beauty secret with you. Make a game of it. Get your family to join in with you, and let each member of the family see how quickly he can detect a change in your appearance, proving to you and to others that this beauty treatment is the greatest one you have ever tried, and the most effective.

And now, as you busy yourself with the application of your beauty treatment, here is one suggestion. Do you hold grudges? Do you think that because some person did you a bad turn a long time ago he would do it again under similar circumstances? Has it ever occurred to you that cherished resentment is like an obstruction in the way of the good that is on its way to you? God is the giver of all good. If you have less of this world's goods than you need today do not blame anyone whom you believe to be your enemy. Clear the way for the good that should come to you by blessing the one you regard as your enemy. You will not find this so difficult if you will take time to realize that the Creator has power above that of the one who injured you and from whom you may anticipate further injury.

Perhaps you have lost a position or something else of value to you. If you have, do not blame any person. Forgive the one who seems to have done you an ill turn, and wait for another door to open, holding yourself ready to enter it with joy in your heart and a blessing for the one whom you may have regarded as your enemy. To forgive with your whole heart is of first importance.

Every time you ask a blessing for another person, you in turn are blessed. Give love and service and you invite love and service. There is something very pitiable about a person who would deliberately injure another or defame someone's character, for this person is surely piling up obstructions that will keep his good from him, and he will suffer until those obstructions are removed and good can flow freely to him again. And since whatever anyone may do to you cannot really harm you if your faith in God's power is steady and deep, why should you cherish ill will toward a fellow man who has not learned what it is that he does to himself when he willfully sets out to bring unhappiness into the life of another or who is so unfortunate as to do great harm instead of just giving vent to passing ill will?

It is a fact that you can readily prove for yourself that anyone who is antagonistic to you, who does not miss an opportunity to belittle you or even spread untruths about you, can be made over into a friend if, instead of directing a stream of resentment toward him, you will silently bless him. You will find a change in yourself first, but presently you will realize that the other person is changing too.

Jesus never rendered evil for evil. He bore all things and continued to believe in His fellow men. He suffered greater humiliation than any of us will ever know anything about, yet "Father, forgive them; for they know not what they do" was

His prayer for His enemies. Could we look for a better pattern or nobler advice than that?

In order to improve your physical appearance, which you can do, and also to improve the appearance of your general affairs, remember your beauty formula and use it every day.

Remember that first you must have love in your heart. It is the softener for whatever hard condition exists. To your love add kindness, which is the lubricator for both skin and knotty problems. Keep up a spirit of good cheer, and feel and express pity where it is needed. Remember that a sense of humor is also important, for it keeps things from becoming monotonous and adds zip to life. Also you must exercise patience, and you must have faith not only in yourself but in other people. Keep hope shining always in your heart, and have courage—courage to follow up your own convictions. Then remember always to smile—whether you feel like it or not. At first your face may give the appearance of a mechanical smile, but keep trying to smile, and as you smile more and more from the inside out your face will actually smile easily and joyously.

Love somebody! Do a kind act or speak a kind word! Be cheerful, help somebody, be patient, and exercise faith in affairs and in people. Face life with courage. And keep smiling!

CLARA MAY ROWLAND

HOW TO BE YOUNG—SPIRITUALLY, MENTALLY, PHYSICALLY

PEOPLE SAY, "I would not want to live forever." No, we would not want to live forever in these bodies and in our present state of consciousness. But most of our ill health, both physical and mental, is because we do not understand the true nature of life. You see, we limit ourselves to the human concept of life. We think of life as limited rather than as endless, eternal.

There is an ancient inscription that reads, "Yet more is to be found in me." The next time you feel run-down or at the end of your rope, remember these words, "Yet more is to be found in me."

"God created man to be immortal and made him to be an image of His own eternity."

We need to get a new premise about life and to work from that premise. For instance, our premise could well be one like this: "Life is continuous and eternal. The life I live and am aware of at this moment is God-life, eternal life." With an idea like this on which to base our thinking we shall come into a new understanding of the limitless, eternal life within us. We shall come to know that there is never any end to this life.

Man has a very limited concept of life in spite of scientific discoveries being made about his capacity for endurance. One scientist has said: "We are only half awake. The individual lives within his own limits."

Even though man has a limited concept of life, he has always

[212]

wanted to live. Even though he submits to death as God's will for him, more than two thousand years ago Ezekiel saw with a flash of inspiration that God says to man, "I have no pleasure in the death of him who dieth . . . wherefore turn yourselves, and live."

Whether we are able to prove eternal life is a different story; but as we turn ourselves and live, as we implant the idea of eternal life in our consciousness, we shall experience a different feeling and a different quality of life and thus start a rejuvenation.

Where did our life come from? The origin of our life is in God. He breathed into us the breath of life, and we became living souls. Surely God thinks of us as He created us, surely He sees His children as living expressions of His life. We need to learn to think of ourselves in the way that God thinks of us.

What are some of the limited concepts of life that keep us from expressing a fuller consciousness of life, from enjoying life?

Are we limited by what we think we have inherited? Do we blame heredity for ill health, lack of vitality, some specific disease? We need to take hold of the idea that our inheritance is from God, that we are children of God, that we have within us His life, His power, His love. We are set free from the bondage of belief in heredity when we continually affirm our freedom, when we claim our divine birthright as children of God.

Have we felt bound by time, have we accepted the idea that our allotted time is three-score years and ten?

Man uses the time system to reckon progress, but the time system is man's idea not God's. We can rise above the thought that we are bound by time by knowing that there is no time in Spirit, that we live in the eternal now.

Perhaps we feel tired, run-down, discouraged, but entertain the hope that next week or next year we shall have more life and energy. Now is the time to do something about this attitude of mind. Now is the time to draw upon the life of God. We live in it, move in it, have our being in it. The power to resurrect is not a supernatural power. In each cell and atom of the body there is life, substance, and intelligence. We speak a word of life, and each cell and atom in our bodies responds. We can charge the cells of our bodies with life, eternal life. They are always listening, always receptive. If we present the idea of life, our bodies take up this idea and act on it. The idea works through the cells and atoms of our bodies and generates life and energy.

The teaching of eternal life is one of the teachings of Jesus and one of the basic teachings of Unity School. When Jesus said, "I am the resurrection, and the life," He knew His identity as a son of life without beginning or end.

Some people say to us, "I am too old to take up these new ideas." But our consciousness about life starts in the mind, and we are never too old to think!

That mental power does not decline with age was proved by Dr. Irving Lorge, eminent psychologist of Columbia University. Dr. Lorge's results from working with an intelligence test devised by Edward L. Thorndike showed that though mental speed declines slowly with the years, mental power never declines at all, that it may even increase with expanding knowledge. His results show that if you could solve a problem in business or science or government or human relations when you were twenty-five, you can solve it just as well even up to ninety years of age.

In an interview George Bernard Shaw, at the age of ninety, stated: "Death is not to be regarded as natural and inevitable. We die because we do not know how to live and kill ourselves by our lethal habits."

Let us forget the idea of growing old and commence really to live. We should not let inactive ideas clog the mind, but let new, creative, life-giving ideas express themselves in and through us.

When we go along in the same old way for a long time it is sometimes a little difficult to act on new ideas. We need to get into the habit of acting on our ideas.

Let us act on our impulse to express love and joy; let us act on our impulse to do good to our fellow man; let us act on our desire to make changes in our way of living.

Let us make up our minds that we are not going to let ourselves get into a rut. Let us not be afraid to make changes in our lives, to try new things, to attempt to do something that is new and challenging.

So many of us sit and watch life go by. We sit back and think that we have no part in it. Youth never watches anyone else do something; youth always tries to do that thing himself;

youth always takes part in some activity. We need to cultivate the habit of action, the habit of becoming a part of the picture rather than merely watching life go by.

It is not so much what comes into our lives that matters as what we do about it. We have the ability to take life as it comes and make something of it.

We should not let inactive ideas clog our minds. One of the things that classifies us as old is thinking of all the happiness and good things as being in the past and longing for the "good old days." Living in the past is a sure way to become old.

In order to stay young and active we must find new interests, we must create within ourselves a love of life; we must be willing to try new things, we must not be content to watch life go by; we must be willing to take part in it.

We need to say to ourselves, "I dare to be young!" We cannot be young unless we feel young. It is not the way we dress or the way we act that makes us young. It is our consciousness of life, youth, and joy that determines this.

Any one of us can learn to love life, to love people, to love beauty. Any one of us can stir up a new spirit of interest and en- thusiasm within. If you start to think of yourself as being too old to make a new start, check yourself, for this is merely an excuse. Make up your mind that you are not going to stay in a rut. Youth is a matter of attitude, not of calendar age. Rather than thinking about life running out, affirm this idea, *"I am alive, alert, awake, joyous, and enthusiastic about life,"* or *"I am the ever-renewing, the ever-unfolding expression of infinite life and youth."* Do not talk about your rheumatism, your poor eyesight, your failing health. Remember that there is "yet more to be found" within you, that the very source of life is within you, renewing you in mind and body.

We cannot live life to the fullest unless we begin to live now. We need to lay hold of life now, to stir up new interest and en- thusiasm, to let go of fear and limiting beliefs. We need to know that we have the life of God in us now, that at this moment we are living in the very midst of eternity.

"God created man to be immortal, and made him to be an im- age of His own eternity."

ERNEST C. WILSON

"HE GIVETH HIS BELOVED SLEEP"

Do YOU FIND it difficult to sleep through the night? Do you toss on your pillow and as a result approach the new day wearied rather than refreshed? Truth can help, and will. Remember the promise of David: "He giveth his beloved sleep."

Lying awake can be as refreshing and renewing as falling asleep if your thoughts and feelings are right, if you are at peace with yourself and the world. So begin by seeking such peace.

If thoughts of the day's activities harass and trouble you, do not fight them or try to drive them out of your mind. Instead make the remembrance of them an opportunity to bless them. Patiently and lovingly go over them in your thought. Examine them with love-filled eyes. Instead of pushing them away from you, look at them more closely, more inwardly, until you discover the inmost good that they contain. If you find bitterness, fear, resentment, or discouragement in any of them, forgive the experiences, anyone connected with them, and yourself. If there is anything you can do to correct a mistake or to adjust a misunderstanding, resolve then and there to do it. Even make a memorandum of it for attention next day. Then dismiss it.

Be practical. If going over and over the problems and opportunities of the day that is closed, or the day that lies ahead, is likely to do any good, yield to this thought process and impartially consider the matters that concern you. Beyond that release them. Merely being unhappy or troubled about them never helps.

[216]

This is an indulgence that is in a class with other harmful human dissipations. You are working against the good when you permit the indulgence.

You say that you do none of these things and sleep still eludes you? Very well. Agree with that condition. Do not fight it. It will do you no harm to lie awake if only you keep relaxed. You will find rest and refreshment while awake as well as while asleep if your thoughts are right. Make your waking state a time of meditation upon Truth. Memorize and repeat some of the affirmations and prayers that especially appeal to you. Say over to yourself the lines of some beautiful poem, or one of the Psalms, particularly if you are fearful, afraid of danger during the night hours. Place yourself in God's care, and know that His love watches over you and those dear to your heart.

While you are resting, enjoy the luxury of unhurried, leisurely thought. During the active hours of the day you may not always have the opportunity to do this. Make the most of it. What a blessing it is that you can keep awake long enough to enjoy it. Ideas will come to you, ideas that are elusive during the hurried daytime hours. Again have recourse to a memorandum pad. Jot down these ideas. Thank the Father that He brings them to your consciousness.

Does it seem that we are avoiding the issue, that instead of offering help in getting sleep we are recommending that you stay awake comfortably and profitably? No. Sleep will come if you do not resist wakefulness. Your agreement with wakefulness is itself conducive to refreshing slumber.

"In peace will I both lay me down and sleep;
For thou, Jehovah, alone makest me dwell in safety."
"Rest in Jehovah, and wait patiently for him."
"My presence shall go *with thee,* and I will give thee rest."
"Sleep on now, and take your rest."
"When thou liest down, thou shalt not be afraid:
Yea, thou shalt lie down, and thy sleep shall be sweet."

MARY BREWERTON DEWITT

THE CONSECRATION OF
THE ROOM

THE BLESSING of consecration, or purification, given here
for house or room has been used for a number of years, and many
have been benefited by it. Sit calmly in the room and speak these
words aloud:

*There is only one presence in this room. This one presence is
the presence of God, or good. No evil can enter here. There is no
evil in God. God, the good, dwells here. Whoever enters here will
be conscious of the one divine presence of good.*

*There is only one presence here. This presence is the presence
of life. There is no death here, nor fear of death. There is only
life here. All fear is cast out. Whoever enters here will be conscious of this life, the pure, holy life of God.*

*There is only one presence here. This presence is the presence
of Truth. No untrue thing can enter here. There is no falsehood,
no deception, no envy, no jealousy, no selfishness, in this room.
Every untrue thought is cast out. Whoever enters here will be
conscious of the presence of Truth.*

*There is only one presence here, the presence of health. No
sickness can enter here; no impurity or fear can enter here. All
weakness and sickness are cast out. Whoever enters here will be
conscious of the presence of health.*

*There is only one presence here, the presence of purity. No
impure thought can enter here. I live and dwell in the pure and*

[218]

holy presence of God. Whoever enters here will be conscious of the pure and holy presence of God.

This room is filled with peace and harmony. I dwell in the presence of peace. No restless or discordant thought can enter here. No irritation or fear can enter here. The presence of God is peace. Whoever enters here will be conscious of the presence of peace.

This room is filled with prosperity. I cannot lack for any good thing. There is no dissatisfaction here. Whoever enters here will be conscious of contentment, satisfaction, and prosperity.

This room is filled with beauty. There is one presence here, the presence of beauty. In God is all spiritual beauty. My room is glorified by His holy presence. Whoever enters here will be conscious of the beauty of holiness.

There is one presence here, the presence of wisdom. All foolishness, ignorance, doubt, and superstition are cast out. God is here, and God is wisdom. I live and move in the presence of wisdom. Whoever enters here will be conscious of wisdom.

There is only one presence here, the presence of joy. Joy radiates here, filling this room. No sorrow can enter here. All depression is cast out. The joy of the Lord is here. I am surrounded by joy. I am filled with joy and happiness. Whoever enters here will be conscious of the presence of joy.

Only love dwells here. This room is filled with the presence of love. God is love, and love is here. All anger, hatred, and revenge are cast out. Love fills these walls. In love I live, move, and have my being. Whoever enters here will be conscious of the pure, holy presence of love.

I am thankful to Thee, O Father, that this room is filled with Thy presence. I am thankful that I live and move in Thee, O God, Thou holy One. I am thankful that I live in Thy life, Truth, health, prosperity, peace, wisdom, joy, and love. I am thankful that all who enter here will be conscious of Thy presence.

This blessing may be enlarged upon and added to; all those who use it realize the Truth in the word, for every good word is a power.

Note—These blessings may be used also as prayers for spiritual development, peace, harmony, health, or prosperity, either for self, friend, or relative, or for business firms, institutions, the city, the country, or the whole world. Ideas as to the best methods to follow will present themselves in each individual case. A plan that has proved helpful is to begin with the first statement, and use each prayer for one week, holding the thought several times daily. The following form will show beginners how to adapt the prayer to various needs:

"There is only one presence in me (you—this room—this institution—this city—this country—the world). This one presence is the presence of God, or good. No evil can enter here (come near me—you—this institution—this city—this country—the world). There is no evil in God. God the good, dwells here (in me—in you—in this city). Whoever enters here (this room—this store—this building—this institution—this city) (comes near me—you) will be conscious of the one divine presence of good."

MARY MAE OESCH

BEATITUDES FOR A HOUSEWIFE

BLESSED IS SHE whose daily tasks are a labor of love; for her willing hands and happy heart translate duty into privilege, and her labor becomes a service to God and all mankind.

Blessed is she who opens the door to welcome both stranger and well-loved friend; for gracious hospitality is a test of brotherly love.

Blessed is she who mends stockings and toys and broken hearts; for her understanding is a balm to humanity.

Blessed is she who scours and scrubs; for well she knows that cleanliness is one expression of godliness.

Blessed is she whom children love; for the love of a child is more to be valued than fortune or fame.

Blessed is she who sings at her work; for music lightens the heaviest load and brightens the dullest chore.

Blessed is she who dusts away doubt and fear and sweeps out the cobwebs of confusion; for her faith will triumph over all adversity.

Blessed is she who serves laughter and smiles with every meal; for her buoyancy of spirit is an aid to mental and physical digestion.

Blessed is she who preserves the sanctity of the Christian home; for hers is a sacred trust that crowns her with dignity.

PRAYER FOR PROTECTION

The light of God surrounds me;
The love of God infolds me;
The power of God protects me;
The presence of God watches over me.
Wherever I am, God is!

MY HAND IN GOD'S

Each morning when I wake I say,
"I place my hand in God's today";
I know He'll walk close by my side
My every wandering step to guide.

He leads me with the tenderest care
When paths are dark and I despair—
No need for me to understand
If I but hold fast to His hand.

My hand in His! No surer way
To walk in safety through each day.
By His great bounty I am fed;
Warmed by His love, and comforted.

When at day's end I seek my rest
And realize how much I'm blessed,
My thanks pour out to Him; and then
I place my hand in God's again.

WILLIAM H. FRAZIER

BLESSED HOME

God lives with me my home to bless
With peace and love and happiness;
His presence dwells in every room,
And thoughts of love replace all gloom.

His blessing rests upon the walls,
The basement, attic, floors, and halls;
My cupboards full shall ever be,
For God Himself is blessing me.

ANNA H. KING

CHEERFUL RESOLVE

I've reached my threescore years and ten,
The Bible limit; so what then?
I've still ten fingers, all my toes,
See with my eyes, scent with my nose.
Should I bring walking to a stop,
All my activities let drop?
Have I delayed my flight too long,
Or should I go on with a song?

For still I love to laugh and joke
And play at games with friendly folk.
Perhaps the good Lord wants me here;
Thinks maybe I can spread some cheer
In all this time of want and gloom;
Feels that there still is lots of room
For greetings gay and laughter sound.
So maybe I'll just linger round!

7. Love Is the Magnet

"Love is the magnet. You must have love.
You cannot live without it. Then begin to live
in the thoughts of love. Center your love thoughts
upon God and you will find love for your fellow
man growing marvelously."

—*Charles Fillmore*

LOWELL FILLMORE

THE POWER OF NONRESISTANCE

WE SOMETIMES TRY to make ourselves believe that memories of bygone mistakes are valuable. The other day I heard a true story about a small-town merchant who has been successful through both lean and good years. He always did well even when other merchants had difficulties. A friend once asked him why he was so successful, and he replied that it was because he did not kid himself. He explained that statement by saying that when at the end of a season he had a stock of out-of-date goods left over, he charged off his loss on it at once instead of carrying the old valuation on his inventory. In this way his books showed what his sound assets really were, and he conducted his business successfully on the basis of the actual value of his assets, forgetting all fictitious values.

If we would charge off from our mental inventories those experiences which are no longer valuable and would give our attention to the business of the present, we should be able to keep out of mental and physical bankruptcy even under strenuous circumstances.

That nothing plus nothing equals nothing, and that nothing plus something equals something, everyone will agree, but few of us realize that this law holds true in all our affairs. If something happens in our daily program that we realize is unprofitable—perhaps a quarrel, a lie about us, or gossip—the question arises, What can we add to such an experience to give it value? Can we avoid thinking, saying, or doing something else that is equally unprofitable? If we can, we are in a position to contribute something to the experience that is valuable. We can express something by thought and word, if not by deed, that will promote love, forgiveness, and good will, so that the final results of the occurrence will be worth while.

There is a universal principle of nonresistance that if properly applied will add value to every negative experience. This principle may be stated in several ways: Agree with your adversary. If somebody asks you to go with him a mile, go with him two miles. If you are struck on one cheek turn the other. Do not resist evil. The meek shall inherit the earth. Satan cannot cast out Satan.

He who expressed these ideas understood the principle of nonresistance. He proved the power of the principle and by its use He made a lasting impression upon the human race that no amount of selfishness has been able to efface.

The only way to overcome evil is to replace it or redeem it with good. By fighting evil with evil we merely add evil to evil, and the result is more evil. But good overcomes evil as light overcomes darkness. Darkness added to darkness results only in darkness.

We sometimes feel that we should like to thrash an offender. This is an immature idea. Reason tells us that two wrongs cannot make a right. The wrong done cannot be corrected by a thrashing. It can be corrected only by something constructive. Something true and good must replace the wrong. A pupil's mistake in working a problem can be corrected only when he learns the right principle or idea. The teacher helps the student to correct his mistake by giving him a correct idea. Giving him another mistaken idea would not help. If I have taken upon myself the responsibility of correcting an error made by my neighbor I must give him a correct or true idea and not another wrong idea. Thrashing him will never show him the right way, but will only confuse him the more. The world moves on ideas. False ideas cause wrongdoing. Only right ideas can produce righteousness.

Wars are based on the fallacy that strife added to strife will make peace. It cannot be brought about in that way. Strife added to strife will produce superstrife. Strife is caused by ideas of disorder, ignorance, hate, and the like. It can be overcome only by harmonious ideas backed up by intelligence and love.

There is a barbaric notion in the race mind that good will has no power to change adverse will, and that evil must be fought with evil. Through thousands of years we have been trying to work out our problems according to this notion, and have always failed because every fight stirs up more ill will. Jesus Christ has shown us the true principles, but we are as yet not courageous enough to use them. We are afraid to do the loving, generous thing; so we fight. We are too weak and ignorant to stand up in our divine right and prove that we are real civilized men and women instead of untamed barbarians.

It requires true bravery to express nonresistance and love. When we are truly brave we shall overcome the strife of the world. The world will never know peace, and men will never be happy in association with one another before they learn that evil must be overcome with good. There is no other way.

WILFERD A. PETERSON

THE MASTER'S TEN LAWS
OF HUMAN RELATIONS

FOR A LONG TIME it has seemed to me that someone should endeavor to set down briefly and consecutively the words of Jesus of Nazareth that apply most specifically to industrial relations. These words could then serve as a guide to labor and management in the practical application of Christian principles to what may be called human engineering.

With this objective in mind I have read through my New Testament several times, marking the words of the Master that seem to me to have the most significance for industry. Reading the New Testament in this light, I discovered that it is the world's greatest manual on human relations. To present the teachings of Jesus in full as they apply to industry would require a sizable book, and sizable books on serious subjects are read by too few. So I have endeavored to select the ten statements that summarize, in my opinion, the application of the Christian principles to human relations in business and industry.

1. *"Agree with thine adversary quickly."*

You must get in step with a man and start moving in his direction, with him, to influence him to go your way willingly. The tugs that pull the giant steamships out of the harbors into the open sea do not crash head-on into the sides of the giant ships. They ease themselves alongside, heading in the same direction as the steamships, and soon the little tugs work the miracle of pulling the majestic ocean liners in the desired direction.

Head-on human collisions cause many wrecks in industry. Arguments are won at the cost of friendships. The wise foreman or executive knows the power of suggestion. He rubs the fur the right way. He gets results by indirection. He mentally disarms his adversary by first agreeing with him and then gradually swinging him in the direction he wishes him to go. He uses the soft answer to turn away wrath. Instead of throwing dynamite into the fire of ill will, he uses the fire extinguisher of tact and understanding to put out the fire. He gets into the other fellow's shoes before he passes judgment. He knows that honey catches more flies than vinegar. Instead of driving men he draws out the best in them. He makes them desire to go his way by making his way their way also. When Jesus said, "Come ye after me, and I will make you fishers of men," He was talking the language of the men He wished to win to His cause. He was using the technique we are outlining here.

2. *"And whosoever shall compel thee to go one mile, go with him two."*

Someone has defined a genius as a man with his heart harnessed to his task. The first mile that a Roman soldier could *compel* a Jew to carry his burden was drudgery for the Jew. It was something he was forced to do; his heart was not in it. But when a man goes the second mile of his own accord, because he wants to render the service, that is when he finds happiness. One of the big tasks of industry is to glorify work, to inspire workers, to put the thrill of heart interest into work.

In his famous sermon on "The Second Mile," Harry Emerson Fosdick said:

. . . Underneath every other practical necessity is the elemental "must" of the breadwinner. Now this compulsion may be faced in one of two ways. If he will, a man may accept it doggedly, skimpingly perform the bare requirements, and bitterly trudge that one scant mile.

Thousands of men work that way, with their eyes on the clock. Or a man may welcome the necessity of work, recognize the dignity of honest toil, and in that way go the second mile, translating duty into privilege. Work, greeted like that, loses the frown of compulsion and begins to smile. When a man works that way he feels that it is his meat and drink, wishes there were more hours in the day than twenty-four, and dreams of heaven as a place where a man can work all the time at his best and never be tired. All the slavery of work vanishes for such a man.

Sweat and toil and labor have been considered ugly words, something to dodge. These words must be given new and inspired meaning by industry. We must revise the definitions. Industry should go the "second mile" to make working conditions safer, easier, friendlier, cleaner, more enjoyable. Give the worker more than he expects and you will get more than you expect from the worker. "Give, and it shall be given unto you."

3. *"Every tree that bringeth not forth good fruit is hewn down, and cast into the fire."*

To succeed, men must be creators, not parasites. They must bear the fruits of energy, ideas, ideals, methods, plans, designs. They must produce, achieve, contribute! Thus only do they grow and serve. Success must be earned; it must be deserved. There are those who seem to get by without giving forth good fruit, but they are riding for a fall. Sooner or later they will be cast into the fire. To get from life we must give to life. The richer our gifts the more we will receive in return. The law of compensation works for us or against us, depending on the kind of material we furnish it to work with.

A business organization may also be likened to a tree. It must serve the public, it must give forth good products, honest products, quality products, if it is to grow and flourish. It must perform a useful function and give value "pressed down, shaken together, running over" if it is to survive. In the years ahead business competition will be intense. The consumers will demand only "good fruit." The firms that fail to deliver will be cast into the fire of failure. Like individuals, a business must give or go! The only sound basis on which to build a life or a business is to bear good fruit.

4. *"All things therefore whatsoever ye would that men should do unto you, even so do ye also unto them: for this is the law and the prophets."*

I purposely did not put the Golden Rule first in my list of the Master's words, because that is where you would expect to find it. Everyone agrees that the Golden Rule expresses life's highest idealism. So much has been said about the Golden Rule that talking about it has become somewhat commonplace. But there is nothing commonplace about its application. Somehow I think we have come to think of the Golden Rule in its national and international applications to such an extent that we have missed applying it in the many little ways in which we could put it into daily use. There would be no wars if all nations practiced the Golden Rule, we say, forgetting that many little wars could be eliminated in the same way, little wars in our home, in our offices, in our factories.

Here is how you can put the Golden Rule into action tomorrow. Make a list of the things you like to have people do to you, then do those things to them. Do you like praise? Then praise others. Praise your wife's dinner. Praise the men under you for the good work they are doing. Praise your children for the good marks they are getting in school. You like to have others greet you with a cheerful "Good morning!" don't you? Then greet them that way.

The Golden Rule is a long rule; it reaches from you here on earth to the highest peak of mankind's ideals. And as we use it today where we are, we best extend its use into all spheres of life.

5. *"Not that which entereth into the mouth defileth the man; but that which proceedeth out of the mouth, this defileth the man."*

The ranting, hysterical words of hatred and bitterness issuing forth from the mouth of Adolf Hitler plunged the world into what was perhaps the most terrible war in all history. And in those words and the ideas expressed were the seeds of his own doom. They set into motion mighty forces of retaliation to bring about his destruction.

Hitler is the world's number one example of the destructive power of negative thinking. He sought victory through hatred, he poisoned the thought life of his people, he created world-wide ill will, and he reaped what he sowed. The law must work.

Almost all the trouble in the world is created by things people think, say, and write. Words of anger, malice, hatred, resentment, jealousy, like physical blows, cause people to hit back. Overbearing, demanding words create determined resistance. And the attitudes of mind back of them, even though we do not speak the words, are sensed by others. For the telepathic power of thought is no longer merely a theory. Thoughts are things.

Abraham Lincoln is a glowing example of one who in thought, word, and deed endeavored to express the goodness of God. What came out of his mouth and his heart united men, created understanding, established teamwork and harmony. He expressed justice, calmness, quietness, tolerance, good will, love. What a contrast to the wild, excited, angry words and attitudes that separate men and create wide seas of misunderstanding between them.

Hitler's attitudes and words have defiled him and made him one of the most hated men of all history. Lincoln's attitudes and words have made him one of the most beloved men of the ages.

That which comes out of your mouth, your expression of ideas and attitudes, the visible and audible expression of what goes on in your mind and heart—this paints your portrait for the world to see! This determines in a mighty measure your success in your contacts with others.

In Tibet, when the natives meet, they stick out their tongues at each other. This is to show that there are no evil words on their tongues! It should also mean that there are no evil thoughts in their heads. Labor and management should sit down at the conference table in the same spirit.

6. *"And whosoever would be first among you, shall be your servant."*

These eleven words express the ideal of leadership in a democracy. Not the great dictator but the great servant is the symbol of the leader. Such a philosophy of leadership involves not so much a sense of power as a sense of obligation. Such a leader does not hold people down; he lifts them up. He does not repress people; he endeavors to express their wishes, purposes, aims. He does not tear men down; he builds men up. He seeks out their undeveloped capacities and helps men and women to grow and expand their personalities.

A business builder today must also be a man builder. He duplicates himself in others. He serves his employees by helping them to succeed, and in doing this he also best serves his business, helping it to grow. He realizes that many big men in a business make a stronger business than a business with only one big man at the head of it. Employees are jewels to be polished.

The totalitarian concept of leadership considers the people

the slaves of the State. The great servant concept considers the people as the ones to be served.

The top executive of a business should think of himself as a master servant of employees, customers, and stockholders. He is working for them. In the measure that he wins their loyalty and devotion he will create a spirit of teamwork and harmony, and lead the business along the road to true prosperity and success.

Labor, too, should consider itself as a servant. From top executive to janitor, all who work are paid by customers. The customer is the big boss of all of us. The amount of money in our pay envelopes depends on how well we serve the customer and how many customers we hold year after year.

Service is the key to true leadership of both men and institutions.

7. *"Feed my sheep."*

The wise executive feeds the whole man. Much of our lack of harmony in industry has been due to the fact that we have thought in terms of physical hunger alone; we have concentrated on the monetary return to the worker. Men have many hungers to be satisfied. Men hunger for appreciation, praise, recognition, acceptance as worth-while personalities. Adler, one of the major figures in modern psychiatry, said that most of all a man wants to feel significant; he wants to feel that he counts. Another psychologist lists four things that men live by—work, play, love, and worship. When these four factors are balanced in a man's life, he attains happiness. The modern executive broadens the scope of his work to include all the factors that make for human happiness.

Leland Stowe, famous war correspondent, told a group of us one of the secrets of Russian morale. Almost every regiment has a newspaper where the names of men doing heroic deeds are listed. By satisfying this hunger for recognition great soldiers are made. Medals and insignia of rank in all armed forces serve a similar purpose. Industry should adopt similar techniques.

A sales research organization checked the motives of salesmen. Monetary return was fourth in the list! Ahead of it came the desire to excel, the desire to be a leader, the desire to win a prize—often of little monetary value.

Many of us have been amazed at the "foolish" reasons for

calling many strikes and walkouts in industry. Often the strikes have not involved wages or hours. Psychologically the hidden factors have been pride, exhibitionism, loyalty to fellow workers, desire to be recognized.

A new day will dawn in industry as executives heed the command of Jesus, "Feed my sheep." When men are given something more than bread to work for, when the pay is expanded beyond the satisfying of physical hunger alone, to include the hungers of mind, heart, and spirit, then we shall be drawing near to the goal of brotherhood in industry.

8. *"But if ye forgive not men their trespasses, neither will your Father forgive your trespasses."*

I talked with an executive recently who is intensely bitter and resentful toward his employees. He feels that they have been traitors to the management, that they have let him down, that they walked roughshod over him and took advantage of the war situation to gain their ends. He is waiting eagerly for revenge. He intends to get that revenge as soon as unemployment looms on the horizon.

The future of industry depends in large measure on executives' being big enough, great enough, and noble enough to forgive and forget, to wipe the slate clean of malice, intolerance, and bitterness. Now as never before in the history of industrial America the times call for true greatness. It is my opinion that the great majority of industrial leaders will rise to the occasion. They will meet the challenge to be big enough and great enough to turn from the misunderstandings of yesterday and walk gallantly into the future.

Labor, too, must be big enough to forgive. At times it has been exploited, ignored, and taken advantage of. It must be great enough to forgive the sins of management, as management forgives the sins of labor. Each must humbly acknowledge its own shortcomings and not attempt to blame the other for all the discord and friction. Both have sinned and come short of the glory of God.

The only effective antidote for the poison of hatred and bitterness is forgiveness. Forgiveness is a mental sulfa drug, a miracle medicine, which can do much to restore industry to spiritual health and vigor.

Hatred, bitterness, and resentment build barriers between men which can only be melted away by forgiveness. Forgiveness sweeps the way clear for a fresh start.

When Peter asked Jesus how many times he should forgive his enemies the Master's reply was that he should forgive his enemies "until seventy times seven" times. That is four hundred and ninety times! That is something to shoot at for both labor and management. Only if we are big enough to forgive shall we be saved.

9. *"Every city or house divided against itself shall not stand."*

When labor and management sit down at the conference table, God should be on both sides of the table! With God on both sides of the table the decisions made will be for the mutual good of management and labor.

Labor and management live in the same house. Their interests are identical; they play on the same team. What hurts the business as a whole hurts both labor and management. What is good for business as a whole is good for both labor and management.

A professional union leader of the old school confided to me his working philosophy. He believes that it is his job to fight management constantly. He does not agree even when he knows management is in the right, for to agree would be to acknowledge weakness and lose face with his followers. He treats management as an enemy, not a friend. Off the record he will admit that he is often just putting on an act, but he says that only by picking flaws and finding fault and waging constant war with management can he make a job for himself. This type of leader is unionism's greatest enemy. He divides the house and brings it down on all our heads!

The new union leader considers labor and management a partnership. He believes that by fighting together for a common cause labor and management will go much farther than by fighting each other. He recognizes that the earning power of a business depends on cutting costs and increasing production, and that only as a business earns more can it pay more. Therefore he believes that it is to labor's advantage to help cut costs and increase production and that to do anything else is to kill the goose that lays the golden egg. He sells labor on uniting with management, pulling in the same direction, working together. He is the creator of industrial harmony, not discord. The future of unionism depends on the multiplication of this type of leadership.

The only way for a business firm to get its house in order for the future is to make it a house united! The "Men Working" sign should be changed to read "Men Working Together!"

10. *"Stretch forth thy hand."*

When Jesus healed the withered hand of the man in the synagogue He commanded, "Stretch forth thy hand!" And the hand was restored. It seems to me that the command of Jesus to this generation might well be summed up in those words. They radiate the spirit of Christianity, dynamic Christianity in action among men. "Stretch forth thy hand!" Stretch it forth in friendship, in sincerity, in good will. Executives, stretch forth your hands to labor. Labor, stretch forth your hands to management. White men, stretch forth your hand to the Negro! The open, outstretched hand harbors no knife of treachery! It is the universal symbol of peace, harmony, co-operation.

Don't wait for the other person to step forward and stretch out his hand to you first. *You* start it! To make a friend be a friend. To win good will give good will. "Stretch forth thy hand!" The outstretched hands of men and women of all groups, classes, races, and colors can restore and heal all America and make us a strong and united nation.

"Stretch forth thy hand!"

CLEDA REYNER

THE WAY THROUGH
GETHSEMANE

IF WE WERE asked to name one of the most important
aids to individual, family, community, or world happiness we
should not have to think hard or long to decide on forgiveness.

Imagine if you can the troubles and the squabbles of the
world being carried over and added to from day to day without
the leaven of forgiveness intervening. The awful weight of human
woe, hate, and condemnation would very soon annihilate all life
and its expressions. Forgiveness is essential.

On the very small scale of your own life think what a load of
grievances, hurt feelings, and injustices you would have on hand
at the present time if forgiveness had not relieved the burden of
lightening your load now and then. Forgiveness is vital!

In spite of all that forgiveness has done and is capable of
doing, however, we are much too sluggish at times as channels of
its expression. Family rifts have existed for years when forgiveness would have restored harmony and the joyous unity of a
family circle. Friendships that once meant mutual happiness have
been severed interminably for lack of forgiveness. Misunderstandings between partner and partner or employer and employee have existed to the disadvantage of all concerned when
forgiveness would have meant all-round prosperity. We could
well devote a portion of our time to learning more than we know
about forgiveness.

A doctor of divinity said in a recent sermon that if Jesus had not found it in His heart to say, "Father, forgive them," as He hung on the cross, there would have been no Resurrection. We can see that there would not have been. A spirit that was bound in any measure by a sense of injustice, or that harbored harsh judgment or condemnation could not have transcended all earthly things. Only a soul that was entirely free and unhampered could have accomplished that.

All forgiveness is divided into two parts. One part is the experience of those who have not yet been through the garden of Gethsemane, and the other part is the experience of those who have entered and passed victoriously to the other side. Let me illustrate.

Some person has treated us shabbily. We had had great faith in him. It seems inconceivable that he could have done to us the things he actually has done. It is not pleasant to be disappointed in one who has displayed such qualities as integrity, friendship, and loyalty. But it is not easy either to carry a load of disappointment on our heart day after day. It interferes definitely with our health and with the orderly progress of our affairs. Life has to go on, so we are almost compelled to forgive. But we do so with reservations. We will forgive but we will remember. And we promise ourselves that we shall not lay ourselves open to any more experiences like that. We shall be more alert next time to the possibilities of human weakness. We are on this side of Gethsemane.

As we go on we find that we are faced again and again with the need to forgive. Seventy times seven times we have occasion for doing so. But in time we have come to the place where we can quickly release all bitterness from our mind and heart. No matter how cruelly we have been hurt we can quickly reassert our poise, our mental and emotional equilibrium. The things that used to eat at our vitals for days very seldom reach our deeper feelings now. We do not expect people to live up to a standard of perfection any more. We can even understand in many instances their reasons for not doing so. We are still on this side of Gethsemane.

As time goes on, however, we learn more and more about the forgiving love of Jesus Christ, and we truly desire in our heart to become more and more like Him. We find that we can look at the people in the world, their selfishnesses, their greed, their money-making schemes, their thoughtless search for pleasure, with a great tolerance in our heart toward them. We see a great mass of people hungry for happiness and satisfaction. A deep pity and compassion fills our heart for those who so ignorantly, blindly, and futilely feed their souls on empty outer things when they are starving for reality. Even yet we are on this side of Gethsemane.

Then finally we come to the garden that isn't located at the foot of the Mount of Olives so far as we are concerned but at the foot of a very high place in consciousness. Whether we ascend to it or not is another matter. It is here that the soul makes known its great desire for freedom and for victory. It is here that the outer, personal man fights for his life, his identity, and his power. There have been issues to meet and decisions to make all along the way, but the time has now come when he must grant supremacy either to the human or the divine. It is in the mind where all victories and defeats take place. What happens in an outer way after the inner unfolding has occurred is merely the law fulfilling itself. This fulfillment is an effortless thing as far as man is concerned. It was within the garden that the resurrection was actually achieved, for it was there that Jesus drew from the Spirit in the midst of Himself the courage to face crucifixion, the power to defy all known laws of the grave, and a divine resistance to all human reasoning. Beside the struggle that look place in the mind of earth's greatest man the experience on Calvary was easy. We know in our own small way that the greatest hardships we have to meet are the ones that take place in the mind. If we meet them there, actual experience is only incidental.

Well, let us assume that we are victorious in our garden too. Then we encounter someone who treats us far from honestly. We have had every reason to believe in him. We have depended on him in many, many ways. Now he has in fact acted contrary to our every expectation. Do we forgive him? We have nothing to forgive. The man that we see has not failed us, nor disappointed us, nor shamed us. He is a potential son of God. To be sure, he has stumbled while crossing our pathway, but our concern is only for him. We see him for what he is, a son of the Most High God who has temporarily lost his course and his bearings. Our only impulse is to steady him and to set him right. It does not occur to us that our own progress has been hindered; we give ourselves no part in the picture. We are on the other side of Gethsemane!

Seventy times seven times do we encounter people who stumble in front of us. They may brush us off our feet in their intensity or preoccupation as they hurry to some selfset goal. They may even strip us of what we consider to be ours if it will further their own progress. I mean by this that they may accept honor and credit and praise that we feel belong to us. I mean that through political influence or some kind of favoritism they may obtain a position we feel we have earned by honest effort. I mean that they may intrude upon friendships and cherished relations. I mean that they may claim any number of things that we value.

But so completely did the human part of us merge into the divine while we were in Gethsemane that we are not conscious of any necessity to forgive. The divinity in us beholds only the divinity in others. We bless the eyes that look down instead of up. Through the power of thought and prayer we share the knowledge that individual progress does not have to be gained at the expense of another. And we remain both calm and happy if our possessions seem disturbed. We know that no one can take from us that which is truly our own, and we know that what is ours will come to us. We are conscious of our oneness with all good and we bless our fellows with the same knowledge concerning themselves. We are on the other side of Gethsemane.

"Father, forgive them" was not uttered by one who at that moment had just purged His mind and heart of human reactions to ignominious treatment. It was love full and perfect asking a blessing upon people that He understood more fully than they understood themselves. Instead of madness and frenzied cruelty He saw only the Father's image. Forgiveness is essential, and forgiveness is vital as long as the bright sun of righteousness is eclipsed by even a shadow of the mortal mind. As long as we entertain even briefly in our heart a feeling of hate or dislike for our fellow men we need to give for it a feeling of love. If misunderstanding has been a barrier to oneness with another of God's children we need to exchange that feeling for one of full comprehension. But love such as possesses the soul when it has passed through Gethsemane victoriously has nothing to forgive. It loves all, understands all, blesses all.

LOWELL FILLMORE

CONQUERING JEALOUSY

REMEMBER that jealousy is a soul disease that causes its victim to suffer mental torture and also adversely affects the functions of his body and his harmonious association with other persons.

Jealousy works on a person's mind in such a subtle way that its unhappy victim often blames other persons for his plight instead of himself, the real culprit. It is almost unbelievable that there are so many good and well-meaning persons who are suffering from this mental malady not knowing what ails them.

Jealousy is often so deeply hidden in a person's subconscious mind that he does not realize that he is jealous. Sometimes others are aware of his condition while he is ignorant of it. He realizes that something is wrong and that he is not happy, and so concludes that outer circumstances are to blame. The question of how or when jealousy entered his consciousness does not matter so much as how he can be rid of it.

He may have acquired it in childhood. Perhaps he became jealous when he thought his parents were showing greater affection and attention to his brothers or sisters than to him, and he told himself that they were getting something that he wanted and he must find a way to get even with the favored ones. Seed thoughts of hate were thus sown among the thoughts of love in his consciousness. These may have grown unnoticed in his subconscious mind, influencing his thoughts and acts without his consent. This does not explain the cause of every person's jealousy, but the point is that no matter how a person acquired it he should not allow it to spoil his career. God's plan for every man and woman is that they are to be happy in serving God and man unselfishly.

If you are unhappy and you have any reason to believe that possibly your unhappiness is being caused by a hidden feeling of jealousy, you should face the problem and analyze your motives carefully. If you find that you are jealous, admit it and cast out the feeling by forgiving yourself and asking God to forgive you also. Then begin forgiving those who have aroused jealousy in you. Forgiveness is the most effective method of removing this kind of trouble. By forgiving all the mistakes of the past, be they your own or those made by other persons, you free yourself from unhealthy weeds that may be growing in your subconscious mind.

I ask you, "Is it reasonable that you should be unhappy when something good comes to another person instead of to you?" When you are sure that God is your unfailing source of supply you feel so rich as you abide in His love that you rejoice when you see someone receiving something good whether you think he deserves it or not.

We should form the habit of giving thanks when we hear that good has come to someone. This habit brings us closer to the source of all blessings, which makes it possible for us to enter into the Spirit of blessing so that blessings greet us on every hand. No matter if another person has attained something good that we desired but failed to attain, we should rejoice anyway; because it shows us that good is possible of attainment, and if he attained it so can we.

If someone who works with you seems to have more favor in the eyes of the boss than you do, do not worry about it. Worry and hurt feelings only make it more difficult for you to succeed in doing what is pleasing to God and man. The way to success is made easier for you when you think thoughts of success and praise rather than thoughts of resentment and discouragement. Make friends with success by giving thanks for it wherever you see it.

Do not be afraid that somebody will take your good away from you. When you are afraid, worried, and resentful you cut down your own power to receive good. Do not surround yourself with a thought aura of negative, vengeful, hurt feelings, for this will make all your associates shun you.

Even a boss may at times suffer from jealousy, which may cause him to fear that his helpers will receive credit for their good suggestions and thus discredit his ability. When he trusts God instead of nursing a jealous heart he knows that every good work that comes out of his department is a credit to him, and he should thank God for it. A department head's greatest value is his ability to encourage and advance his subordinates. When we would render our best possible services we must not allow jealousy to becloud our vision.

If our success is so insecure that it cannot stand up when other persons succeed it is not true success.

We must practice putting all our affairs into the hands of God while we rejoice in the success of every person, even our competitors. It cannot help us to grieve when others succeed. But it does help a lot when we rejoice in their good fortune, for this puts us in friendly relationship with success.

By being forgiving and thankful always, you will become a magnet to attract good to you. Therefore you do not need to worry about anyone else's good fortune. Back of material good fortune is spiritual good fortune. Build up your spiritual reserve of good fortune, and then go forward in the faith that God will supply all your needs bountifully and that there is nothing to fear from competition.

Realize that when you are loving, forgiving, and happy you are keeping close to the divine source, God, from whom all your good comes. No one in all the world can take away your good when you keep close to God in spirit. Hate, self-pity, resentment, and suspicion never helped anyone to attain real success and happiness.

Truth students should never allow hidden jealousy to cause them unhappiness, because they know the law of the creative power of thought. Good thoughts bring good results. Jealous thoughts are not good thoughts. Therefore jealousy is unprofitable and unnecessary, and it can be cast out by the power of God.

COMPILED BY SILENT UNITY

HELP FOR ALCOHOLICS

To EVERYONE faced with the problem of alcoholism, either his own or someone else's, Unity gives this assurance: Alcoholism can be healed! When we pray for those who seem in bondage to the drink habit we go beyond the surface appearance and pray for the whole man. To pray only for the overcoming of the habit of drink is to deal with the end result, not the cause. The alcoholic needs help not for alcoholism alone but for all that is behind the alcoholism, which is but the symptom of the real need.

We know that even in the person who seems far removed from the image and likeness of God in every way there is a spark of divinity, there is the Spirit of God innate in him, however unaware he and everyone about him may be of this fact. His hope lies in this spark of divinity: "Christ in you, the hope of glory." The help that can be given him through prayer lies in the realization of this Spirit in him.

We do not condemn the one who is considered an alcoholic any more than we condemn the one who asks for help in regaining his health. We know that there is a need of healing in both cases, and we have faith that all things are possible to God, that there is nothing too hard for Him.

Even a person who feels that he cannot help himself, that he is in hopeless bondage to the habit of drink, has something in him that responds to the idea that he is a spiritual being, that he is a child of God, that he has been given dominion and mastery

[248]

from the beginning of time. It takes but a little faith to rekindle the divine fire in man. Prayer can rekindle, reawaken the spirit in a man so that he will come to himself, as it were, so that he will realize that he is greater than circumstances, stronger than habit, that he can begin again. Like the prodigal son he can say to himself, "I will arise and go to my Father."

In God's sight there are no alcoholics, there are only souls seeking light and freedom and peace, God's children on the road of life searching for the way of happiness.

If you would help someone who seems in bondage to drink, cease thinking of him as an alcoholic and think of him first and foremost as a child of God, think of him as possessing a divine spark that can be quickened into a strong fire of courage and faith. Bless him in your thoughts, give him your love and faith and understanding, and trust the Father in him to bring him safely through. What you cannot do for him, what no other person in the world can do for him, the Spirit of God in him can do. The Spirit of God in him can lift him out of the self that has given way to defeat and despair and reawaken his spiritual nature. What your prayers and faith do is to help to quicken the Spirit of God in him.

If you who read this have considered yourself an alcoholic, begin to change your thought about yourself. Say to yourself again and again until the truth of it stays with you: "I am a spiritual being. I am created in the image and likeness of God, and through His Spirit in me I am able to meet everything in my life. I am strong in the Lord, and in the power of His might."

Unity stands ready and willing to help you or your loved ones. We are with you always in Spirit, and our constant realization is that the power of God is able to do all things, that there is no person beyond His help, no condition outside His healing power.

RICHARD J. LYNCH

THE ART OF APPRECIATION

EVERY PERSON recognizes the psychological effect of appreciation in his own experience. It adds zest to work and joy to
life, inspiring willing, devoted service, whereas ingratitude on the
other hand is "sharper than a serpent's tooth" and just as deadly.
One attracts, the other repels. One opens the floodgates of enthusiasm, the other closes and barricades the sluices of plenty.

Other qualities of spirit are included in appreciation. It has
clear insight, correct judgment, the beauty of harmony and good
will. Only the little, narrow soul is concerned with envy and its
ugly brood of jealous, critical self-seekers. Appreciation springs
from fineness of character and high spiritual motive, from depth
of understanding and unselfish purpose. It is the positive motive power behind gratitude, and its dynamic energy, set in
motion, is both constructive and reactive. It is one of the most
important and at the same time one of the simplest acts of the
mind. The appreciative spirit is in closer touch with its source in
All-Good than the one that takes its blessings for granted or ha-
bitually bewails its misfortunes.

Real appreciation cannot be compelled. It springs from an
inner impulse, is inspired by love and coupled with justice and
understanding. It is the very foundation of continuous harmony
in all human relations, whether those of the family or of the social or the business world. Love and friendship are lighted at its
altar, for our friends are those who value us for what we really
are. They are not blind to our faults, but they see them in relation

to our virtues, and on this they base their judgment and build their appreciation.

The tender child mind cannot thrive in a coldly critical atmosphere of distrust and faultfinding. Fortunate indeed are the children whose parents understand the value of appreciative praise. Even though they may at times stray far from home, like the prodigal son, they will always remember, as he did, that in the Father's house are love and understanding: "I will arise and go to my father." How sure he was of his parent! How well he knew what he might expect!

Appreciation and its expression are valuable assets in the life of an employer. In a way those who serve him are as children, looking to him for guidance. They depend upon his recognition and valuation of their efforts and are responsive to his genuine praise. The service he obtains by fear of criticism or loses from consequent lack of interest is a poor, negative thing, without the fire of enthusiasm that is kindled at the altar of appreciation.

Appreciation is a fine art involving one of the most important principles of mental action. It also includes one of the simplest laws of physics—one that even a child can understand—the equivalence of action and reaction. For every force set in motion there is an equal and opposite counterforce. There can be no action without its corresponding reaction.

Appreciation releases its stored-up energy as gratitude, which in turn feeds the activity of thanksgiving. Force thus expended must, according to principle, react or rebound in proportion to its motive power. The life, the love, and the success we appreciate, whether in our own life or that of others, come back to us in exact proportion to the gratitude that we ourselves have set in motion.

On the other hand, if we have neglected to be grateful for our blessings, if we have taken them for granted or perhaps criticized them, we have liberated a force just as powerful—the negative force of ingratitude. Its rebound is just as inevitable as that of its opposite. The secret of so many failures lies in the tendency of most people to fix their thought upon negative conditions. They are always ready to rehearse their troubles at length, to emphasize lack and limitation, sickness and old age.

In one of his letters to his pupil Timothy, the apostle Paul wrote, "Stir up the gift of God, which is in thee." We all need this advice. We need to appreciate, not only that which God has placed within us as individuals, but all the good that has come to humanity. If we have but one talent, we need not envy another who has two or perhaps five. By recognition and use we may double and redouble, indefinitely, the one we possess. Appreciative interest and enthusiastic effort will work miracles for us, but a thought of limitation may deprive us even of that which we now have.

In relating the parable of the talents Jesus made it plain that each man received according to his ability. To one the master gave five talents, to another two, and to the third a single talent only. Appreciative endeavor soon worked miracles for the first two stewards. Grateful for their master's confident belief in their ability and honest loyalty, they at once set about the business of increasing his substance. Neither complained because he had been given *only* five or *only* two. Each fixed his attention upon his own portion and soon each doubled its amount.

But the poor, fearful steward with no sense of appreciation in his mind and no buoyant sense of gratefulness in his heart, went "and hid his lord's money." To him the master was a hard man, selfish and unfair. What was one insignificant talent when others had been given more! So he dug in the earth of envious ingratitude and hid his trust fund. And the law worked for him also. The thought of limitation that he placed upon his portion reacted upon him in due time, for he lost even that which he had.

There is nothing mysterious about what we call good luck. It is the working out of principle. It is an answer to the prayer of grateful appreciation expressed in praise and thanksgiving. For that prayer is a prayer of appropriation. It woos the hidden potentialities of the universe into visible form. As the spring sun invites the hidden seeds and bulbs until they burst forth in exquisite expression, so the acknowledgment of blessings attracts and magnifies the value of our God-given heritage of life and its infinite possibilities. Appreciation was the magic that Jesus used in the realm of the miraculous. "Father, I thank thee" was His habitual prayer.

Jesus was continually calling attention to the rewards of gratitude, yet He was amazed when He unexpectedly contacted the depth of appreciation shown Him by a certain centurion who requested healing for one of his faithful servants. The Master certainly did not need the comments upon the worthiness of the man from those who stood by, He soon found it out for Himself. Among the demands made upon Jesus—demands for help and requiring His personal presence—this appeal of the Roman captain must have astonished Him.

Accustomed, as Jesus was, to being summoned at any hour and expected to sacrifice His comfort and contribute His time and energy to all who claimed it, He said to the centurion who asked healing for his servant, "I will come and heal him." With what surprise He must have heard the centurion's reply, which was something like this: "Oh, no, sir. I appreciate Your position. I know how many demands are made upon You. I realize this because I too have responsibilities. My trouble is no greater than the troubles of others. I believe in You so implicitly I know that if You will but speak the word of truth, my servant will be healed."

When Jesus heard this He marveled at both the faith and the understanding of the man, which were greater than any expressed by even His close friends and followers. We are told how in that very instant His response went out to meet the request, for "the servant was healed in that hour."

The record of the incident ends here, but we need no report of that centurion's gratitude. He was so deeply versed in the art of appreciation, so considerate of the Master, so worthy and generous that any further report of his dealings with Jesus is unnecessary. We often hear it said that the spirit of appreciation and the sense of gratitude have grown feeble and very nearly dropped out of life. There are times when we almost believe this; circumstances make this seem true. But we are often surprised, as Jesus was, to find the quality where we least expected it.

Every art requires distinctive training and steadfast practice, and that of appreciation is no exception. Of all arts of the spirit it stands closest to the soul of being, as it affects every thought and qualifies every act of its possessor. It is one of the secrets of personal charm and the first attribute of a truly great nature.

He who would be versed in this finest of fine arts must learn its technique and live and work accordingly. He must have "the hearing ear, and the seeing eye," the wisdom to judge fairly, the love that does not envy or seek its own selfish ends or take account of evil, the desire to praise whatever is worthy both in others and in himself. As he understands life from this viewpoint, he cannot fail to recognize its privileges and its possibilities. Appreciation of these inspires his theme song, making it a psalm of praise and thanksgiving.

The grateful heart is a magnet that draws to itself ever more and more for which to be thankful. Let us magnetize ours to attract our full heritage of good.

GOD BLESS THIS AUTOMOBILE

THIS IS God's car. It neither gives nor receives offense in all its journeyings. God's hand is at the wheel. His wisdom chooses the way. God's law of order and right adjustment is manifest in all its mechanism. No fear alarms its occupants; for God's presence blesses them with the spirit of peace.

The driver of this car is an emissary of Spirit. God's wisdom inspires in him alertness, good judgment, and quick decision. God's patience gives him temperance and courtesy. The Spirit of the Lord is upon him and directs him in all his ways.

AIRPLANE BLESSING

THIS IS God's airplane. His intelligence is in every part of it. As He keeps the stars in their courses and the sun and moon in their paths, so He guides and directs this plane. He knows every highway and byway of the air even as He knows the highways and byways of the earth. I rest secure in His protecting presence, and all is well.

8. The Light Shines in the Darkness

"We are not to be too concerned

with the appearances of inharmony, lack,

and imperfections about us. These things

are not real, and they will pass away quickly

as Truth takes hold in the consciousness. We are

to remember that the Light shines in the darkness—

and that in the very midst of the darkness,

man's mind opens to the Light, and for him

there is no more darkness."

—*Myrtle Fillmore*

WILLIAM A. CLOUGH

BE NOT DISMAYED

THERE IS a solution for every problem. There is a cure
for every ill. There is nothing in your life, absolutely nothing,
that cannot be changed, corrected, and cured. There is no difficulty anywhere on earth that cannot be set right.

Truly this is a tremendous thought, but it is more than a
thought. It is the Truth. If you know and accept the Truth, the
Truth will make you free. You may not be able to understand or
believe it now, but it is absolutely true that the present condition
of your circumstances, your mind or body can be completely
changed.

Your misery can become happiness. Your fear can become
faith. Your confusion can become clear understanding. Your illness can become health. Your trouble can be taken away and no
longer exist. Though you cannot possibly see any way out, there
is a way. Though you are certain your trouble is beyond any possible cure, there is a cure.

Whoever you are, wherever you are, whatever your difficulty
may be, to you this is the word of truth: Be not dismayed; there
is help for you. You may be plunged in the deepest despair. You
may be engulfed in a depth of depression into which no flicker
of light shines. You may be torn by the terror of one great fear or
a multitude of fears. There is hope, and light, and assurance, and
sweet peace for you. There is a cure for you.

You have done something that you believe cannot be undone.
Someone you love has hurt you seemingly beyond any possible

[259]

mending. You have an illness of mind or body that has been pronounced incurable.

Still the answer comes with all the force of Truth behind it:
there is change, mending, cure complete and utter for you. Lift
up your head; lift up your heart. There is a dawning light, there
is a safe and sure retreat, there is an overcoming and a victory,
there is happiness and peace for you.

No empty, idle promise is this, no false illusion, no mirage to
lead you toward still deeper despair. It has the power and reality
of the universe behind it. It rests on the one great law of life. It
is the word of God.

You want to be free from the difficulties in which you find
yourself. You have cried out in agony of spirit for relief; but the
darkness does not lift, the sorrow does not go away. You cannot
get away from it.

Will you try this method then?

Start with the premise that you have been created by God,
the Father Spirit of all life. Believe that God is infinitely good,
that there is no wrong of any sort in Him. He created you, and
gave you life from Himself. He made you in His own image. The
life in you is God's life. Therefore it is good, just as He is good.
The real you, the spirit that God created, is good and perfect.
Try to believe that.

God took the real you, the spirit, and gave it a body and a
mind. He left your mind free to think as you direct it. Whether
you realize it or not, it is your mind now that is causing you your
trouble, and it is your mind reaching inward to the true you and
bringing it out that can cure it.

No longer blame any other person or circumstance for your
condition. No longer blame yourself. Have done with making
your problem the center of your thinking. Think instead that actually God is the center of your life, the core, the primary reality.
The circumstances that crowd around you, the thoughts that
twist and tear you, are not the true reality at all.

If you can get to the real you, which is God in you, and start
expressing your true self in your thinking, you will slowly but
surely see the change coming. Thought by thought, step by step,
day by day, you will see your mind changing. And miracle of
miracles, as your mind changes conditions change, other people

change for you. Your whole life changes. That is the amazing truth.

Cease to say to yourself: "I am unhappy. I am miserable. I am ill. I am in the grip of conditions and circumstances from which there is no release. I have been injured beyond repair. I am unable to rise above my fears and troubles."

Say rather: "I am made for happiness. I am made for health. The Spirit of God within me is perfect in every detail. I am that Spirit. I am the conqueror of all things through God who is in me. I am not weak. I am immeasurably strong. I am able through realization of the God power within me to rise above my difficulties, whatever they are. I am able, and I will."

Do not dismiss this as something you cannot understand. Do not say it is foolish theorizing. Try it. Give it an honest trial. It will work. It is God's everlasting Truth.

LOWELL FILLMORE

HEALING THE PAST

REMEMBER that you can be master of your past, present, and future if you will cultivate your faith in Christ within you.

If something that happened in the past troubles you today you are not exercising your divine authority. Through your words you can call your divine authority into action. "Thou shalt also decree a thing, and it shall be established unto thee" is the promise.

Vain regrets concerning past mistakes, remembrance of injustice done to you, loss of friends, these things are depressing only to the degree that you permit them to rule your emotions. They exist only in your mind. You can fill yourself so full of Christlike thoughts that the old memories will be crowded out. If you feel that you need forgiveness because of past misdeeds you can do something about it this minute. You can put the forces of divine forgiveness into operation by faithfully using the right affirmations.

There is no need for you to suffer any longer for what has happened in the past. Today is your opportunity for mending the past and preparing for a happy, prosperous future. The power of Jesus Christ is able to remove the sting of past mistakes and bring healing to your soul.

Repeat the following affirmation seven times every morning, seven times every noon, and seven times every night before you go to bed:

"The forgiving love of Jesus Christ has wiped out the mistakes

of the past, and I am comforted and cheered. All things are for-
given, and love and good will permeate all the affairs of my life.
Old things have passed away and I am a new creature in Christ
Jesus."

Use this affirmation faithfully until the old unpleasant memories are swallowed up and dissolved in the love of Jesus Christ.
They will be rendered helpless ever to torment you again. You
will be free and happy every day as you do the will of Christ.

Remember that you are a child of the living God and that
therefore only good can come to you. You are forgiven and your
mistakes are forgotten the minute you forgive and forget the
mistakes of others. "Forgive, and ye shall be forgiven." * This is
the divine law. No matter how serious and real the wrongs of the
past may seem to you to be, through the help of Jesus Christ you
can overcome them all and be forgiven if you will ask the Christ
within you to help you forgive.

To one who lives in the presence of Christ, every day is a
new beginning. Great possibilities lie before you today. They
will be revealed to you to the extent that you make yourself receptive to them and free your mind from the thought burdens of
the past by denying their reality in Christ. Declare the truth by
making affirmations of Truth; then rejoice because all things are
made new and you have been forgiven to the fullest.

Many of the bodily infirmities that are torturing mankind
today are the outgrowth of concealed unforgiving attitudes of
mind. The memory of an experience of the past may hold us in
bondage because we will not "forgive" it and let it go. We cannot afford to carry the poison of unforgiveness about with us,
and we do not need to be burdened by it. Christ can help us be
free from it.

You remember how the man sick of the palsy had to be let
down through the roof into the presence of Jesus Christ because
of the crowd that filled the house in which Jesus was teaching.
Jesus healed the man by saying: "Son, thy sins are forgiven."

Here we learn that Jesus recognized a connection between
sickness and sin. When his sins were forgiven the man was healed.
Of course he and his friends had great faith, which was proved
by their method of getting past the crowd that filled the house.

* Scriptural reference quoted from the Authorized Version of the Holy Bible.

Faith in Christ is necessary if we wish to invoke His forgiveness. His forgiveness frees us from the limiting, destructive memories of the past, but there is a divine law upon which this help depends. We must do our part. Here is a statement of the law as Jesus gave it:

"Forgive, and ye shall be forgiven."

This means we must forgive ourselves as well as other people if Christ is to forgive us. If you are condemning yourself for a past error stop and forgive yourself, asking Christ's help. Speak good words about yourself as well as other people. Think of yourself as a child of God. Know that a child of God cannot do wrong and that the past can have no detrimental power over a child of the living God. Forgive all men, and then become a co-worker with Christ. You will become master of your thoughts and ruler of your past, present, and future.

FRANK B. WHITNEY

THE CHALLENGE OF THE DAWN

EACH DAWNING of a new day is in a sense an entirely new experience to you. At this morning's dawn a strange thing happened in your life. The curtains of night that had seemingly hid you in a vestibule of darkness were opened wide and you looked upon a new world. Some of the things of your past life— unpleasant things perhaps—were forgotten and your soul was purified of all that was sordid and unholy. The dark experiences of yesterday you found in the darkness and stillness of the night to be as nothing. For a while possibly all your past became as nought while in the darkness of night your soul breathed a prayer heavenward and your spirit touched your heart with a sense of love and desire for the things of God, the things of reality. Such may be the experience of night and of sleep if we infold ourselves in prayer and know that "underneath are the everlasting arms."

This vestibule between yesterday and today, the past and the present, then and now—is it not a vestibule between two worlds? In it do we not cast off the unholy tatters of an old existence only to be clad in the raiment of holiness, newness, and youthful expectancy? On the unseen side of life, the side unseen by eyes too heavy to behold things of dazzling brightness, are we not prepared for a new day, for a glorious dawning, for the fulfillment of new hopes and of our prayerful desire?

Are not dawn and sleep but some sort of purgatorial cleansing to free us from earthly and heavy and darkened thoughts of yesterday only to instill in our minds and hearts something of heavenly beauty, ecstasy, joy, and shining glory—the dawning of a new day? What a joy for the soul to take up that which is seemingly a burden and know that it is light! What an opportunity to be the new man that you hope to be in a new world! What a chance to say good-by to habits of bondage and good morning to a new life free from all sense of bondage and limitation!

Possibly in some mystical sense there is something of our own spirit abiding in the sun as it looks at us from the horizon and says good morning to us, something that would expect to see us arraying ourselves in high and holy thoughts, clothing ourselves in wisdom, joy, love, courage, and faith. If we have caught the vision of a new day, the challenge of its dawn, we greet it purified of yesterday's mistakes and enthused with today's promises and opportunities.

Persons with leaden and clouded vision awaken with the thought of just another day. Those who catch the high vision see a new world of rare delight and behold themselves as both guest and master of the world, its victor and its lord. The spirit of the new day—and surely the new day has its spirit just as does everything of freshness and vitality—the spirit of the dawn sounds a trump and a note that heralds the approach of new opportunities for us, the fulfillment of some righteous desire, the answer to some cherished prayer.

Shall we carry into the new day yesterday's grief and loss and pain? Shall we let yesterday's limiting thoughts of ourselves and others be our thoughts for today? Do you not see that today would be but yesterday to you if today you lived in yesterday's thoughts and experiences? There are those who never experience the joy of a new dawn because their minds are so firmly fixed on the unhappiness and defeat of yesterday.

The dawn challenges you to behold yourself in a new day, a new world, a new life. In order that you may meet this challenge you need to greet the new day in the spirit of prayer that has power to purify your thought and regenerate you in mind, soul, and body. Pray in the spirit of being ushered into a new existence where you are so taken with ecstasy at what you behold that you are speechless—unable to speak of evil, unpleasant memories, disappointments. You can but voice the joy of beholding the presence of God within and about you. Your new world lies before you. In the triumphant spirit of the Christ within you, you find that after all this new and beautiful world is just something at your feet.

The despondent, the tired of life, the discouraged need to be directed to the new dawn, their new world. They need to behold in the greeting of the sun the smiling face that answers the dismay in their inner heart of hearts: "It can be done. You can achieve. You can succeed." They need to be as a newborn babe bringing with it nothing but its life and its spontaneous marveling at a panorama of delightful surprises.

The new dawn is your time for reincarnation, for laying hold of a new consciousness of your body, for a new appreciation of your health and perfection. The happy memories of yesterday have place in your today only as they have place in Truth and love and life. Yesterday's weaknesses must give place to today's strength. Yesterday's defeat must be lost sight of as you anticipate today's victory. Today's dawn proclaims with all its fervor that you are born again. You are born of Spirit—the Spirit of newness, freshness, vitality.

Do you see the possibilities of a dawn, the opportunities of a new day, the joy of beholding your new world revealed to you at the beginning of a new day? If only all the world could grasp this message of Truth and hope and newness! If every heart at dawning would but catch the vision of all things made new! Do you not see that in Truth nothing of yesterday belongs to you today save that which is of Spirit, of Truth, of God; that which is the eternally substantial of you, that which in Spirit is permanent and enduring?

Take the attitude that this morning you were given a new mind, a renewed consciousness. Possibly yesterday you believed that there were things you could not know. Possibly yesterday you cluttered up your mind with thoughts of darkness, ignorance, sin, evil, fear, hate, and disease. Your new-mindedness must be dedicated to that which is of Truth, holy, good, ennobling, beautiful. You must realize that at dawn your mind became so charged with Truth that there is no room for any belief that is of darkness, fear, and disease.

Take the mental attitude that at dawn your body was charged with new life, health, and strength. Of course you must not hark back to the negative and adverse beliefs about your body that you may have held yesterday. Today is no time to recall yesterday's pain. Today is a new day unrelated to the pains of the past. Each new moment of the day serves to introduce you to new experiences and new victories. Even the moment just gone now belongs to the dead past!

Have you not felt that a new gospel is being proclaimed by teacher and prophet, in church, in school, in the market place, calling all men to a new vision? Do you not see that to be in the vanguard of a new civilization you must hear the voice and message of new hope and accept its bidding? Even as another civilization will sometime replace that of today so must your culture of new ideas replace the old and useless beliefs of yesteryear.

In your heart of hearts you will be called upon to decide today whether or not you have caught the vision of the new day and have met its challenge to be born anew. Today's sunset and nightfall will reveal to you whether or not you have lived to the full the life offered you today. You will ask yourself whether or not you have been true to your indwelling Spirit of truth, whether or not you have been faithful to Christ in the midst of you. To those who catch the message of the dawn even the thought of nightfall belongs to the remote future; so our thought at the close of today must be but relative to that of dawn.

At each dawn a bright and shining path opens before you. It reveals to you new friendships, new occasions to give expression to love, new opportunities to put into practice what your indwelling Spirit of truth has taught you and bid you do. There will never be another day just like this. Today alone can offer today's opportunities and today's joys. Each second of the day will give you a new opportunity to prove to yourself that you have met the dawn's challenge.

Even this message, since you took it up, has given you a new outlook upon life. You have been strengthened and encouraged in your determination to take a new hold on life. The sinews of your mind have been given spiritual power to keep out objectionable beliefs and to entertain only such thoughts as inspire and illumine you. Your new day, your new life, dates from the second when you catch a vision of Truth and try to plant your feet on higher ground.

The consciousness of new life calls upon you to live life anew. Gone forever will be every limiting belief, every thought that you cannot progress and succeed, if you only hold to this vision to the exclusion of all contrary thought. Even as in the past you may have hobbled yourself to some belief or pattern of despair and failure, so must you today catch the high vision of your soul's supremacy and your spirit's victory.

If you answer to the dawn's challenge, you set your feet on a new path and go the way of light and peace. New forces of the dawn attend you and buoy you up and exalt you. A new note of optimism and hope sings in your heart. You feel a new life surging through you to dissipate all that would call you back to things of old. A new sense of victory fills your consciousness, and you know something of what it means to let the world serve you with joy and gladness without being bound to the things of the world.

Man can know springtime in the heart any time that he can catch a vision of the eternal spring of Spirit. He can know eternal youth if he can but behold the great truth of youth's eternity. He can possess the power to be master of all things if he can but catch the meaning of the great secret that the Spirit of God within him is master of all of the world about him.

There are no limitations upon the Truth and Spirit of God and consequently there are none on you, God's perfect child. You need to behold yourself in God's mirror of Truth and to behold there a reflection of what you are in God's sight. You need to reflect often upon the divine idea of man, for you are this perfect idea brought into manifestation. You need to keep out of mind every thought that would limit or bind you in order that you may go forward and upward into the glories of your new day and glorified life.

You will lose all sense of mental and physical darkness and heaviness as you hold to the vision of the new day, the new dawning of your soul's supremacy over things of the world. No walls can confine you when you effect a union with the great universal Spirit of life and freedom. No adverse condition can bind you to itself when you realize your freedom and perfection. Yesterday cannot call you back to it when you feel the call to go onward and forward.

The purpose of the new dawn is to call you away from the shadows of yesterday and bring you into the light of higher truths. You are called upon to walk the path of light, to sing the song of joy, to hear the voice and call of spiritual obedience. You must be faithful to all that would inspire and elevate, all that would exalt and glorify.

Your soul's cry of the past finds its answer in the good that is offered you today. Your ideals of yesteryear become the realities of today's dawning if you can but behold them as your own. Your prayers and aspirations and yearnings find in today's dawning the advent of blessings beyond compare. The great moment of anticipation has arrived. You are now at the threshold of open doors and unlocked treasuries. Will you enter in?

Today will you behold your associates as new companions in a new world, freed from your sense of their limitations? Today will you see neighbor and relative freed from blemish and stain, released from fault and accusation, taking a higher road, heading for the goal long visioned? Today will you release from mind that tense thought which has bound you and yours to tension, nega-tion, distrust, jealousy, and strife? The new day has no place for such thoughts as these. The new day is heaven's miracle in which your own miracle can take place.

To you who may have placed one faltering foot upon the higher pathway hands and love are extended. To you who may have given up hope in the present life, straining to reach beyond, comes the message of light and exaltation. Catch your vision here and now. Live in Spirit right at this moment. No longer delay and anticipate. Today is your day of fulfillment. From this morning's dawn to this evening's close great joys can come to you. Be ready for them. To try to live in the future is as much of a sin as to bind yourself to the past. In Truth there is only today, in fact only the present moment, with its attendant joys and answered prayer.

Keep your vision clear. "Lay aside every weight" and "run with patience the race" before you. Count over and over the joys that today can give you. Take a new lease on life. Keep your face turned toward the light, the shadows behind you. Find in today's promises the fulfillment of whatever joy and blessing you seek.

You cannot be mistaken in following this way of joy and hope. Nothing must be sacrificed, nothing denied you. You go forward with assurance and confidence that the Spirit of God within and about you will bless and serve you. You confidently expect and joyfully receive. You discover the great secret of life that you need only turn to God in order to have Him turn to you. You need only anticipate and expect joyfully the blessings of God in order to have them poured out at your feet. Such is the way of those who catch the higher vision, who believe in the mystical unity between God and man, who are constantly grasping the opportunities of the soul's great dawning, who claim the promises of God and please Him by expecting much of Him in their personal life.

Nothing in all this world has power to challenge you save that Spirit within you which inspires you to move onward and upward. The beginning of a new day sees this challenge given you that you may make the most of your day, that you may find inspiration to make your life fuller and richer. Accept the challenge. Feel that you have within you that which cannot know defeat, that which cannot keep you from gaining higher visions and making newer conquests. The Spirit of God within you is your constant inspiration to do all things to His glory. When you accept the challenge of the dawn, you feel the Spirit of God within you is mighty to do all things through you.

GARDNER HUNTING

THE COME-BACK

WHY NOT HAVE what you want? Have you settled down
with a notion that you can't get it?

Are you accepting a disappointment as something you *must*
suffer?

Do you look at the thing that you really desire as being far
beyond your reach?

Do you carry around with you a heartache because you think
your heart's desire is finally and forever denied you?

Do you look on yourself as being down and out, with no
chance to get back?

Do you think you are too poor to buy the things you like or
even the things you need?

Have you done something that you think has brought a penalty on you—sickness, poverty, loss of freedom, grief?

Well, before you give it all up as hopeless won't you just read
along a little way in this discussion to see if your case is as bad
as you think it is? I am not writing to sell you anything or to
teach you anything or to persuade you of anything, but just to
share with you the ideas that changed the life of a man who used
to think as you do and who thought he had good reason to think
so, but who has found out that he was mistaken and that life is
not hopeless at all; and who believes that what helped him may
help somebody else who is under a cloud similar to the one that
he once lived under. Many things you want most are now within
your reach.

It has been said that if a man were to offer twenty-dollar gold pieces for sale on the street at fifty cents each, there would be few buyers, because nearly everybody would leap to the conclusion that he was a fraud. If you will study the real reason why people instinctively feel that way, you will find in it the very secret of success in getting what *you* want.

You have heard it said a thousand times that "you can't get something for nothing." You may or may not think that you believe this to be true, but it is true, whether you believe it or not; and everybody deep down in his inner nature knows it is true. That's why he is shy of any promise that promises too much. That's why you are probably skeptical about the promise of this little piece of print. But just let this idea get a foothold in your mind: if it is a law that I cannot get something for nothing, then it must be true of this law, as it is of all genuine laws, that it works both ways; it must be true that *I cannot give anything without getting something for it.* Ever think of that?

Have you ever been surprised to find that when you liked or disliked a man or woman, that person was sure to return the feeling you had for or "gave" to him? Have you ever noticed what a railroad company does that enables it to take in money? It gives transportation that is needed by people. Have you ever wondered why Henry Ford and John D. Rockefeller were so rich? Whatever else you may think of them, you must see that the world gave them money because they gave something to the world—the one, a good low-priced car; the other, good oil at a reasonable price. What does a department store do before it gets regular customers? It gives service, courtesy, good will, a square deal, accommodation, and so forth, to a community, which brings in the trade as the direct and inevitable result. What does an employee do before he gets wages or a salary? He gives a day's work or a week's or a month's. What gets him a raise? Giving a little more than he is paid for, nothing else. What does a farmer do before he gets a crop? He gives the seed to the ground and gives it water and care. How does an artist or a writer win fame? By giving the world a work of art or some great literature. How do I win a friend? By giving him friendship, and in no other way.

Sometimes people say—and maybe you are one of them just now—that there are people who get something for nothing; who give nothing for what they receive. Did you ever study such cases or do you take somebody else's word for it, as most of us do in such matters? Well, are you from Missouri? If you honestly want to be shown, you are on the only sound ground that there is.

Now, who gets something for nothing? The man who finds an oil well in his back yard? The woman who marries a rich man? The miner who stumbles upon gold? The fellow who wins in the lottery? The thief who takes a purse or the contents of a bank vault? The swindler who cheats the unwary out of his property? The real estate shark who sells worthless lots for big prices? The bootlegger who makes his own liquor with wood alcohol, puts bogus labels on it, and sells it as "just off the ship"? The heirs who destroy the old Will or forge a new one so that all the property comes to them? The counterfeiter who makes hundred-dollar bills out of mere paper and ink? The chap who raises a thousand-dollar check to $10,000? Do any of these get something for nothing? I used to think they did. Often it looks so.

But the more you watch the individuals who do these things, the more you'll see that the law works with them just as it works with you and me. It's law—just as truly as the law of gravitation is law—and I can't break it. Neither can you. Neither can anybody else. Did you ever know a gambler who got rich? Did you ever know a burglar who had anything left after his pals, his fence, and his lawyers got through with him? Did you ever know a counterfeiter who had a country home and a yacht? Did you ever know a woman who married for money and was happy?

"Maybe not," you say, "but they got away with the profits of the crooked deal!" Did they? How long did the profits last? Do you know?

Did you ever know anybody to keep the money he won in a lottery? Did you ever know the "lucky" finder of oil or gold, who hadn't given something for it, to profit by it?

If you will let go of the rumors and fabulous stories about riches coming to people for nothing, and get right down and investigate, you'll be surprised. Study the history of "depressions."

What is success in business made of? I mean any success in any business. Some persons will say, "Hard work." But that is not always true. Hard work alone will not insure success. You know plenty of persons who have worked hard but have gotten almost nothing for it. Does honesty make success? Not necessarily. Does dishonesty pay? No! Terribly upsetting, isn't it, to be told that neither crookedness nor honesty succeeds? Well, that's where you and I have been making a mistake. We have swung like pendulums from one extreme to the other. First we've tried to succeed by one method, then by the other. When crookedness fails, men preach honesty; when honesty fails, the preachers are dumbfounded and other men turn bitterly back to crookedness. What is the reason? Simply that neither mere dishonesty nor mere honesty pays; nor mere laziness, nor mere hard work. Nothing really pays but obedience to law—not man's law but God's law.

Gravitation is one of God's laws, isn't it? Who uses the law of gravitation? Anybody? Does it make any difference whether he is good or bad, honest or dishonest, crooked or straight, saint or sinner, rich or poor, fat or lean, white or black? It does not; the law of gravitation works for him infallibly, invariably, inflexibly, eternally, regardless of who or what he is. Who uses the laws governing the burning of gasoline to drive a car? Who uses the laws of friction to stop a car? Who uses the laws of electricity? the laws of light? Does it make any difference whether one is handsome or homely, whether he is freckled or pallid, whether he smokes or drinks or swears or goes to church or fights or steals or kills or loves? It does not. A murderer can drive a car or stop it. A clown can ride in an airplane. A fool can start or stop a dynamo. An idiot can set a fire. A preacher or a moron can explode dynamite. A sister of charity or a woman of the street will burn a hand on a hot stove. Good or bad, saintly or vicious—law works alike for all, and everything works under law.

But some laws seem to be greater than others, to include others, to transcend others. For instance, the laws controlling the airplane seem to enable us to break the law of gravitation. Of course, they don't; they simply enable us to counteract the force of gravitation. The laws of the radio release us from conditions to which we have thought ourselves limited by other governing laws—laws of sound transmission. By studying these things I see that so soon as I begin working by *any* law I begin to benefit by it, and no other law can stop me; because all the laws of nature fit together, work together, help one another—they never work against one another. The law of gravitation helps me to use the airplane, it holds me down against the air. If it did not, I'd be flung off the world into space, airplane and all—not to mention other things that would happen. When I start my car, the laws governing the action of the engine seem to overcome the laws of inertia and friction—but no law is broken. If it weren't for inertia there would be no momentum; if it weren't for friction my clutch would not grip and my tires would not take hold of the road. I do not break laws; I use them.

Now, a law that works at all always works. You say conditions affect laws? No; fog, for instance, only obscures the light of the stars to my eyes—the stars still shine. Static interferes with the radio only as it obscures the broadcasting for me; the broadcasting is there just the same. Law *always* works—anywhere—everywhere—now and forever. Two and two make four, by mathematical law, in New York or Kansas City, in Paris or Tokyo, in the cathedral or the prison, in the home or the dive, on Earth or Mars, today or in Caesar's time, now or in eternity.

If this law that I cannot get something for nothing, and that therefore I cannot give without receiving, is law, then it works with the same infallibility and continuity as all other laws. It makes no difference who I am, where I am, how much I weigh, what color my hair is, or what my character is, this law works for me just the same. It is commonly called the law of giving and receiving, and it can be stated this way: What I give out comes back to me—multiplied—always. The "come-back" is like the yield from seed.

Now, if you agree so far, don't you see where this has led you? It has led you to recognize that you are where you are today because of what you have given out. You are getting it back multiplied, just as I'm getting mine. But what else does it mean? It also means that what you start giving out now is also going to start coming back to you—multiplied. You can change the crop you are reaping, but there's just one way to do it: you can change the seed you are planting—change the sort of thing you are giving out. I did. It works, and nobody can stop it; nothing can stop it, no circumstance, no apparent handicap, no apparent misfortune, no "bad luck," no enemy, nobody who "has it in for you." What you give out comes back to you—what you begin giving out begins coming back. Any man, woman, or child can transform his life by transforming the thing he gives out.

Of course the first question that comes up in your mind (it was the first in my mind) is "How long must I suffer for what I've already done?" That's an interesting point. Suppose we think a minute about law: If I am working a problem in arithmetic, and I have been getting the wrong answer over and over and over again; and I suddenly find that I've been trying to work the problem by the wrong method—contrary to principle—in opposition to law; and if I stop going contrary to law and work with law, how long does it take me to get the right answer? Suppose that I am learning to drive a car, and I try to start it by stepping on the gas without putting it in gear; the car does not start. But when I put it in gear—in other words obey the law governing the case— and then "step on the gas," how long does it take the car to start? Suppose I have a boat with a hole in it; I find that when I put it into the water, it fills and sinks. Suppose that I obey the law governing boats, and stop the leak; how long does it take the boat to float? If I am locked in a room and don't know how to unlock the door, I stay there till I learn how, do I not? But when I learn how to turn the key in that lock, how soon do I get out?

You may think out as many other examples as you like of how law works for you the moment you begin to obey it, of how obedience *now* cancels the mistakes of yesterday, or of last year. Then come back to our argument and think this one over: So true and far-reaching and fundamental is this law of giving and receiving that it extends into our thoughts. There's a lot of talk these days about the power of thought, and some persons are disposed to sneer at it. But there's more in it than these persons suppose, and they suffer because they don't realize the power of thought. It is true, too, that what you think comes back to you, multiplied. Is there a laugh in that for you? Well, can you do anything without first thinking about it? Is any discovery or invention, any work of art or book, any newspaper or tool, any manufacturing or any crime, any deed good or bad ever performed without someone's first thinking about it? In other words, everything that you do is first an idea in your mind. That is where it is first "created." If you make a chair, or a plan, or a steamship, or a printing press, or a bomb, or a broom, it must first take shape in your mind, as an idea. As a matter of fact, the idea of a thing is the real creation of it; the physical putting it together afterward is a mere copy of the idea in your mind.

We are accustomed to think that a certain amount of time and energy is required to make the visible copy of the idea—the visible chair, or plow, or broom. But the more perfectly we think it out—that is, create it as a complete idea in mind—the more quickly and perfectly we can create it in visible form; and as we think it out better and better, we find that we require less and less time to make the visible thing—and less and less energy. Newly invented machines, for instance, are usually crude, cumbersome, heavy, and require a lot of power to operate them. But as they are perfected—that is, as they are thought out—they become lighter, simpler, more efficient, are operated by less power, and do their work more quickly. In this process the time always comes when the thing that once took a long period and much labor to make is made at a speed so high that the production is in some cases almost instantaneous. If when we began making this thing we had understood all the laws of its making, we could have made it instantaneously without learning how.

But that would have been a miracle! Exactly! The difference between what we call a natural process and what we call a miracle is largely a matter of the time required to reach the desired end. But doing a "miracle" is merely a matter of understanding the laws by which it is done. The first Ford car required months of grueling labor to build; today the Ford plants can make about five and one half cars a minute—or one about every ten seconds. Is that a miracle? Wouldn't it have been a miracle to produce a Ford every ten seconds, say thirty years ago? What makes it possible today? Knowledge of the laws.

Knowledge of the laws involved in anything is not only the most valuable knowledge that we can have but it is absolutely essential. Mr. Ford never would have made a car if he had started with no knowledge of the law. But he began by using what he had—probably by using something that he had been told, or had read, about the laws of mechanics. As he used the knowledge that he had, his knowledge grew—just as your muscle grows as you use it—or as intelligence grows by use—or anything else. And

wouldn't Henry Ford have been foolish not to try out his first bits
of knowledge about law?

Think this over and you'll see that anything men ever achieve
is accomplished by knowledge of the law. Health, wealth, happiness, success, prosperity, freedom! Anything you want literally
will come to you if you will obey its laws just as literally as you
obey the law of gravitation.

Now, of course you see the direction of this argument. A
man's work or a woman's work is not primarily to do something
hard that brings the sweat, breaks the nails, tires the muscles,
and exhausts the wind—something that is drudgery. Not at all.
The secret of getting what you want lies in obeying the law governing getting what you want.

What is that law? Why, it is just what we've been talking
about—the law of giving and receiving.

Now, what is your first thought at this suggestion? You think,
"What have I to give?" Perhaps you conclude that you have
nothing. But Henry Ford had nothing—at the start—nothing but
an idea. Heinz, the pickle man, of "fifty-seven varieties" fame,
had nothing at the start—nothing but an idea. Woolworth, the
five-and-ten-cent-store man, had nothing at the start—nothing
but an idea. Golden Rule Nash, the tailor, who built a business
up from nothing to $12,000,000 in six years, had nothing at the
start—nothing but an idea. But the curious thing about it is that
these men all had the same idea. What was it? It was the idea of
giving the world something that it needed—something of value.
When they began acting on the idea by giving what they had to
begin with, they learned how to give more, and so received more;
and when they gave that, more came—until every one of them
reached the point where he was successful and famous, and
money rolled in upon him faster than he could use it.

It will work for you—this law. It has worked for me. It is
working for you and for me whether we know it or not—whether
we believe it or not. What you give out comes back to you—multiplied. If you don't get what you want, it's nobody's fault but
your own. If I don't get what I want, it's nobody's fault but mine.
The law works. If it works for me slowly at first, that is because
I must learn by giving what I have, before I can get more knowledge of the law and thus have more to give. But if I will give

what I have, where I am, to someone who needs it, I'll gain the knowledge and the things that I need. As I go on giving, I rapidly rise toward the point where I shall do easily and instantaneously the thing that now takes me a long time to do—just as my hand gains skill and speed and ease with a hammer, or a drill, or a needle, or a baseball, or a boxing glove, or a hoe, or a tennis racket, or a camera, or a motor car, or a dynamo. Eventually, by using all the knowledge I have of law, in giving service to the world, I shall gain the ability to do seeming miracles—as Henry Ford, Ty Cobb, Barney Oldfield, Mary Pickford, Thomas Edison, and Luther Burbank have done.

If you believe that the foregoing argument is sound, has it occurred to you that the conclusion is not new? It's at least as old as the year 33 A.D. In other words, it has been taught to the world more or less ever since the time of Jesus. In fact it was and is His teaching. Many people overlook the real teaching of Jesus of Nazareth. But listen: Didn't He say, "Give, and it shall be given unto you; good measure, pressed down, shaken together, running over"? Whatever you think about Him religiously, did He know what He was talking about? Did He state a law?

We believe that Jesus of Nazareth did not merely found a religion, but that He taught a way to live—to live happily, successfully, prosperously. Didn't He say, "I came that they may have life, and may have it abundantly"? In other words, He taught not merely a way to be good and moral and honest and industrious and all that, but a way to live by the law that brings success and money and fame and love and all the other things that we want. And the law He taught was give—and give first—if you want to get anything. He voiced the Golden Rule: "Whatsoever ye would that men should do unto you, even so do ye also unto them." The wisest of the world's cynics say that you have to pay sometime for whatever you get. Jesus of Nazareth says, practically, "Pay as you enter." Select what you want, and pay first.

Maybe this sounds impracticable to you. It did to me. But try it out. I did. You'll get results. I did. It won't fail you. It hasn't failed me. Why? Because there is just one maker of law in the universe and that is the power we call God, and that power made the law of giving and receiving. Give the best you have and look for the best in return. God challenges you and me to prove the promises He makes in the Bible, and these promises are simply statements of law that never fail of fulfillment. "Prove me now," says God, "if I will not open you the windows of heaven, and pour you out a blessing, that there shall not be room enough *to receive it.*" His only condition is that we shall "give first"—that's all. Commonly we do not take this sort of promise seriously; but it is sound and true. Is there anything wrong about the foregoing argument? God *is* the law. He is the law of love, which is only another name for the law of giving and receiving. If you will stop thinking of God as a joke, or as a terror, or as a myth, or as a dream, or as something far off and outside everyday life, and will think of Him as the Maker of the law of gravitation and of the law of love, one of which is just as real as the other—you'll get somewhere.

If you want to know how, the whole secret lies in beginning. The way to do it is to do it. Right where you are, now, begin to give something good to the person nearest you, and keep on doing it, no matter what you seem to get back at first. *Do!* Don't talk! And you'll lift yourself out of your troubles, no matter what they seem to be or how deeply you seem to be sunk in them. Try it. You'll be surprised. I was. Try it patiently and as hard as you would try to get a drink of water if you were very thirsty. You'll get a return, a reward, that you don't even dream of yet. You *will!* Don't let anybody fool you about it.

And besides, if it doesn't work, you don't have to keep on with it. But you will keep on—if you give it a fair chance to prove itself. Because—it works.

RALPH E. JOHNSON

YOU CAN DECREE YOUR GOOD

IN ONE of her poems Ella Wheeler Wilcox points to a
paradox of the sea:

> One ship drives east and another drives west
> With the self-same winds that blow.

What makes the difference in their courses? "The set of the sails."
Mrs. Wilcox applies the lesson to human life, showing that the
direction we take in life, whether we drift with the winds of adversity or use their power to guide us into the port of satisfaction
and joy, is determined by the set of our sails.

Whether we realize it or not, we alone have the power to decide the direction our life is to take. We are not puppets, to be
driven ahead of every wind, unable to choose our port of destination. The gales may blow about us, but our ship can always be
guided into the port of peace, health, and success.

We can decree our "port of destination" long before we meet
any "winds" by learning the power we possess to set our sails
rightly. The set of our sails will make every experience an aid in
reaching our goal.

We have all known persons who quailed at almost everything,
who believed life was made up of hardships, injustices, and en-
mities. They were doubtful, fearful of everything. Even before
anything occurred, they had set their course toward disappointment, failure, and distress, had decreed the direction they were
to take, by their fearful and pessimistic expectations. Is it any
wonder that what they fear comes upon them?

[282]

We all know people of the opposite type, people who face life with courage and daring. Such people have an assured and confident approach to life. They think in positive terms, in terms of their power to overcome. They are aware of obstacles to be met, but they meet each one with the assurance that they can overcome it. Such an attitude makes them receptive to the wisdom, courage, initiative, and creative guidance that insure success. They have decreed their good by the way they face life.

In Job we read, "Thou shalt also decree a thing, and it shall be established unto thee." This scriptural passage refers to the power we all possess of determining what we shall think, how we shall feel, and how we shall approach life. To think and feel according to the highest standard is to "set our sails" in the way that will insure our reaching the most desirable port regardless of what winds may blow. We need only set our sails aright; then our destination will be unerringly determined and our good firmly established.

A knowledge of our relation to God will enable us to chart the course of our life and direct it perfectly. Assured that God is all, over all, and through all, and that we are part of Him, we shall not look out upon the world as a scene of capricious uncertainties to which we are subject. We shall know that every problem can be solved, every illness healed, good always made manifest; because "one on God's side is a majority."

We can decree the manifestation of good. Because of this we can determine our joy and peace and freedom. The power of decree we possess is the power to direct our thought and speech in channels that make us receptive to our good. Our decree is not a command made to God, who is forever giving good without stint; our decree is a command to our own consciousness that we become fully receptive to His bounty.

A man's consciousness is his kingdom. The real self, the Christ within, is king and ruler. To decree any good, we must command the subjects of our kingdom, the thoughts we think and the words we speak, to be obedient to our decree. The feelings and ideas we entertain and express prepare the way for our good to be established.

If we would decree health, we must decide to have nothing more to do with thoughts of weakness, incurable disease, or pain.

Instead we must resolve to think in terms of strength and wholeness, of our expectancy of perfection and freedom from pain. Such a decision invites health and makes ready the way for God to work in our body to transform and renew it.

We decree prosperity by thinking, speaking, and acting prosperous. We do not complain of difficulty, nor do we express any form of discouragement. We cast out doubt and confusion by believing strongly that nothing can stand in the way of God's promise of abundance. We expect success and the best from every experience. The ability thus to dictate to and direct our thoughts and acts is proof that we are in command of the kingdom of our consciousness.

Let us no longer allow every wind to buffet us. Knowing that we have the power to set our sails for the port of radiant health, joy, peace, and abundance, let us use this power to direct every thought and word wisely and so bring forth good.

The following affirmations you will find helpful:

In the name of Jesus Christ
I decree for myself health, purity, wholeness.
I decree for myself energy, strength, power.
I decree for myself joy, happiness, harmony.
I decree for myself life, light, enlightenment.
I decree for myself wealth, plenty, riches.
I decree for myself true activity and service.
I decree for myself a spiritual mind and a spiritual body.

RUSSELL A. KEMP

THIS IS THE YEAR!

Wonderful, wonderful, fortunate you,
This is the year that your dreams come true!
This is the year that your ships come in;
This is the year you find Christ within.
This is the year you are glad to live;
This is the year you have much to give.
This is the year when you know the Truth;
This is the year when you find new youth.
This is the year that brings happiness;
This is the year you will live to bless.
Wonderful, wonderful, fortunate you,
This is the year that your dreams come true!

MARTHA SMOCK

NO OTHER WAY

Could we but see the pattern of our days,
We should discern how devious were the ways
By which we came to this, the present time,
This place in life; and we should see the climb
Our soul has made up through the years.
We should forget the hurts, the wanderings,
    the fears,
The wastelands of our life, and know
That we could come no other way or grow
Into our good without these steps our feet
Found hard to take, our faith found hard to
    meet.
The road of life winds on, and we like
    travelers go
From turn to turn until we come to know
The truth that life is endless and that we
Forever are inhabitants of all eternity.

9. The Only Bond That Endures

"We who are following Jesus Christ in the resurrection know life as a spiritual thing, and that we live spiritually, if we understand the law of life, and that we shall continue to live in Spirit, 'whether in the body or out of the body.' And we know that this spiritual bond is the only bond that will really endure."

—*Charles Fillmore*

WILLIAM A. CLOUGH

THE ROAD BEYOND

Not long ago I received a letter from a friend telling me of her grief and loneliness after the loss of a dear one. "I feel so utterly lonely," she wrote. "How can I go on without him?"

Such expressions of grief touch the heart, and friends offer comforting words and tokens of sympathy to those who sorrow. All who have had a similar experience understand the feeling of emptiness and heartache that comes when the physical presence of a loved one is gone forever.

There are times in the life of all of us, whatever our age or place, when grief is heavy upon us. Grief is not inevitable, but it is common to us all. Grief at the loss of a dear one is one of the most common and certainly one of the most difficult of human problems.

But as in the case of all problems great and small, there is an answer. There is comfort and compensation and joy for every heart that sorrow shakes. To the lonely and bereft friend and to every grieving soul comes the word of truth from the Sermon on the Mount: "Blessed are they that mourn: for they shall be comforted."

The Master did not say, "They shall not mourn." He said, "They shall be comforted."

Grief is not a sign of weakness, for the greatest men have known deep grief. But they have manifested their greatness by rising above and overcoming their grief and claiming the joy that is their rightful heritage. Grief is human; joy is divine. Grief is a part of our human nature, but joy is a part of our divine nature.

I cannot say to my friend, "You must not grieve, it is wrong." But I can say: "You must not continue to grieve. That would be wrong." Those who mourn are blessed, because there is comfort that takes away their sorrow and leaves them on higher ground where the vision is clearer and the view is wider. Failure to accept divine comfort is wrong.

Prolonged mourning may be an indication of too great self-concern. We are mourning then not for the one who has gone but for ourselves. When the letter *u* is taken from the word *mourning* the word becomes *morning,* the dawn of a new day:

Is it not significant that the verse telling of Jesus' grief is the shortest one in the whole Bible? "Jesus wept." Sorrow touched Him. He was a "man of sorrows, and acquainted with grief," but sorrow's stay with Him was short. He saw the morning, ever bright, and came through the little night to its great dawn.

You and I can do the same no matter how irreparable our loss may seem to be. Others have done it again and again. Though from the depth of our grief we may say with the writer of Lamentations, "Behold, and see if there be any sorrow like unto my sorrow," we can leave it behind and go forward. Grief may leave its mark, but for those who overcome grief it is a mark of victory. The Cross is a symbol of victory, not defeat; of joy, not sorrow.

How can I overcome and rise above my grief, you ask, just as the friend asks, "How can I go on without him?"

"Every one can master a grief but he that has it," Shakespeare said, so it would be presumptuous of us to attempt to answer the questions of one who knows grief unless we ourselves have a real appreciation of his feelings.

I seek to put myself in the place of my friend. I try to realize how I would feel if my wife or only child should suddenly be taken from me. Could I overcome my grief and find new and higher meaning in life? Could I see through the shadows of night to the morning light?

My answer is yes, for I know that my loved ones can never be taken from me, can never be lost to me. I know that God would lead me through grief to greater spiritual understanding, and in my greater understanding my loved ones would be nearer and dearer to me than ever. I would see them through the eyes of Spirit and feel in my spirit their living presence.

Since beginning this article I have received word of the ongoing of a very dear friend, a beautiful wife and mother, who left two young children and a husband who leaned on her with more than the usual degree of dependence. The husband is a minister, and the couple's life had been earnestly devoted to doing good.

Probably in his hurt he will say as Job might have said, and as you and I might say, "Why should this blow fall on me when I have been doing the very best I know?" Yet the pull of faith is stronger in him, I know, than the pull of sorrow. He will go on to greater good as, with an earthly prop removed, he leans more heavily on God.

My father and mother had been married nearly fifty years when my father reached "journey's end." My mother had nursed him night and day for weeks, but she never broke down and never shed a tear, at least in the presence of any of us.

"I know he is not really cold and alone," she said. "He has gone into an upper room where it is warm and where he is well again. He is still close to me. I shall not grieve."

It was neither will power nor empty theory that kept her spirit up. It was no lack of deep feeling, for she was keenly sensitive. It was faith—strong, sure faith. It was strength she drew from an infinite source. It was the real substance of life. She knew in the depth of her being that both he and she were safe in God's keeping.

When years later she, too, moved into the "upper room" she left no legacy of grief to us. She left an example of triumphant faith. She left the imprint of victorious spirit upon everyone who had come under its benediction. It never leaves and it never will. What place is there for grief when nothing has been lost?

> Death's but an open door;
> We move from room to room.
> There is one life . . .
> No dying and no tomb.

Living Spirit is forever living Spirit, even as God is God, whatever our thought may be.

The basic chord of the melody of life is affirmation, whether life be here or hereafter. It is saying yes to the so-called mysteries of birth and death alike, yes to immortality, yes to the imperishable substance of Spirit in the departed and in us, yes to the perfect will of God.

Most of us can look at the circle of our acquaintance and find examples of varying reactions to the loss of a loved one. Where one person in his grief permits the shadows to close down about him, another uses faith to sweep the shadows away.

I know two women of approximately the same age who were left widows with small children. One wore a long face, complained continually of her loss and of the harsh way in which life was treating her. She complained of her inability to take care of the children, and she accepted financial help from relatives without a show of gratitude. She lived negatively, fighting against life. Her children grew up with little supervision and few privileges. Embittered and unhappy, she grew old prematurely.

The other woman immediately faced her loss and its obligations, prayed, studied, obtained a full-time teaching position, entered into betterment work in church and community, and became an influence for good, bringing up a splendid family. She took a stand on faith and was strengthened and comforted.

Both women faced the same circumstance. One took the way of negation and self-pity, the other the way of affirmation and self-help. One said no, the other yes.

Faith and work will ease and take away the deepest grief. God's will for us, His children, is happiness. God does not visit sorrow upon us. He does take it away when we bring it upon ourselves and when it comes from causes beyond our comprehension. He never hurts. He heals.

Faith is the answer to the question we fling out in the poignancy of our grief. Faith is the overcoming and the victory. Faith tells us the truth that all is well with our loved one and all is well with us. Faith tells us that Spirit is immortal, that love outlives the grave and transcends time.

Faith tells us death is not the terrible thing, not the final great calamity we so often consider it. Faith tells us it is the gateway to a new life, a phase in the continuing process of spiritual ascension.

Your departed loved one lives, and spirit with spirit may speak in the language of Spirit, the language of love. We do not know what form the spirit takes when it is gone from here. We may have theories, but we do not know. One thing we know, that life goes on with God.

I do not know what tomorrow or even the next hour holds for me. But I know I have nothing to fear, for God is in it. I do not know what life after mortal death is like. But I know it is good, for the eternal Father is in it. I do not know what happens to my spirit when it leaves this body, but I know it is moving in accordance with divine plan and that it lives and grows.

> I know not where His islands lift
> Their fronded palms in air;
> I only know I cannot drift
> Beyond His love and care.

Jesus went to a mourning Mary and Martha and said in effect: "Stop grieving. I'll prove to you that life has not ended. I'll recall it into the cold body of Lazarus." Jesus did the same for the grieving widow.

The whole emphasis of Jesus' teaching was on life. It is the essence of God's will toward us—life, abundant life. In our lack of understanding we have placed too great an emphasis on a phase of life that we falsely consider its end. Life is continuous, uninterrupted by change.

Your loved one is alive, gloriously alive. Do not continue to grieve. Do not lift a hurt and sorrowing face to his shining, radiant countenance. Do not shut yourself in and your loved one out with a wall of grief.

Take up your tasks in prayer and faith. Think of your departed dear one lovingly, gratefully, happily, still with the Father of all, changed but unchanged. Lift up your face to the light. Behold him in the choir invisible. Say yes. It is the word of faith. Yes, I know he is in God's care. Yes, I will face life myself in God's care. Yes, I know that my Redeemer lives.

For myself I am not concerned with what the future life may be like, for I believe with all my heart that life is a great continuous experience, a part revealed and a part unrevealed, and all to be revealed in God's good time.

When a loved one travels beyond my mortal sight, far down the road beyond, I see him still through the inner eye of faith, alive and well and hand in hand with God.

ERNEST C. WILSON

HOW TO MEET BEREAVEMENT

THERE ARE three truths that can be of great help to us if we are called upon to meet bereavement.

I. Life Is Eternal

"The free gift of God," said Paul, "is eternal life." Life did not begin when we were born, nor does it cease if we die,, any more than we begin to live when we put on a garment, or cease to live if we lay it aside. It is true that a part of our spiritual growth is to learn to exercise our God-given dominion over the body, but the last enemy to be overcome is death (I Cor. 15:26). We take a great step toward that overcoming when we overcome the *fear* of death. We cannot overcome death by dwelling upon the thought of death, any more than we can overcome weakness by dwelling upon weakness. To overcome weakness we must use the strength that we have. The better we use it, the more it will increase. To overcome death we must place our emphasis upon life. The more completely we express life the more will our life increase.

We should not wish to perpetuate the body as it is. We wish to overcome its manifest imperfections. We seek to do this not by dwelling upon these imperfections, but rather by dwelling upon God's idea of the body, created in His image and of Spirit substance. "For this corruptible must put on incorruption, and this mortal must put on immortality." It is not by death that man puts

I

on this incorruptible body, but by growth and unfoldment into the Christ likeness.

We should think of the body as the temple of God. We should behold the body as created of spiritual substance and amenable to the powers of Spirit.

We should not think of the body as being the self of us. I am not my body. I am not my mind. I have a body. I have a mind. I am Spirit. I am a son of God. "The Spirit himself beareth witness with our spirit, that we are children of God: and if children, then heirs; heirs of God, and joint-heirs with Christ."

"God himself shall be with them, *and be* their God: and he shall wipe away every tear from their eyes; and death shall be no more; neither shall there be mourning, nor crying, nor pain, any more: the first things are passed away."

This was the vision of one whose sight was clear, and who perceived things as they are in Truth, and as they shall be in manifestation when man has learned to express Truth completely.

As yet, however, death and mourning are still in the world: death as a means of escape from bodies that men have not yet learned to redeem to health and well-being; mourning because men do not clearly perceive that death is not the end of life, nor birth the beginning.

Even though the Truth student looks toward the ultimate overcoming of death as God's supreme and loving will for man, yet he will also recognize God's love in seemingly hard experiences along the way toward that overcoming. He knows that one has not necessarily failed if he is not evolved enough to partake in fullness of God's will for him. Through all life's experiences he retains his divine identity, and though he may change the form that clothes him, he extracts the essence of spiritual life and substance that will contribute to the building of the perfect, incorruptible body.

II. Love Is Mightier Than Death

We read in fairy stories of the magic cloak of invisibility. The body is the opposite of this. For us it is a cloak of visibility. It enables us to be visible to one another. It is the instrument by which the divine in us can express itself on the physical plane of being. It is a very valuable, wonderful, and important gift to us from the Father. But if it is laid aside, we do not thereby cease to be, any more than we cease to be if we lay aside any other garment, or if we disappear to the sight of our friends by going to some distant place.

Our nearness to or distance from others is not determined by physical proximity or remoteness. We may be very far distant from those whom we can actually touch with our finger tips; very close to dear ones who are many miles away. We are close to those who are dear to us because they are dear to us, because we have much in common, because our attachment to them is not an attachment of the body but of the mind and the spirit. We sense that nearness when our letters cross in the mail and answer questions before they are received, and when without outward means of communication we are subtly aware of one another's deep feelings and thoughts.

It is natural for us to like to have near to us those that we love, but just as we are willing to let them leave us to go away to school, or to take up some new work, or for some other good reason, so too we should not seek to bind to us those who surrender their physical bodies. We should love them unselfishly enough to free them from our personal will or desire, but we should positively declare and believe that they are alive forevermore, thereby giving them support and strength and understanding that will help them overcome the "last enemy." We should bless them with our realization that they are safely held in the love and wisdom of God, and that He leads them step by step into that which is for their highest good.

We should not fear death, either for ourselves or for others. We do not fear it if we are firmly established in the understanding of God's love for us. We wish for those whom we love only that which is for their good. If we knowingly had the power, we would insure that good to them. If our human love would do so much, how much more will the love of God do! We readily forgive the errors of those whom we love. We help them to overcome weakness, to manifest wisdom and strength. How much more does God forgive us our human mistakes, and help us to be strong and wise!

III. Grief Is Selfish

Our grief for the departed is not usually grief for them. Seldom do we grieve because we realize that they have not made the final great overcoming that Jesus made, but rather because we shall miss them, and because we seem to be separated from them. We take from bereavement its greatest power to distress us when we realize that in fact our grief is for ourselves.

There are many ways in which our love for those who slip out of our life can be expressed more practically than by grief. A mother made desolate by the passing away of her little son, and realizing this fact, courageously laid aside her grief and consecrated her life to helping hundreds of children who had been deprived of such affection and care as she had showered on her own child. A husband, turning to practical Christianity for comfort in the loss of his wife, not only regenerated his own life, but helped, by his example and the sharing of his wealth, to bring many others into the realization of the Truth that had helped him.

Better than grieving for those whom we love is the making of our life a noble testimony to our love for them.

JAMES DILLET FREEMAN

THE TRAVELER

He has put on invisibility.
Dear Lord, I cannot see—
But this I know, although the road ascends
And passes from my sight,
That there will be no night;
That You will take him gently by the hand
And lead him on
Along the road of life that never ends,
And he will find it is not death but dawn.
I do not doubt that You are there as here,
And You will hold him dear.

Our life did not begin with birth,
It is not of the earth;
And this that we call death, it is no more
Than the opening and closing of a door—
And in Your house how many rooms must be
Beyond this one where we rest momently.

Dear Lord, I thank You for the faith that frees,
The love that knows it cannot lose its own;
The love that, looking through the shadows, sees
That you and he and I are ever one!

HELEN S. CARPENTER

I AM CONTENT

BY THY GRACE, O God, lover of my soul, strength of my body, light of my life, I am sustained in my sorrow. My heart is at peace, for I am one with Thee. My faith has told me so. I draw nearer to Thee, dear Father, that I may be nearer to my loved one who is with Thee. Help me to know perfectly that life is eternal and death but a shadow that hides from my earthly sight the unseen world into which my dear one has stepped. Love knows no boundaries, and the love of my heart reaches into the beyond.

Thou didst not lose when Thou gavest this dear one to me, and I cannot lose when my beloved returns to Thine eternal home. "In my Father's house are many mansions." Still in the shadow of Thy protection, still in Thy loving care, only into another room has my dear one gone. This I know, even as I know Thou art ever watchful over me.

As to life in this other room, I trust that to Thee. I know that when the mists of uncertainty are fully lifted from my vision I shall see clearly into this room; know perfectly all that is now hid.

Help me, dear Father, to understand the mystery of eternal life. Some day I shall understand. Until then I am content to know that my beloved is with Thee, safe in Thine everlasting arms.

10. Your Child Is God's Child

"Your little child is God's child. God is both father and mother to him. The divine Father-Mother has created him and given him a perfect pattern for his life and placed in him intelligence with which to build a perfect body. God is also the unfailing and abundant supply of everything that is needed by the child for his spirit, soul, and body. God has not only created him but is ever abiding in him as his very mind, life, wisdom, and substance. Isn't that a glorious thought?"

—*Myrtle Fillmore*

MARTHA SMOCK

"WHO WILL TAKE CARE
OF THE CHILDREN?"

IN THE EARLY days of Unity, when Charles and Myrtle Fillmore were just beginning their work, Mrs. Fillmore had a vision. To quote from *The Household of Faith*, by James Dillet Freeman: "It had seemed to her that she was one of a vast congregation of people, many of whom were children. The children were completely undisciplined; in great confusion they were pushing and squirming through the crowd. As she watched them, the thought came to her that they needed someone to look after them. 'Who will take care of the children?' she asked.

"Even as she asked the question, it seemed to her as though a tremendous force took hold of her and impelled her to the front of the throng. As she was thus thrust forward, a voice spoke to her and said: 'You are to take care of the children; this is your work.'"

This vision led Myrtle Fillmore to start the Sunday-school work and to begin the publication of Unity's magazine for children, *Wee Wisdom*. All her life she was devoted to the welfare of children and wrote and taught for their benefit.

Most parents want above all else to see their children grow into happy, successful adults. Many times the parent finds himself surrounded by articles and material on child training, and he is beset with suggestions and ideas. From his reading and listening it would seem that the parent knows all the answers; and yet in spite of all the wonderful ideas he has read about in books and heard discussed from the platform, there are the children, pushing and squirming through the crowd, oftentimes completely undisciplined. The parent may feel like giving up; he may ask himself, as Mrs. Fillmore did in her vision, "Who will take care of the children?" The answer is already there for him: "You are to take care of the children; this is your work."

Sometimes the parent seems so unqualified for the job of rearing children that he hesitates to use his own ideas in teaching and training them. He searches for advice and information. He feels that if someone in authority sanctions his reasoning, then it may be right. But "if the trumpet give an uncertain sound, who shall prepare himself?" The parent should not be an "uncertain trumpet," and he need not be.

A leading journalist has said that we do not need to be child authorities in order to understand children and their needs. She says, "I remember me." So every parent was once a child; he remembers himself as a child; he remembers his longings; he remembers how he learned and grew. He remembers that he did not love his parents and teachers less because they expected him to abide by the rules, because they expected him to control his emotions and his disposition, because they did not allow him to continue in destructive or foolish ways.

We are "uncertain trumpets" as parents when we waver in our decisions, when we are swayed by our fear that the child will not love us if we do not allow him to be unruly and disobedient.

If we remember ourselves as children, we remember that we knew when the adults around us were "uncertain trumpets." We did not respect the authority that was not really authority; we did not respect the rules that were laid down with great emphasis one day and ignored from then on.

When we remember ourselves as children, what stands out most vividly? Most of us cherish the memory of the persons or the experiences that made us feel capable and worthy even as little children. We think with thankfulness of the ones who took time and had the patience to teach us how to conduct ourselves, who took our hands as we crossed new thresholds of learning and living, who opened our eyes and our ears and our hearts to the wonders of the world about us and the world within us.

The child who screams if you try to make him mind, who has

temper tantrums, who is noisy and destructive, needs and wants to learn how to live happily and peaceably with his family and with other persons. He will not love you less because you teach him that his way is not the right way; he will love you more because he will love himself more.

When do we begin to teach children how to act, how to think, how to live? From the moment they draw breath we are teaching them. A tiny baby soon learns how to get attention; he discovers that the world seems to revolve around him. Even with a tiny baby the parents can help him to get the feeling that there are other persons in the world besides himself, that the world has not been created just to do his bidding.

But even if we feel that we have somehow gotten off to a wrong start with our child, that he has already formed negative patterns of behavior, it is never too late to begin changing, first, our own thought about him, and then our own thought about ourselves as parents. As we pray for light and guidance, we will be shown what we can do to help our child; our understanding of him will increase; we will become more aware of his needs; we will begin to see him as a growing and unfolding soul rather than as a "problem child."

The child is an all-important part of the family, of course, but he has to learn to make himself an important and valuable part of life. If he does not learn it as a child, he has to learn it eventually; and the way is harder for a "grown-up child."

"To whomsoever much is given, of him shall much be required." Certainly this is true of parents, for a parent is given the greatest gift of all, the gift of a life to guide and help, the gift of a living soul to love. But with such a gift come requirements. To be a parent calls for wisdom, strength, understanding, patience, love, for all the best that any human being can give. But every parent should remember that he can meet these requirements, for he has the love of Christ within him.

Children respond to our unconscious influence as well as to our conscious influence, sometimes more so. The more loving we are, the more patient we are. The more understanding we are, the more we will influence our children to follow our unconscious example.

And children are very receptive to true ideas; they accept a belief in God easily and unquestionably. They long, even as we long, to feel beloved of God, to know that God watches over them. Faith comes naturally to them, and our own faith in God and His goodness is one of the greatest blessings we can give the child. That child is fortunate who has parents who nourish and encourage the spiritual self of him, who help him to come to the place where he discovers for himself the living, loving Christ presence.

In all our teaching and training and guidance of the child, we should never lose sight of the truth that he is more than a child—he is God's own creation. He has powers and abilities in him beyond any we could pray for or imagine for him. He has everything in him that he requires for perfect growth and fulfillment. Our part is to nourish and nurture him in his growing period.

Are our children in need of help and guidance? Is our home in need of peace and order? Are our lives in need of happiness and love? Something in us will not let us stand back. Something in us will not let us continue to feel helpless and hopeless about the situation; something in us pushes us forward and says to us: "You are the one. This is your work."

CLARA PALMER

HERITAGE OF THE LORD

THERE IS ONE special privilege that Jesus Christ shares
with all of us, the privilege of blessing children, even as He
blessed them so long ago. We ask you to join with us in blessing
in His name all children, all boys and girls everywhere, and if
possible to do some act of love and kindness that will add to the
health and happiness of some child somewhere.

If in your heart you desire to help children, we know that
Jesus Christ, the lover of all children, will open the way for your
desire to be fulfilled. Nothing can give your Lord greater joy,
nothing can give you greater joy, nothing can prove of greater
benefit to all than the service you render to children in His name.

No matter who you are or where you are, there is a definite
work that you can do for children. Even though you may not see
the results of your work, they will be written in terms of divine
love and faith upon the hearts of tomorrow's men and women,
recorded forever in the kingdom of God.

The work that you can do is one of prayer.

Scarcely an edition of a newspaper is printed that does not
contain some item about children. You can read the list of births
and send to each newborn baby a thought of love and blessing
as you lift your heart in prayer and thanksgiving to God for the
wellbeing of the little one.

Almost daily the newspapers carry an account of some child's
unusual ability, his heroism, or his need for healing. They also
carry reports of juvenile delinquency, heartbreaking stories of

boys and girls whose misguided imagination led them into trying to re-enact the exciting crime they had seen pictured in the movie, the comic book, the detective-storybook, or television, or heard about over the radio, or through the conversations of others.

What can you do to help these children? You can pray faithfully, regularly, lovingly. Prayer should always be the first step in the solving of every human problem, for prayer unifies the one who prays with the infinite Father who answers prayer. Your prayer makes your life an open channel for the outpouring of God's blessing. You may or may not be called upon personally to help in bringing to pass the good you ask for. In any event you can always be very sure that your prayers, your affirmative words of Truth, praise, and blessing are a vital factor in helping, healing, uplifting, and redeeming those for whom you pray. In all the world no prayer can be more pleasing to God or more helpful to the universe than the prayer you offer for a little child.

Who can say that the children of today are not the children of the new race that is to establish the kingdom of God on this earth? Have you noticed how beautiful these children are, how quick in understanding, how keen in intelligence? They are indeed a choice creation, these children of today, and they deserve the very best that can be given them in the way of prayer, blessing, recognition, spiritual instruction, and understanding. It is a very great privilege to follow in the Christ way of loving, healing, helping, and blessing these children.

Was ever higher honor given anyone than was given by Jesus Christ to the little child whom He took and set in the midst of the encircling multitude, saying: "Whosoever shall receive one of such little children in my name, receiveth me: and whosoever receiveth me, receiveth not me, but him that sent me." And again Jesus Christ said, "Suffer the little children, and forbid them not to come unto me: for to such belongeth the kingdom of heaven."

The Scripture does not describe the little child whom Jesus Christ so honored. In the neighborhood where the child lived he was just one little boy among other children. Possibly there may have been neighbors who thought of him as a very annoying or mischievous child. But Jesus Christ with eyes of love looked to the heart of the child and beheld divine qualities and potentialities in him, qualities and potentialities that may also be found this day in the heart of every child by persons who love children as Jesus Christ loves them.

"Lo, children are a heritage of Jehovah," a heritage shared by us. What joy it is to know that "to such belongeth the kingdom of heaven." Can any words more joyously describe the resilient, ageless life that is ours in the kingdom of God?

As long as this earth exists there will be children to bless, children to love, children who will help us grow in love, patience, and understanding, children who will bless us with happiness even as we would bless them, children who by God's blessing and ours will become strong, courageous, illumined, and helpful men and women.

Children are a responsibility; that is a fact. Possibly they do make work, but when a little child comes to you for a blessing; when with wide eyes and wide-awake mind he plies you with questions; when, right in the midst of your busiest hours, he wants to be cuddled and loved a bit, do not brush him aside with the feeling that you have not time to bother with him. Just recall the service-filled days of Jesus, the urgency of the demands made upon Him, and then remember His words: "Suffer the little children, and forbid them not to come unto me: for to such belongeth the kingdom of heaven." Remember His attitude when, while the thronging multitudes were made to wait: "He took them in his arms, and blessed them."

Emulating Him, you shall be blessed and your duties divinely adjusted; and the children will love and recompense you.

Bless God for the children!

ZELIA M. WALTERS

THE CHILD'S RELIGION

"I WAS WALKING with my grandmother late one summer afternoon. There had been dry, hot weather for two weeks. Grandmother had been looking at her garden and remarking that her garden needed rain. As we walked she looked up into the western sky where a few small gray clouds were gathering. There had been clouds like that for several evenings past, but by moonrise they were dissipated without bringing the wished-for rain.

" 'Let us thank God for the rain that the gardens and farms need,' said Grandmother.

" 'What, before we get it?' I cried in surprise.

" 'Why, certainly, didn't we ask for it?' said Grandmother tranquilly.

"We walked in silence a few minutes, Grandmother, I suppose, thanking God for the rain that had not yet come. But I couldn't do that. It was too much for a boy of thirteen.

"At about nine o'clock that night Grandmother called me to the door. A gentle rain was falling. It rained all night, bringing the incalculable blessing of a soaking rain to farms and gardens.

"No lesson in faith—no sermon, no book, no so-called demonstration—has ever done for me what my grandmother's answer did: 'Why, certainly; didn't we ask for it?' Whenever I falter now, in my adult years, I remember that. Of course I asked many questions, and Grandmother explained so that my immature mind could grasp it. You got what you asked for if you were in line with God's will and believed. You must be careful what you asked. If you asked something that would harm another, you would hurt yourself too. You must always add 'in God's way and according to God's will' to your prayer of request. Then you would be sure you were asking only good. Remember to be thankful. Unthankful people shut the door on their own blessings.

"That summer I learned too that my grandmother lived by faith, that she never worried in the face of seemingly impending disaster; and no stroke of misfortune ever did fall. She had asked God. She never talked about what her faith had done. There was no talk of 'demonstration,' no bragging of what she could accomplish. After all these years I shall not talk about it either. But I learned faith by living that summer with my grandmother."

A man who would seem to have gone far on the road of faith himself told me the foregoing story of his childhood; and I can think of no better introduction to the study of the child's religion.

We have changed our ideas of child training in religion. We no longer expect to do it by sending him to Sunday school for an hour once a week and possibly to a class in the catechism when he is preparing for confirmation. We know now that a religion like that, fenced off in a little separate compartment of life, is of no practical use; and unless religion works in connection with the everyday problems we have to meet in this common life of ours. it is not worth having. We know now that real religion permeates and interpenetrates every moment of life as the universal ether permeates space. We take religion with us to the ball game, to the picnic, on the automobile ride, to the theater, to every social meeting. We take it into factory, office, bank, store. We use it on the farm and in the kitchen. We use it in schoolroom and studio. We take it into the hospital. We even take it to church! That is, we take it into all these places if we have any religion.

It is this religion—which means always feeling the presence of God—that we should like to teach our children. There will be very little formal instruction in a religion like this. In a well-conducted home there is very little formal instruction in courtesy or in the use of good English. The children merely live with their parents, and grow into courteous gentlefolk. So in teaching religion the points we wish to impress upon the child mind will arise in the hourly events of the day. As we deal with them the child will form his ideas of God and of his relation to his world.

But while the instruction will come spontaneously from the events of the day, we should have in our mind as parents some clearly defined plan of what we will teach under the general name of religion.

Perhaps most of us will agree on some such outline as this:

Love is power, whereas hate or violence is surely doomed to failure.

Faith is a working force, not a vague impractical sentiment.

God is our Father and cares about all that we do.

The world is a brotherhood and, as in the family, its members rise or fall together.

We are in the world as children of God to do His will, and in that we shall find our happiness and fulfillment.

With this as our objective, let us use the happenings of the child's day to prepare him for life as a child of God. There is no day that does not give the child opportunity to practice courage, faith, patience, industry, kindness, truth. As he learns that he is practicing his small virtues in accordance with universal laws, he will grow in mind and spirit.

But, says the doubter, how much can a young child understand about universal law? Anyone who deals with children will answer that they do understand. Sometimes their intuitive grasp of a situation makes us gasp in astonishment.

Sandy, aged six, was having a serious talk with Mother. He had been lagging in obedience on several occasions, and she was explaining to him why a child must learn to obey promptly and cheerfully. It was to prepare him for the time when parents and teachers would no longer control him, but he must be strong and wise enough to obey the laws of the universe. Mother explained that the laws of the universe must be obeyed. They cannot be argued with. If we disobey, they make us pay. If we put a hand in the fire, we shall be burned, no matter what excuses we may make to the law. So it is very important to learn to obey parents while one is young. She went on to say we need not bother about these laws; they take care of themselves. If someone treats us badly, we need not try to repay them. We can ignore it; the law of the universe will take care of it.

When Sandy had left the room another member of the family laughed good-naturedly at Mother. "How much of that do you suppose that child understood?" "Oh, quite a good deal," said Mother serenely.

Next day a smaller cousin was teasing Sandy. After a while the child's mother felt interference was necessary.

"Jimmy, what are you trying to do?" she said. "Do you want to make trouble?"

"Oh, never mind about that, Aunt Ruth," said Sandy with an air of tolerance. "The law of the universe will take care of him."

Had Sandy grasped the sense of the lesson?

Another true incident: Bob came home from the playground very much ruffled. A custodian had reminded him in a disagreeable manner of some rule he had inadvertently transgressed.

"But, Bob," said Mother, "they are the same rules that were in force last year. You didn't feel hurt at being asked to obey them then."

"That's just it, Mother. We want to obey the rules. Last year if we did anything we shouldn't, Mr. Lee would tell us, but he was nice about it and we didn't mind. But Mr. Blank is so mean about it that we'd just like to break all the rules." He thought it over for a while and then came to his own bit of philosophy. "Just think, Mother, one person can make you like the rules and get you to try to keep them, and another person can make you hate the very same rules."

"Yes; and which kind are you going to be?"

"I'll make them like the rules. I'll be polite when I have to tell people things."

That was a good conclusion, but Mother did not stop at that. Had she done so, he might have gone to the playground next day set on annoying the disagreeable Mr. Blank. She tactfully drew from him the admission that the playground rules were good, designed to keep the children harmonious and happy. Would we be foolish to let a disagreeable person have the mastery over us to the extent of leading us to break rules that we believed good, or to do anything else against our better judgment? To repay Mr. Blank with defiance or more disagreeableness to match his would make the playground an unhappy place. Was it not better to forget that it had happened and treat Mr. Blank with courtesy?

The questions with which children meet the puzzling matters in this strange new world to which they have come are usually enough in themselves to furnish the background for the children's religious education.

"What is the soul? Where is it? How do I know I have one? Why can't I see it?"

How shall I answer so as to tell all I ought and impart no wrong notions?

One mother used the natural manifestation closest at hand.

"What is it that is lifting the leaves of the trees?"

"The wind."

"Can you see it?"

"No, but I can see what it does."

"That is the way with the soul. We cannot see it, but we can see what it does." From this analogy she went on to answer the questions about the soul, making it all seem natural and reasonable. A sunbeam would have carried the lesson equally well, or the mysterious impulse that travels in the form of radio waves.

But we have to keep on searching into the depths of our own spirit for the answers to these searching questions. For answered they must be.

"Why is it wrong to tell a lie?"

Well, do you, parent or teacher, know why? It isn't enough to say as parents once did, "I do not want you to tell a lie"; or even to say that God forbids lies. Still the child wants to know. Why does he? You must find simple words to explain to the child that truth makes a dividing line across the universe. On one side is everything that is straight and fine and noble, in a word, true. All art, science, invention, leadership, trade, or labor that is worthy to endure stands on the right side of the line. On the other side are the lies of every kind, all the false things, all the distorted shadows and errors that cloud the mind of mankind and lead our feet astray.

"Why must I not strike that boy?"

Do you know enough of the law of love to make this clear to the child? All your teaching and all that the child has observed of you up to this point should be a reinforcement of what you now have to say to explain why the way of violence does not work.

"What does it mean when God forgives me?"

Has the child learned from the forgiveness he has experienced in the home what the forgiveness of God is like? When an error has been dealt with in the home, set right as far as the child can do it, is it then forgotten as if it had never been? In some homes the memory of a childish misdeed is held over the child's head day after day. He is reminded of it, reproved for it again and again, perhaps the punishment for it is even repeated. Of course there is a mistaken notion in the parental mind that this impresses the child with the danger of doing the thing again. But how would you like that sort of forgiveness from God? Have you ever rejoiced in the promise "I will forgive their iniquity, and their sin will I remember no more"? Give your child that kind of forgiveness too, and you need do very little explaining about God's forgiveness.

"Is God mad at me when I'm bad?"

Happy is the parent who can reply, "No; no more than I am mad at you when you are bad," and from that can go on to explain that love lasts always even though one removes oneself out of the circle of its blessings.

"Why doesn't God make me be good?"

From here you can begin to give the child a glimpse of the large liberty that is his as a child of God. He is not made like a doll or a puppet, so that someone can pull the strings and decide his actions. He has free will. He must choose between good and evil.

Thus we will go on as the daily questions arise. Some we can lead the child to answer for himself. But we will not evade or put him off, or answer in any way but truthfully. We will not try to whittle the Truth down to our notion of his understanding. It is better for him to have his mind stand tiptoe to reach up to what we are teaching.

Years ago I heard a mother give a large dose of Truth to two small children. And not long ago one of them told me that she did understand it then and had never forgotten it. The mother had taken her children to a picnic, which turned out to be rather dull. The children came to their mother saying that they were not having a good time.

"Of course you're not," said the mother. "You didn't bring a good time with you."

How much did they understand? At least they stopped whining and began to turn over in childish minds this idea that you must take your good times with you. Certainly in the years that came they returned to the idea again and again until they knew its truth from experience.

Though the child may thus wander far afield, he will come back to the simple Truth again and again.

Be sure that you teach the child early the law of giving. No one has any real religion until he understands that "with what measure ye mete, it shall be measured unto you." This is the law of love and faith in action.

There are two points in the religious training of the child of yesterday that were considered of first importance: regular attendance at religious services, and daily reading of the Bible. There will never come a time when we can discard these.

Regular attendance at some religious service gives aid to spiritual growth. There is something strengthening in being a part of the worshiping multitude. We catch a contagion of devotion from one another. To be so situated that we must miss this is to miss a very real means of grace. It matters not what kind of worshiping multitude; it may be a small multitude, perhaps only the scriptural two or three gathered together in His name. We might kneel with devout pagans and all of us lift our souls together toward God. We enter a cathedral, crowded to the doors with the faithful, and beauty and holiness wrap us round. We feel the prayers of these hundreds. Perhaps we enter a bare little church on the frontier. The few communicants are sitting in hushed silence before the service. We join them and come face to face with God. By all means teach the child the habit of regular attendance upon some service of worship.

And teach him too that there is a proper deportment for church. How often are the devout shocked by stepping into a church that appears like a jolly club meeting. The hum of voices will bar meditation. There is a sort of spiritual etiquette. Some bodies of Christians teach it to their children from infancy, others seem to neglect it entirely. The few minutes before the hour of worship are an opportunity for meditation and prayer, and a social conversation with one's neighbor is quite out of place. Teach the child from his first attendance at church that he is "in his holy temple," and that all the earth keeps silence before

God. Do not teach him that this silent reverence is irksome but that it is a joy. In God's house we listen for His word.

Have him read and memorize from the Bible. In it he will find wisdom, inspiration, comfort, strength. His soul will be attuned to beauty. He will find there the way plainly marked so that he need not stumble. He will read the records of weak and erring men and women who yet found their way into the presence of God. And do not forget that the Scriptures are not finished. As in the past, men of God today are speaking and writing as they are moved by the Holy Spirit. There is much to read that will help us build a firm foundation under our virtues, and much that will give wings to faith.

JANE PALMER

"WHO IS GOD?"

(Some years ago a grandmother wrote to Jane Palmer,
editor of Wee Wisdom, asking for help in answering her
four-and-a-half-year-old grandson's question, "Who is God?"
Miss Palmer's answer follows.)

    I HAVE DELAYED answering your letter asking for an ex-
planation of God that would be understandable to a young child
until I should have time to give the explanation careful consideration. "Who is God?" is a difficult question to answer satisfac-
torily. Then there is "Where is God?" "Can He see me?" and
"Why can't I see Him?"
    I believe the whole matter will be straightened out easily
if we begin when the child first asks by simply telling him that
God is Spirit. He will not understand at first what Spirit is any
better than he understands what God is, but he will accept it, and
this gives us a basis for further comment and explanation. Everything and everyone has spirit, just as he has life. We do not see
our life, but we know it is there because we can run and laugh
and play and love one another. We cannot see love, but we know
it is there because we are happy when someone loves us.
    We can say that God is love instead of God is Spirit if we like
that better, or God is wisdom, or understanding. A very young
child will accept the explanation that God is love readily because he understands the word love. Mother and Father love

him. He loves baby sister. It is easy to slip from love as expressed by parents to love as expressed by God.

Once I helped a very small girl, less than three, overcome her fear of the dark by taking her by the hand and leading her into a darkened room. She was familiar with the room and everything in it, so she was not afraid of the dark so long as I held her hand. Then I turned on the light and showed her that everything in the room was just as she had known it to be. Then I switched off the light. She was not afraid because she knew there was nothing in there that had not been there when the light was on. I then let go of her hand and walked across the room from her. She felt secure because she knew that I was there although she could not see me.

She knew that I loved her because I did things for her. I played with her when she was ready for play, fed her when she was hungry, comforted her when she was hurt. She accepted my love because of the evidence, not because she saw it.

A child cannot see God any more than he can see Mother when she is in a darkened room, but he can accept God as love because He does things for him. He gives the sunshine to warm the earth, the rain to slacken thirst; daytime for work and play, night for rest. He clothes, feeds, and cares for animals and birds; He gives men the wisdom and understanding to build homes for shelter and comfort; He gives us fruit and vegetables for food. Just as Father's and Mother's love for their children is evidenced by their care for them, God's love is evidenced by His great and gracious gifts to all His children.

You can elaborate on these ideas by using your own examples of little homey things that the child is familiar with.

I should try to disabuse the child's mind of the idea of God as a man with the explanation that a man would not be able to be in all places at the same time. The conception of God as love will help you with this. Mother loves Father when he is at the office or in the field. At the same time she loves Big Sister, who is married and lives in another city, and she loves Brother, who is in school, as much as she loves the little child who is in the home, and she loves them all equally and at the same time. She does this through her spirit of love. Because God is Spirit or love He understands us all and loves us all, no matter where we are or what we are doing.

I hope that this explanation will prove helpful. I know that God's Spirit of love and understanding guides your daughter in the training of her little ones in the Christ way of life.

WHAT IS PRAYER?

(The following short articles, compiled from the Unity *Truth Lessons for Boys and Girls, are included here with the thought that parents will want to read them to their children.)*

"PRAYER IS talking with God." That is what we said when we were very small and we were right too. Prayer is talking to God, but prayer is also listening to God. A prayer does not have to be said out loud. It does not even have to be said at all. Sometimes prayer is just feeling very close to God, thinking of God, loving God, and listening to God.

We do not listen to God with our ears, for God does not talk to us with words that we can hear. God talks to us by putting pleasant thoughts in our mind. He talks to us by making our heart feel happy and loving, and by causing us to think of kind things to say and do.

Prayer is talking to God either silently or out loud and then listening for the message or direction that God sends through our thoughts. Prayer is feeling the warmth and the joy and the closeness of God in our heart.

But how do we know that the thought in our mind is a message from God? Here is a good way to tell. If the thought in our mind is like God; if it is kind and loving and unselfish and the kind of thought we should expect God to think, then we can believe that it came from Him. We know what God is like. We know that God would not send a thought of jealousy or deceit or cowardice. So when we are listening for God's message, it is best to remember what God is like.

[321]

When we are first learning to pray, we say certain words or prayers out loud because the words are about God and make us think of God. Then we learn to think the words without saying them at all. This is helpful, for many times we want to pray without having other people hear us. Next we learn that we can pray without saying or thinking any special words. We can just talk naturally to God as we would to any other friend about anything we like.

It does not greatly matter whether we pray silently or out loud. It does not matter whether we pray memorized prayers or make them up ourselves. What does matter is that we mean what we say to God with all our heart; that we feel His presence within us and let God's thoughts fill our mind. This is prayer.

Why We Pray

We pray because we are children of God, and the quickest and most direct way of getting what we want is to ask our Father-God for it. We pray because we are children of God, and we get homesick or lonely for our Father when we stay too long away from Him. We pray because we are children of God, and we do not know what to do or say or how to live without His direction.

We eat food to keep our body renewed and satisfied, and we pray to keep our spirit renewed and satisfied. Prayer is spiritual food. No matter how much fine food we eat, how well we are clothed, how beautiful our home is, or how many friends we have about us, we still feel hungry and cold and lonely unless we take spiritual food.

No matter how long we go to school or how smart and quick we are, we still make blunders and mistakes that keep us troubled and unhappy unless we let God direct our thoughts. There are many things that we need and want that no one can give us but God. Such things as hope and courage and love and joy must come from God within ourselves, and they come much faster and more freely when we open the way through prayer.

There is nothing in all the world, either things for the body or things for the spirit, that God cannot give us. And we pray because prayer is the pathway to God, the best and surest way to reach Him.

When We Pray

A certain man once said that the best time to pray was late in the afternoon and the best way to pray was standing on one's head. This man had fallen into a well head first late one afternoon, and he had found that particular time and position a very, very good time and position in which to pray. This is just a funny story of course, and it proves nothing to us except that the best time and way to pray is any time and every way.

Some people like to kneel down when they pray, as people do before a king. This helps them to remember that God is the king or ruler of their life.

Some people like to fold their hands to show that they depend on God more than on their own skill or strength. Others like to open their hands as if to receive all the good their hands can hold.

It does not matter what position our hands or body are in when we pray as long as our mind and heart are open to God and we do not just repeat words like a parrot.

All of us pray when we go to church. That is partly our reason for going. Most of us pray before we go to bed to fill our mind with God's love and protection before we go to sleep. Most of us like to pray when we awake, because we are so happy, so filled with the love of God, and because we want God's guidance through the day.

Most of us like to thank God for our food every time we eat. It seems to taste so much better when we pause to remember that it came from God. We like to pray before we start to school or on any journey so as to remember that God goes with us.

We like to remember God with a tiny prayer of thanks when we are very happy, and to ask His help when we are sad or lonely or afraid. We like to ask His guidance when we have some hard lesson or task to do and to thank Him when our work is done.

There is never a moment day or night when we cannot pray, even if it is only with a thought or a wish in our heart.

The place to pray is any place, and the time to pray is now.

How We Pray

There is nothing too big or too small for God to give you, but God has nothing to give but good. No amount of pleading or begging can change God's wonderful plan of good. We do not pray to change God or to get God to be more interested in us and our affairs. We pray so that we may come closer to Him, to understand His great plan of good and do our part in working it out.

We do not pray for food and clothes and fun and friends. We pray so that we may always know how to find these gifts of God and how to use them.

We know that God's plan is for life and health for all of His children. We do not pray to Him to give them to us or to our friends; we pray so that we may become more convinced or aware of them.

We do not pray God to make our teacher or some friend love us more than he loves some other child. We just pray to be more loving and more lovable ourselves and to know how to work with God's great plan of love.

We know that God has a place where everybody can work and grow. So when our father or some friend needs a place to work, we pray that he will come close enough to God so that God can show him or direct him to his own place.

We do not pray to win contests or make high grades. We know that these things have all been worked out in God's plan for the greatest good of everybody. So we pray that we may do our very best to use all the skill and knowledge we have.

Every prayer is heard, and every prayer is answered. If they are not always answered in just the way we planned for them to be, we remember that God's plans are better than ours. We know that God has planned to give us more good than we can know or ask for. And we pray to understand God's plan and prepare to receive greater good.

JAMES DILLET FREEMAN

CHILDREN ARE LIKE A BANK

Children are like a bank in which we store
Faith in the future and all human lore,
The ideas and ideals of our race.
In the bright wonder of an upturned face,
We see the whole hope of man's betterment.
Children are savings but cannot be spent.
It is a joy to hold the helpless, small
Armful that is a babe, yet best of all
Is this: to give our children back again
To life, grown up, young women and young men.
Life lets us have our children as a loan,
Ours to enjoy and guard but not to own,
To increase like our talents, not to hoard.
Children are an investment of the Lord.

11. The Spirit of Youth in You

"The spirit of youth in you is the Spirit of God in you. You are of the Infinite and there is no failure for you—the only apparent failure is your failure to see and to claim as yours this truth of your being. The moment you catch the vision, you let flood your soul and your body that light and life which make you to know that all things are possible with you, now."

—*Myrtle Fillmore*

JAMES E. SWEANEY

BETWEEN THE LINES

(Excerpts from a monthly department in You magazine)

Not for Grades

*Whatsoever ye do, work heartily, as unto the Lord, and not unto men—*Col. 3:23.

Do your school grades bother you?

When asked this question, one young man replied, "They don't bother me, but they sure bother my dad!"

Many students worry about their school grades. They worry about the effect of these grades on their parents and on their teachers and the subsequent reaction on themselves.

Do you find your grades a subject for worry? Perhaps you have tried to please your parents and your teachers and tried to make better grades, but seemingly have not succeeded. Perhaps you are discouraged as well as worried and resigned to the feeling that to get good grades is hopeless.

If you want to solve this problem, take a tip from the best and happiest workers in any organization. They are the workers who follow the Biblical advice, "Whatsoever ye do, work heartily, as unto the Lord, and not unto men."

Do your schoolwork as unto God and not just to please your teachers and your parents. This is the secret of making grades that will please both your teachers and your parents.

[329]

Does this seem like "double talk"? Actually, it is a spiritual law that is referred to time and again in the Bible and that we are applying here to your schoolwork.

In the over-all plan of your life, where does attendance at school fit in?

Why are you giving time and attention to school?

To learn, of course, so that you may better fit yourself for a successful, happy life. Do you think that school is part of God's plan for you?

Leaving your teachers and your parents out of the picture entirely, how would you please God in regard to your schoolwork?

God is interested in whether you are learning the things you need, whether you are making the habits of industry part of your character. God is interested in you and your progress.

So when you start working for God and not just for grades the focus of your attention and effort is changed. You put your attention on actual learning, not on impressing teachers. The teachers become your guides; whether or not you learn your lessons becomes the important thing to you.

Do you see the difference? Once understood and followed, you have made a principle your own that will be invaluable to you in later life as well as in your schoolwork at the present time.

Whatever you study, dismiss the thought of the grades you are to receive from teachers, and study for God, who sees beyond your recitations and examination papers into your mind and heart.

If you can actually do this, you will be surprised how the problems concerning your school grades will be solved!

Accepting Parental Leadership

And he went down with them, and came to Nazareth; and he was subject unto them—Luke 2:51.

The teens are years of rapid growth and development.

Because of this rapid growth, there sometimes may arise difficulties between you and your parents. Much of your growing is within—in your mind, your emotions, and your understanding—and, therefore, your parents are not always aware of each stride that you make forward and upward. Conflicts in the outer may arise where actually none should exist, because both you and your parents are working toward the same goal: acceptance for you in the world as a fine, mature young man or woman.

You are making rapid strides in increasing your wisdom and understanding. This growth is recognized by your teachers and by others. But your parents may not seem to notice it. Perhaps they seem to look upon you still as a child.

Jesus must have had a similar experience. When He was on the threshold of His teens, He went with His parents to the annual feast of the Passover at Jerusalem. While there, He engaged in discussions with the teachers in the Temple, and they were amazed at His understanding and His answers to their questions.

Meanwhile, His parents began their return journey to Nazareth and, thinking Him to be among their kinsfolk or acquaintances, had traveled a whole day before they missed Him. When they discovered He was not "in the company," they returned to Jerusalem, where, "after three days they found him in the temple, sitting in the midst of the teachers, both hearing them, and asking them questions: and all that heard him were amazed at his understanding and his answers."

His parents' words to Him show us that they did not understand the import of His discussions with the learned teachers and that they were more aware at that moment of their own personal feelings. "Son," His mother said, "why hast thou thus dealt with us? behold, thy father and I sought thee sorrowing."

Jesus said, "How is it that ye sought me? knew ye not that I must be in my Father's house?"

He was expressing what seemed perfectly obvious to Him. He was "filled with wisdom: and the grace of God was upon him." He felt it and knew it, and others recognized it. He may have felt a keen disappointment because His parents "understood not the saying which he spake unto them."

Here is a situation that is repeated in various ways in our present-day world, and it often leads to inharmony and misunderstanding.

We acknowledge Jesus as our Way-Shower. How did He meet this familiar teen-and-parent situation?

"And he went down with them, and came to Nazareth; and he was subject unto them."

The sensible attitude of Jesus is the one for you to take as you go through your teens. Even though Jesus was filled with greater wisdom than His parents apparently understood, He submitted patiently to their leadership and guidance during His youth. And we know that He learned much in these years with His mother and father, for in His later teachings are illustrations taken from His early life.

Be patient; and even though your parents do not seem always to understand you, they are trying to, even as Jesus' "mother kept all *these* sayings in her heart." Your parents observe the things you do and say, your capabilities, your growth, and they think about them and try to estimate and understand. At least, you can know that they have your good interest at heart at all times.

If you meet your own situation in this way, you, too, will advance "in wisdom and stature, and in favor with God and men."

Keep Faith in the Midst of Lack

For though the fig-tree shall not flourish,
Neither shall fruit be in the vines;
The labor of the olive shall fail,
And the fields shall yield no food;
The flock shall be cut off from the fold,
And there shall be no herd in the stalls:
Yet I will rejoice in Jehovah,
I will joy in the God of my salvation.

—Hab. 3:17,18.

Poverty and lack are hard for young people to endure. Of course poverty brings misery to everyone who experiences it, but it seems especially hard on young people because it can so easily distort their future life.

Perhaps one reason why it is hard for young people to endure poverty is that there seems to be so little they can do about it while they are dependent upon their elders for sustenance and support. And young people tend to feel things very deeply.

The young person who feels the pinch of lack in his home often becomes ashamed of his parents, his clothes, and the place in which he lives. He is embarrassed and mortified by everything that reveals his condition of lack.

If young people are not careful, a home of limited circumstances can warp their thinking and actually start them on the road of life believing they are "inferior," not so good as their more prosperous friends. Or it can embitter them and make them feel cheated and hopeless about life.

Yet a background of limited means need not affect a young person adversely as he faces life. Indeed many of the great men of our nation have come from homes where there was want and privation.

If you are a young person in such circumstances, do not lose hope or faith in God and yourself. Instead know that no matter how dark or how limited your present circumstances may seem to be, you can work your way out of them.

Remember that God is for you. You are just as precious in His sight as anyone else, regardless of how much money you have.

Keep your faith in yourself. Finish your schooling so you will be prepared for the work you want to do, even though at times it may seem difficult. If possible do something to add to the family income, and try to make the best use of the money and other resources that are available.

Above all, do not let present limited circumstances embitter you or make you feel inferior. You are *not* inferior. It is the potentialities in you that count, not your family's income.

And know that you have within you the ability to overcome lack and poverty. Do what you can to the best of your ability, and keep faith in God, and you will be richly rewarded.

Your Future Home

For this cause shall a man leave his father and mother, and shall cleave to his wife; and the two shall become one flesh.—Eph. 5:31.

The family is a very important unit in community life. Likewise the stability or instability of families plays a major role in the stability of nations.

You probably are a part of a family group now, although it may not seem to you to be the traditional picture of one. Perhaps there are things about your family that you feel are far from perfect, perhaps the group has been broken up in some way.

Whether you feel that your own family life is perfect or imperfect, it can be your training ground for the more active role you will play in the future home you will share.

The teens is not too early an age to begin thinking about marriage and what it means. Not, of course, in the sense of getting married immediately, or for the purpose of searching for the right mate among your present friends, but in order to prepare yourself mentally and spiritually for a happy marriage at the right time.

It seems to me that the most important fact to remember about marriage is that when you marry you establish a new home. To realize this fact and all it implies will help you see marriage in its true and most wonderful aspect.

Marriage is not just a lifetime "date," it is not just a honeymoon that lasts forever, it is not just being with the one you love from now on. Marriage is the establishing of a home.

A home is a place where members of the family work together for the common good, where the needs for food, shelter, clothing, companionship, and love are fulfilled. Maintaining a home involves the earning of income, housecleaning, taxes, obligations to the community, and loyalty to the other members of the household.

Realizing the responsibilities of marriage will help you to decide for yourself many things in connection with it. You see that in selecting a mate the characteristics in a person that contribute to the happiness and well-being of those around him will be important in making home life agreeable. But a person who is selfish and has a bad disposition is not likely to be willing to help make a home happy.

Physical attraction, dancing ability, ability to make jokes, and to entertain, are all good and have their place in life but they are not necessary qualifications for establishing a happy home. Homes are founded on love, wisdom, common sense, understanding, tolerance, dependability, willingness to work for the common good.

A life partner can have all the extra abilities that may seem desirable, such as dancing, entertaining, and the like, but the basic, solid qualities are much more important.

Understanding that the purpose of marriage is to establish a home will help you to know the right time to get married. It will keep you from a hasty, ill-advised marriage, for you will realize that before you marry you must be willing and able to establish a home.

Remember that sooner or later you probably will want a home of your own. Your present and past experience as a member of a family can be helpful to you. If you will keep in mind that in marriage you are establishing a home, it will help you to get and keep the right perspective about marriage.

JAMES A. DECKER

WHAT SHOULD I SAY TO GOD?

(Sometime ago the editors of You *magazine received a letter from Evelyn M——, a teen-age reader who said that she did not know how to pray and asked what she should say to God. The editors gave the letter to Mr. Decker, a frequent contributor to* You *and other Unity periodicals, and asked for a practical, down-to-earth answer to Evelyn's question. The accompanying article is his answer.)*

EVELYN HAS a problem. Life is, generally speaking, a wonderful adventure for her, as it is for most teen-agers, because she tries to live it constructively as best she knows how. And therein lies her problem: She wants to know how to get more out of these wonderful years, and sometimes she feels that she does not know exactly how to go about it.

"I've just begun to realize that I don't know how to pray in the true sense of the word," she writes. "When I go to church on Sunday I pray, but I still don't feel that I understand what I should say to God."

If you want to pray, there are not many mistakes you *can* make, because wanting to pray is the most important part of praying. One mistake that can keep you from getting the most out of prayer, however, is to regard it as complicated or mysterious or difficult.

Prayer means many things to many persons. In the minds of some, solemn rituals and ceremonies are part of prayer. We who

[336]

make simple prayer part of our lives can also respect and partici-
pate in the language and rites of formal worship. But we feel,
through our own experience with simple prayer, that a quiet talk
with God is the finest kind of refreshing, uplifting interlude in
today's busy living.

If you feel that you must have certain conditions and surroundings before you pray, you are sometimes unable to go to
God when you most need to talk with Him. That is why the first
step in learning how to pray is to understand that prayer is,
simply and wonderfully, talking with God.

Perhaps *talking* is not the most accurate word to use, for often
nothing is said aloud. A better word might be *communing*—a
word that does not deserve the air of awesome mystery it often
seems to have. Communing might be defined as "thinking together." The best of friends are those we commune with; they
are ones who are so close to us that we can spend much time with
them without saying more than a few words aloud. Words are
not always necessary among good friends; we learn to share one
another's thoughts and emotions, and we feel an intangible but
very real bond even in the midst of a noisy crowd.

So it is—or can be—in our relationship with God. In fact, the
togetherness can be even more real, because God is closer to us
than any friend; He is within us. The thoughts that we think
come from God originally, so it is just a matter of re-attuning our
minds with His mind. Then we are thinking together with God—
and this is the most effective kind of prayer.

Of course, getting in tune with God's way of thinking is not
something that we can do automatically, as we would switch on
an electric light. We cannot commune with God if some of our
thoughts are miles away—on tomorrow's exam or the Saturday-
night dance. We have to be genuinely interested in God's ideas
if we expect to pray effectively.

Such a requirement is not unreasonable, is it? If you had occasion to ask a banker to lend you a sum of money and kept your
appointment with him disinterestedly, he probably would decide
against making the loan. If, while the banker told you the conditions under which you would be permitted to borrow the needed
money, you kept staring out the window, watching passers-by on

the sidewalk, the banker might be expected to feel that you were not really interested in securing the money.

God has a right to expect as much courtesy and interested attention as we would give to any good friend in conversation. The only way to center our thoughts on God is to approach Him in a mood that is in keeping with His nature: an attitude of reverence and worship. Here again, it is wise to remember that worship does not necessarily mean kneeling in a church, or going through any similar ritual. Worship *may* be formal; most of us find it helpful and inspiring to worship God publicly, solemnly, and with ceremony at regular intervals. But such worship is an extra, or an added dividend of good. The basic good is the good we come to know through informal, private worship. God is never unapproachable or remote. We can go to Him at any time, in any surroundings, regardless of companions or conditions.

Silence is an essential part of prayer; but the silence must be within us, not necessarily around us. Practice will make possible a genuine inner silence that we can achieve whenever we need to commune with God.

"What should I say to God?" We know that it is not necessary to say anything aloud, unless we particularly want to speak. Sometimes it is helpful to speak; it helps us to realize the presence of God. If you feel that you can more surely and reverently approach God by speaking, then you should speak. Even so, you need not speak loudly; a whisper, or even forming the words in your mind, will do as well.

What you should say is whatever seems most helpful under the circumstances. Different situations may call for different expressions. The best way to find out what words you want to use in approaching God is to experiment. You can find different affirmations—sentences or phrases that have helped others to recognize God's presence. Repeat—aloud or silently—one of these affirmations when you go to God. Or use any sentence, phrase, or word that comes to your mind; if you truly want to approach Him, God will come more than halfway to meet you. He will put the right thought into your mind.

I remember one of Gardner Hunting's articles that told of a man who, when he wanted to bring his thoughts into harmony with God's thinking, said simply, "*Now, Lord.*" Another writer,

Emmet Fox, said that a favorite affirmation of his was *"God is with me."* Even the word *God* is a powerful thought in itself.

At any rate, you will find that it is easy to contact God. He is so close—"closer . . . then breathing, and nearer than hands and feet." He is not an awesome, remote deity with whom you must make a formal appointment; He is within you, always immediately available when you need Him.

Once you have learned to recognize His presence, once you know (and it is so easy, so simple to know!) how to approach Him, you are praying. But then, you may ask again, "What should I say?" And again, the answer is: "You can say a great deal or very little. You can bring your most complicated problems, your most cherished ideals and discuss them with Him; or you can just relax in His presence, with the sure knowledge that He is solving your problems, adjusting all your affairs, bringing about what you most want to achieve and be."

Should you pray about specific things? You may if you want to; many persons do, and their prayers are answered. But you are sure to find, as you gain experience in praying, that the wisest prayer is the prayer that lets God make your decisions and choices.

We can pray for the friendship of one certain person, bearing in mind always that God's plans for us include the friendship of all around us and brotherhood that is wide enough to encircle the whole world. We can ask in prayer for the successful outcome of a test or examination, knowing that God's infinite wisdom is ours to use in all that we undertake—that He works with us to bring about good results in all that we study, profitable use of all that we learn.

God is interested in us; He wants us to share with Him every condition, situation, and association affecting our lives. No seeming trouble is too small to bring to Him for adjustment; no dream is too remote, no ideal too high to entrust to Him. No good thing that we want to undertake is farfetched in God's sight. He knows the unlimited power that is within us, even though we may never have demonstrated our talents and abilities.

We should place every detail of our living in God's keeping. We should never think of anyone or anything in a negative, critical way. We should consider not what is wrong but what is right. We should not see any discouraging or inharmonious situation as it appears to be, but as it will be when God adjusts it. We should see good developing out of every circumstance, even though we are not able to see exactly how the development will take place.

I say this not in a manner of preaching or teaching; I say it simply by way of relating what prayer has meant to me. I have prayed in this way many times, in many situations. This simple way of praying—this thinking together with God, seeing the good and letting Him work it out as He sees fit—has helped me in school, in relationships with others, in planning my affairs. There is nothing exclusive, nothing mysterious, nothing complicated about it.

"What should I say to God?" Say what comes naturally; do not wait for special words to come. Do not strive for perfect sentences, polished phrases. Go to God as you would go to any good friend; share your thoughts with Him, and He will share His ideas with you. And almost before you know it, you will come to realize that all your thoughts, all your actions are part of prayer.

There is no more heartening thing to know. It is something to hold in your mind, something you will never lose.

It will make all the hours of your life richer and fuller.

JAMES E. SWEANEY

SO YOU ARE GRADUATING

So YOU ARE graduating!

First of all, may I offer you my heartiest congratulations! You are passing a milestone in your life. It is a milestone you can recognize and be prepared for.

Milestones are rather like the two types of stories in news gathering. One type is the news that everyone knows is going to occur, such as an election, a sporting event, and other scheduled activities. Such events are covered adequately by news agencies. Then there are the news stories that cannot be anticipated, such as earthquakes, fires, and other unexpected events. These are handled as best they can by the news agencies as they occur.

Likewise, milestones in your life are of two types. There are the milestones that can be anticipated; and there are those that are totally unexpected, those that seem simply to occur and must be faced and worked out with the resources that you have built up. Both are capable of giving you a real boost in your ongoing.

Graduation is a milestone that you anticipate and prepare for. Knowing this, it is only wise to be as well prepared spiritually, mentally, and emotionally to meet it as you can. The purpose of this message is to help you prepare for what comes next.

Whether you go on to higher education or enter the everyday, workaday world after graduation, it is a "commencement," the commencement of a new era.

If you go on to higher education, remember that with each passing year you are giving your time to learning rather than to doing, to studying rather than to accomplishing. Therefore, the time you give to your education becomes more precious each year. It will be up to you to make sure that through diligent study and application you make the time worth its investment.

If this is the end of your formal schooling, you may have the thought that your education is completed. But actually if you are going forward in the world, your education is only beginning. You will go on learning and growing in many, many ways. The term "commencement" applies here, too. You will want to be willing to learn new things, new methods, and to keep abreast of the changing world.

Those of you who will not go on to higher education no doubt are looking forward to a job, a career, to marriage, a home, children, to a full and happy life. These things seem desirable to you; and yet because the future is unknown and untried, you may feel uneasiness, even fear, as to how you will acquire them. If you find that you look upon the future with some fear, you will do well to try to overcome it. Fear can only confuse you and cause you to do irrational things.

There is a place for you in the world, a place where you are wanted and needed. Try to know that this is true; try to believe it. Take the prayer, *"The Spirit of the Lord goes before me, and my way is happy, successful, and prosperous."*

As you go forth from school to build your new life, there will be many adjustments and changes to make. There will be times of temptation and discouragement in the future, but also there will be happy and glorious times. Fierce desires will mellow; good will ripen and bring ever greater satisfaction and pleasure in the coming years.

As you go forward in life, cling always to the thought that all things are working together for your good.

Until now someone else probably has assumed responsibility for you and supported you financially. Soon you will assume responsibility for yourself, you probably will be supporting yourself. Do not feel disturbed or apprehensive about this, for it is the natural, normal, and right thing.

You owe it to yourself to take responsibility for your life as soon as you can, and also you owe it to your parents—not necessarily because of financial considerations involved, but because you will want to be developing the right attitudes toward life. Every mature, adult person should walk as independently as he can, accepting cheerfully and joyfully responsibility for his life, his decisions, his achievements in the world. Therefore, to be a fully matured individual, you should assume responsibility for yourself. You should begin to make your own decisions, to plan your own life, to accept the responsibility for results in your life.

This does not mean that you are to turn your back suddenly on your parents and all they have meant and can mean to you. Instead, endeavor to make this maturing process a time of mutual co-operation and understanding. Try to avoid making it a time of strife, but with understanding and graciousness begin to find your inner independence gradually and confidently and let it work itself out tactfully and normally. To break off the present relationship between you and your parents suddenly is not natural and will cause inharmony and unhappiness.

Your parents can now and always will be able to give you much help and advice that can prove invaluable to you. To refuse angrily to consider anything they say is not a sign of maturity but is rather a sign of lack of maturity. The correct way is to begin to think as clearly and responsibly as possible, considering and accepting suggestions and ideas.

An affirmative prayer that will help you in achieving the independence you desire is as follows:

"*I express the independent, mature, reasonable person that I am in my Christ nature.*"

If you are planning to go to work after graduation, you have a very interesting and rewarding experience awaiting you.

You may know already what kind of work you are going to do. You may even know the exact company you are going to work for and the exact job you are going to have. On the other hand, you may not have the slightest idea what kind of work you want.

This is an age of specialization, and the person who goes farthest in business and the working world is the one who has at least some idea of what he wants to do. It is to your advantage to try to decide at least what field of work you desire to enter, rather than leaving all to chance.

Prayer will help you in this. Consider your desires, your abilities, and your opportunities prayerfully. Ask for guidance. Try to get a leading on what you would like to devote your time and energy to.

If you worked at a job before, perhaps after school hours or during summer vacations, you know something of what to expect. Yet there is a difference when you know that your work is on a more or less permanent basis and not for just a season. You have the feeling that "this is it!" and the job means more to you than the short-time or part-time jobs you have had. You will not want to be easily upset if things go wrong, or if raises do not seem to come often enough.

You will need patience in your work, for you probably will not be a thunderous success overnight. New relationships will have to be formed, and more important still, new material values and standards will have to be established. For the most part, school achievements will count for little in the workaday world. Honors and high recognition that were attained in school are likely to be unimpressive and passed over outside of school.

Begin your work with an open mind, expecting that your efforts will bear fruit and that you will be able to accomplish something fine in the world. Let your experiences contribute to your inner progress and growth.

If you are a young man, you may be facing service in the armed forces after your graduation. While it may not appear possible, try to know that even from this experience you can gain something good, something fine. Resist any thought of the uselessness of life, of futility, or that there is no use to prepare for or look forward to a good life. This attitude brings you only discouragement and unhappiness rather than helping to build your character and widen your outlook on life.

Know that wherever you go, God is, whether it be to a neighborhood town or to the other side of the earth. Dissolve your fear by knowing that God is wherever you are and that you can never be separated from Him. He surrounds you, protects you, infolds you, cares for you, and enables you to find the good that is in life.

So you are graduating! You are leaving this school, but what you have learned here, the education you have received here and elsewhere, will go with you wherever you go. It has become part of you.

Actually, it is not what you have learned that will influence your life most, but what habits you have formed, and what attitudes you hold toward life. The kind of person you are is more important than what you know.

This is the real influence that your education has had on you, the lasting influence—not what your education has placed in your mind but the character and attitudes it has helped you form.

Face the future unafraid.

This is God's world, and it always will be. God is good. Good, happiness, and life are before you.

Let graduation be a time of commencement. Commence to claim and enjoy God's good.

CLEDA REYNER

A CAREER OF FRIENDLINESS
IS OPEN TO EVERYONE

I WAS TALKING with a friend of mine the other day, and
among other things I complimented her on her ability to bring
out the best in people, including myself. When I am with her I
always feel that something fine in me heretofore unexplored has
opened up. I seem to grow by contact with her.

"I especially appreciate that compliment," she told me, "for
there was a time when I am sure people were no better off for
having associated with me."

Leaping at conclusions and with a wise nod of my head, I
said: "Oh, an inferiority complex. I, too, have spent much time
in retirement hiding my light 'under the bushel,' so to speak. I
used to be painfully shy."

But "No," she said, "I perhaps did have an inferiority complex, but I reacted to it quite oppositely from the way you did. I
was one of those youngsters who always had to be in the center
of things. My attention was all on putting my own best foot forward rather than on helping others along. It was a memorable
occasion for me when I suddenly developed a 'producer complex.'"

Then she went on to tell me about a high-school principal
who asked her to assemble all the talent she could find for a parent-teacher entertainment. She accepted the appointment with a
will and was both surprised and pleased at the number of unher-
alded talents that she was able to uncover in schoolmates who,

[346]

like myself, kept their light "under the bushel" for the most part. In herself she also found an aptitude for creating a burlesque program plus a few serious turns that gave everyone a moment in the spotlight. She laughed when she recalled that she even found a suitable place in the show for a certain boy who could add a comic note by wiggling his ears, and for another boy who gave an amazing imitation of a cackling hen.

She said that the great success of the program brought her a joy that she had never before experienced. She thrilled to see her schoolmates perform and their parents laugh and beam with pride. She sensed then and there what she could not at that time have put into words, the fact that happiness does not come solely from one's ability to perform successfully oneself but also from one's ability to help others succeed and from one's interest in their success. The triumphant feeling she always had when she put on a successful one-man show was nothing compared with the glow of pride and satisfaction that this "every-man" show brought her. She had not been particularly close to her schoolmates before the parent-teacher show and the great thrill of being on the inside of their hearts and not on the outside gave her a "producer complex" that she has never got over. In fact she is now virtually a genius at seeing beyond the surface of people —through the superficialities to the real—and helping them see and be their most glorious selves. She does extensive work among young people, helping them to understand themselves and others well enough to be harmonious notes in the great symphony of life.

What my friend discovered in her teens, the joy of helping and living close to others, many people go all through life without learning. Without intentionally building walls around themselves, they nevertheless become circumscribed because of their lack of interest in anything but their own performance. The unselfish acts that would keep their life flowing into other lives and vice versa—an interchange that is vital to rich and happy living —are left undone.

Yet I think all people really desire to mingle easily with their fellow men. They desire to stand high in the esteem of others and to have evidence that they do. And I believe that the desire is justifiable, for people have a very real need for one another. The resources of our own life are not enough. For both our happiness and our success we are dependent on our ability to live and work and play with others.

"Life is social in nature," said the speaker at a high-school commencement exercise that I attended recently. "The mythical self-made man does not exist." I verily believe that if we could take apart the components of any man's success and examine them, we should see for the most part simply an assembly of countless contributions from his fellows.

A career of friendliness, which is vital to the success of any other career, is open to everyone. Happy is the man who finds it easy and natural to mix with other people, but far from hopeless is the one who finds it difficult. Everyone has the potential qualities necessary to successful association with others. I believe that the simple acceptance of this truth will eliminate the biggest barrier that the imagination erects against getting along with people. The longer I live the more convinced I become that everyone can be a charmer in his own way. Rich possibilities and talents lie within us all.

My friend found that many different types of people with their different talents can make a very successful show, each one adding his bit to the success of the whole. She looks with interest now at all kinds of people, because she feels that all are necessary to the divine plan of this universe. And I think she is right. Our God and Father, being omnipresent and infinite, surely cannot find complete expression through any one personality, however great. It is easy to believe that it takes us all in our infinite number of ways to manifest Him.

My friend thinks that there is no greater obstacle to the making of friends than a lot of prejudices concerning certain characteristics. "Just as sure as we demand that persons have a mind and manners similar to ours, we cut down the number of our friends and hence our blessings."

My friend, by the way, is one of the most popular people I know, and I believe she likes virtually every person she meets. I heard her say once of a vivid, vital person that he was the kind of tonic that everyone should frequently "take," but she is also especially fond of another friend for the opposite reason: she likes his quietness. She very much likes one ambitious young person because he inspires her in her own line of endeavor with ideals and ambitions toward success similar to his own. But she confided in me one day that she just adores Jane, who is considered lazy. She says Jane has taught her more about relaxing and enjoying the natural, unearned joys of life than any other person.

She likes her sophisticated, traveled friends, but no more, it seems to me, than the ones who talk enthusiastically about their gardens and children and church suppers and family picnics. She never seems to require anyone to be different from what he is. She approves of people as they are. No wonder she draws out people's most charming, natural selves. I wish everyone knew such a person, for her approval does more to chasten one than any number of sermons, and more to encourage than dozens of pep talks. In the presence of her approval timid, quiet folks feel no need to be talkative and clever, and the feeling of being tongue-tied gives way to naturalness and ease. I know she has never rebuked anyone for being egotistical, but in her presence one loses the feeling that there is need for exaggerating one's importance.

I believe it was not until I discovered that I like other people just as they are that I felt wholly free to be myself. I believe that the reason many folks fail to attract friends into their life is because they do not do themselves the justice of expressing themselves truly. People are not attracted to shams. I heard a young man say once that he would like to know what he was really like. Wouldn't we all! So much true character gets submerged by the fear of what others may think or by inherited or thoughtlessly accepted beliefs. A personality may be and often is as ill fitting as hand-me-down clothes. And all the while the real self that is covered up is lovable, gracious, warm, and true, in every sense adaptable and harmonious. If you have worked hard at being something other than you truly are you may find help, as I have, in a little story that I remember from my earliest Sunday-school days.

It is the story of a little old man who had neither home nor friends nor money. Though a sort of vagabond, he was honest in all respects but one, and his single delinquency was unique. He stole flowers regularly from shops and flower stands and made a weekly visit to a hospital for children. He had an intense love for little folks, but he did not flatter himself with the belief that children could love him. However the children all loved flowers, and he always felt repaid for the risks he had taken when little hands reached for his offerings, when young voices said thankful, happy words to him, and when childish eyes and faces were made light by smiles.

But the inevitable day came when his sin overtook him. He was caught in the act of stealing flowers, and there was also evidence of his previous thefts. So the little old man had to be sent away. But at his earnest insistence he was granted the privilege of first visiting the hospital and his little friends. He had no offering for them on this last visit, but at least he could see them and tell them he would not be back any more. He feared that they might look for his weekly gift and be disappointed at his failure to arrive. So in all humility he approached them empty-handed. To his amazement greetings were as loving, smiles spread as readily over faces, and hands that had formerly reached for flowers reached out to grasp his fingers. He was dismayed, overjoyed, and overcome. The children loved him not for the flowers he had been bringing but for himself!

The little man in the story is typical, I think, of many of us. We undervalue the very thing in ourselves that people are hungry for but try on the other hand to make friends by offering gifts that sometimes are not honestly ours. Haven't you seen what could have been lasting and happy friendships grow stale and die because the friends gave only "borrowed" gifts to each other? Borrowed wit and gaiety? Borrowed knowledge that held no core of originality? Haven't you realized that what the friendship needed was simplicity and naturalness and love? Our own gifts, however unassuming, are much needed in the world today. Minds may be awed by our assumptions, but hearts remain untouched. Hearts respond best to simple signs of thoughtfulness and understanding.

We need not be concerned, I think, about our real qualities being acceptable to others. It is true that we are all different in outward expression, but basically we are so much alike that what we like in fundamentals others like too. Shakespeare's articulate little Jew very well covered the similarity of all people when he compared his people with the Christians.

"Hath not a Jew hands, organs, dimensions, senses, affections, passions? fed with the same food, hurt with the same weapons, subject to the same diseases, healed by the same means, warmed and cooled by the same winter and summer as a Christian is? If you prick us, do we not bleed? if you tickle us, do we not laugh?"

To follow somewhat the little merchant's trend of reasoning, are not all persons made in the same image and likeness? Are we not all subject to the desire for happiness? Are we not all warmed by expressions of love and friendliness and cooled by the lack of them?

I find that if I love enough I am blessed with the degree of forgetfulness of myself and my interests that makes remembrance and thoughtfulness of others easy. Love makes us too much interested in others to feel abashed before them, and it furnishes us with intuitions about making others feel at ease with us. Love keeps us interested when others talk and interesting when we talk, because a loving nature is sensitive to the things that are pleasing to other people. Love is the source of all the graces that we seek to gain for ourselves through books and lectures and observation. Love, with its millions of ways of manifestation, is the only magic there is in popularity.

When I was in school I did not know why a boy with a great thatch of unruly blond hair and a multitude of freckles was so very much liked by all the boys and girls .That is, I did not know until he invited me to his party. It was the first party I had ever been considered eligible to attend by the older crowd, and my self-confidence was very much in its embryonic state. When I told him I could come he said, "Gosh, I'm glad." I have remembered his sincerity and his friendliness for—well, a good many years.

If we wonder whether a simple little act of friendliness would be welcome to another, I think we can get the right answer by asking ourselves, "Would we be glad to have the same thing done for us?" If we are concerned as to whether our friend will like the only gift we can afford, we can inquire of ourselves what our own reactions would be. If we are troubled about some thoughtless remark we have made to another, we can usually be comforted by considering whether or not we should understand if the same thing were said to us. If we feel an impulse to tell people they are fine, we need not repress the desire without asking ourselves if we should like it. The things others do for us that make our own heart light and joyous, that give our own heart wings, these are the things that make us known as friends when we do them for others in a way that they can readily accept.

While we learn contentedly to play or sing our own appointed and harmonious notes in life's great symphony I think it is well also to educate ourselves in the matter of recognizing and appreciating the particular type of applause accorded us. One man's "music" makes people tap their toes and sway their bodies and clap their hands while another's calls for more quiet appreciation. It would be entirely out of harmony to reverse the procedure, to beat time to a lovely melody and to sit tranquilly through a piece of swing. But a girl I know has not yet learned to distinguish between the different types of applause. Her closest friend is gay, spontaneous, and rollicking. She therefore calls forth that kind of response from other people. Much "kidding," laughter, and joking are directed toward her. The quiet one—or the "melody," as I think of her—longs to have a part in the easy and friendly banter. It is difficult for her to see that her own "production" is equally appreciated, that the quietness of the reception given her is no less genuine or valued. Our own of anything comes to us inevitably, and when we recognize it, our own is wholly satisfying to us. We have no envy or jealousy to overcome when we recognize our own incoming tide of blessings, each one made to our especial order.

A man whose popularity is still a fact after nearly two thousand years well knew and loved humanity's similarities as well as its differences. So deeply was He aware of the likeness that comes from being knit together by the one great, holy Spirit that He moved with equal grace and love among the wise and the untutored. Some say He made Himself congenial with all kinds of people so that He might teach them the law, but my own heart says no to this. I think it was love of people that made Jesus Christ harmonize Himself with every type of person. And I think that their conviction that He loved them made the devotion He felt toward God so contagious.

As someone has said, "Religion is caught, not taught."

Love for people, interest in them, and joy in their success, that is what makes us happy.

ERNEST C. WILSON

THE STUDENT'S PSALM

I dwell in the secret place of the Great Teacher,
And abide in the light of His understanding.
I say of the Lord, He is my reference and my authority:
My God, in whom I trust.
He delivers me from ensnaring perplexities
And from confusing fears.
He infolds me with His peace,
And I am secure in the assurance of His instruction:
His Truth is to me a fount of knowledge.
I am not afraid of dark or terrifying thoughts that may enter my
      mind,
Nor misled by the rambling ideas that intrude upon my studies.
No matter how many others may fail, I shall be secure,
Because of the Great Teacher who is my help unfailing.
Because I have made the Lord, even the Most High, my instruc-
      tor, I cannot fail.
Trusting in Him, I do my best.
His loving thoughts have charge over me, to keep me in all my
      ways.
They bear me up when I am downcast and depressed.
Through Him I am victorious over dangers and difficulties.
Because my faith is in God He will deliver me.
He will help me to be successful.
He will answer when I call upon Him;

He will be with me in trouble.
He will inspire me and bring honor to me;
With life abundant He will bless me,
And He will show me His ways of wisdom.

CALLIE KIENY

A PRAYER FOR BABY SITTERS

I BLESS the opportunity to serve one who needs my help. I serve to the best of my ability, living up to the trust that has been placed in me. I know that I am letting the Christ in me find expression. As I allow the Christ in me to come forth, the wisdom and the knowledge that I need in a particular situation becomes mine, and I find it easy to do my work well.

THANK GOD FOR LIFE!

"I love life and thank God for it."

You MAY be convinced that the trite expression, "These are the happiest days of your life," just can't be true. But it can be true, depending on you!

Every phase of living has its own particular set of blessings. It is a matter of keeping your focus on the advantages of your present stage of life, of making the most of every good thing that you have now, while you have it.

So be glad that you are young. Thank God for the qualities of youth.

Thank God for:

Your belief in yourself and your abilities, which make you know that you can do and be and conquer all things.

Your curiosity about things; your vision for a more wonderful you; your will power to carry things through to their proper conclusion.

Your boundless energy; your spirited eagerness for accomplishment.

Your capacity for laughter and fun; your natural response to the joy of living.

Copy down and place this prayer where you can see it often: *"I love life and thank God for it."* Make a mental note of it, so that you may be constantly reminded to focus your thoughts on present-day blessings.

Yes, be glad you are young! And when you are older be glad then, too, for God has designed a different but equally wonderful set of blessings for every phase of your life.

NOTES ON AUTHORS

MARCUS BACH focused new attention on religion's relation to education with his work in the Department of Religion of the University of Iowa. His latest book is *The Will to Believe*. "The Lord's Side of the Ledger" was published in *Good Business*.

CLARA BERANGER is a well-known writer, and formerly a teacher at the University of Southern California. Her published books include *Peace Begins at Home* (a Unity Book) and *Writing for the Screen*. "Thou Shalt Not Be Afraid" was published in *Weekly Unity*.

CLINTON E. BERNARD is editor of *Good Business*, and author of several pamphlets. His article "Truth or Psychology?" originally appeared in the Human Relations department in *Good Business*.

H. EMILIE CADY was a homeopathic physician and writer of metaphysical articles when Charles and Myrtle Fillmore persuaded her to write a course of basic Truth study. This became *Lessons in Truth*, Unity's basic textbook. Miss Cady also wrote *How I Used Truth* and *God a Present Help*.

HELEN S. CARPENTER is on the Silent Unity staff. She is the wife of George E. Carpenter, editor of *Unity*.

WILLIAM A. CLOUGH is a former newspaperman who has written extensively for the Unity periodicals and for the publications of the Methodist Church.

JOHN DAVIS is an Atlanta businessman-author whose articles appear in the country's most widely read magazines. "A Formula for Prosperity" originally appeared in *Good Business*.

JAMES A. DECKER is associate editor of *Good Business*, and a frequent contributor to the other Unity periodicals. His article "What Should I Say to God?" appeared originally in *You*.

MARY BREWERTON DEWITT was one of the early-day Unity workers.

CHARLES FILLMORE, co-founder of Unity School of Christianity, was a prolific and brilliant writer on almost every facet of Truth. Unity publishes eleven of his books, ranging from *Christian Healing* to *Atom-Smashing Power of Mind*.

LOWELL FILLMORE is president of Unity School of Christianity, contributor of the weekly feature "Things to Be Remembered" in *Weekly Unity*, and author of two books: *New Ways to Solve Old Problems* and *Things to Be Remembered*.

MYRTLE FILLMORE, co-founder of Unity School of Christianity, was also the founder and first editor of *Wee Wisdom*, Unity's magazine for children. In 1936 a book, *Healing Letters of Myrtle Fillmore*, was published.

CONSTANCE J. FOSTER's articles have appeared in leading American magazines. She is co-author with O. Spurgeon English of the book *Fathers Are Parents Too*. Her article "Nothing Doubting" is from *Weekly Unity*.

EMMET FOX was for many years the minister of the Church of the Healing Christ in New York City. He is the author of many books. "The Golden Key" is reprinted from his book *Power through Constructive Thinking* by kind permission of the publishers, Harper and Brothers, New York. "Life Is Consciousness" was originally an address given to the Unity workers.

WILLIAM H. FRAZIER wrote his poem "Blessed Home" while a member of the Silent Unity staff.

JAMES DILLET FREEMAN is dean of the Unity ministerial training program, and author of *Be!*, a collection of poems and prose-poems. His poems appear frequently in *Daily Word* and other Unity periodicals. In 1951 he wrote *The Household of Faith*, the definitive story of the founding and growth of Unity.

DANA GATLIN was at one time with the New York *Sun*. She wrote fiction for a number of leading American magazines. After her retirement from fiction writing, she wrote extensively for the Unity periodicals. Unity publishes two of her books, *God Is the Answer* and *Prayer Changes Things*.

HILDA GREEN contributed various articles to the Unity periodicals.

R. H. GRENVILLE is a Canadian author who writes for several of the Unity periodicals.

GARDNER HUNTING was formerly a professional screen-writer, and is one of the most popular writers for the Unity periodicals. His most recent book is *The Word beyond Words*. Unity publishes two of his books: *Prove Me Now* and *Working with God*, from which "The Come-Back" is taken.

H. B. JEFFERY was one of the early-day metaphysicians, author of several Unity articles and meditations.

RALPH E. JOHNSON was a member of the Silent Unity staff.

FLORENCE SCRIPPS KELLOGG is a Californian associated with the work of Christ Church, Unity in Los Angeles.

RUSSELL A. KEMP is a Unity center leader.

CALLIE KIENY has contributed to *You*.

ANNA H. KING contributed "Cheerful Resolve" to *Weekly Unity*.

HANNAH MORE KOHAUS wrote several books on metaphysics.

RICHARD J. LYNCH is a former Unity center leader, who now lectures widely. He is the author of the book *Know Thyself*. His article "The Art of Appreciation" was originally published in *Unity* magazine.

MARY MAE OESCH writes regularly for the *Unity Sunday-school Leaflet*.

CLARA PALMER is associated with the Silent Unity ministry in its healing work and writes regularly for *Weekly Unity* and the other Unity periodicals. She is author of the book *You Can Be Healed*.

JANE PALMER is editor of *Wee Wisdom*, the Unity magazine for children, and associate editor of *Weekly Unity*, in which "Who Is God?" was published.

WILFERD A. PETERSON is a Michigan advertising-agency executive, and author of *The Art of Getting Along*. "The Master's Ten Laws of Human Relations," originally a *Good Business* article, is one of Unity's most popular pamphlets.

M. J. READING's "A New Kind of Beauty Treatment" appeared originally in *Weekly Unity*.

CLEDA REYNER supervises one of the correspondence sections

of Silent Unity, and writes for the Unity periodicals. Her contributions to this book were originally published in *Unity*.

CLARA MAY ROWLAND is director of Silent Unity, Unity's prayer group, author of many articles, and a favorite Unity lecturer. Her article "How to Be Young" was published originally in *Daily Word*.

WINFRED RHOADES has been newspaperman, teacher, and clergyman. At the Boston Dispensary, in 1933, he conducted some of the earliest classes in the effect of prayer on physical ills. Author of many books, he contributes frequently to the Unity periodicals. "How Do You Think of God?" appeared originally in *Weekly Unity*.

ELLA SYFERS SCHENCK's "Morning Prayer" has been a favorite of Unity readers since it was first published in *Weekly Unity*.

MARTHA SMOCK is one of the editors of *Daily Word*, wherein "Who Will Take Care of the Children?" and "No Other Way" originally appeared.

JAMES E. SWEANEY is editor of *You*, Unity's magazine for young people, and a former Unity center leader.

KAY SWEANEY was formerly on the Unity editorial staff. She is the wife of James Sweaney, editor of *You*.

ZELIA WALTERS is the author of three Unity Books: *You and Your Child, Whatsoever Ye Shall Ask* and *Dr. Houston Speaking*. Her articles appear frequently in the Unity periodicals.

GEORGIANA TREE WEST is leader of one of the Unity centers in New York City, and author of the book *Prosperity's Ten Commandments*. "Pray Without Ceasing" appeared originally in *Unity*.

FRANK B. WHITNEY was the first editor of *Daily Word*, and author of many poems appearing in the Unity periodicals. His published books include *Beginning Again*.

ERNEST C. WILSON is minister of Christ Church, Unity, in Los Angeles and author of many books, including *The Sunlit Way, Have We Lived Before?* and *The Great Physician*. He was formerly editor-in-chief of the Unity publications.

A LIST OF UNITY BOOKS

Atom-Smashing Power of Mind, by CHARLES FILLMORE
Be! by JAMES DILLET FREEMAN
Be of Good Courage, by FRANK B. WHITNEY
Beginning Again, by FRANK B. WHITNEY
Best-Loved Unity Poems
Both Riches and Honor, by ANNIE RIX MILITZ
Christ Enthroned in Man, by CORA DEDRICK FILLMORE
Christian Healing, by CHARLES FILLMORE
Divine Remedies
Doctor Houston Speaking, by ZELIA M. WALTERS
Effectual Prayer, by FRANCES W. FOULKS
Favorite Unity Radio Talks
God a Present Help, by H. EMILIE CADY
God Is the Answer, by DANA GATLIN
The Great Physician, by ERNEST C. WILSON
Have We Lived Before? by ERNEST C. WILSON
The Household of Faith, by JAMES DILLET FREEMAN
How I Used Truth, by H. EMILIE CADY
Jesus Christ Heals, by CHARLES FILLMORE
Keep a True Lent, by CHARLES FILLMORE
Know Thyself, by RICHARD LYNCH
Lessons in Truth, by H. EMILIE CADY
Let There Be Light, by ELIZABETH SAND TURNER
Lovingly in the Hands of the Father, by EVELYN WHITELL
The Metaphysical Bible Dictionary
Mightier Than Circumstance, by FRANK B. WHITNEY
A More Wonderful You

Myrtle Fillmore's Healing Letters
Mysteries of Genesis, by CHARLES FILLMORE
Mysteries of John, by CHARLES FILLMORE
New Ways to Solve Old Problems, by LOWELL FILLMORE
Peace Begins at Home, by CLARA BERANGER
Prayer Changes Things, by DANA GATLIN
Prayer in the Market Place
Prosperity, by CHARLES FILLMORE
Prosperity's Ten Commandments, by GEORGIANA TREE WEST
Prove Me Now, by GARDNER HUNTING
Selected Studies, by IMELDA OCTAVIA SHANKLIN
The Sunlit Way, by ERNEST C. WILSON
Talks on Truth, by CHARLES FILLMORE
Teach Us to Pray, by CHARLES and CORA FILLMORE
Things to Be Remembered, by LOWELL FILLMORE
Truth Ideas of an M.D., by DR. C. O. SOUTHARD
The Story of Unity, by JAMES DILLET FREEMAN
The Twelve Powers of Man, by CHARLES FILLMORE
Unity Vegetarian Cookbook
What Are You? by IMELDA OCTAVIA SHANKLIN
Whatsoever Ye Shall Ask, by ZELIA M. WALTERS
Working with God, by GARDNER HUNTING
You and Your Child, by ZELIA M. WALTERS
You Can Be Healed, by CLARA PALMER

BOOKS FOR CHILDREN

Adventures of the Seven Spartans, by LAWRENT LEE
Barky's New Home, by GEORGIA TUCKER SMITH
Barky and His Friends, by GEORGIA TUCKER SMITH
Crybaby Kangaroo, by GEORGIA TUCKER SMITH
Jet's Adventures, by BULA HAHN
Jet and the New Country, by BULA HAHN
Jet's Choice, by BULA HAHN
Teach Me to Pray, by BILL and BERNARD MARTIN
Thank You, God, by BILL and BERNARD MARTIN

THE EDITOR AND HIS BOOK

Lowell Fillmore, *oldest son of Charles and Myrtle Fillmore, the founders of Unity, was born in Pueblo, Colorado, in 1882. The Fillmores were cousins of Millard Fillmore, thirteenth President of the United States. Lowell Fillmore, began working for Unity as an office boy in 1899. He graduated from Kansas City Business College in 1901 and in 1909 became editor of the newly-created* Weekly Unity. *He assisted in the incorporation of Unity work under the name Unity School of Christianity in 1914, and became president of the School in 1948, upon the death of his father. Married in 1926 to Alice Lee, whom he met at Unity School, Lowell Fillmore makes his home at Unity Village, Lee's Summit, Missouri. He is the author of* Remember *(Unity, 1929),* New Ways to Solve Old Problems *(Unity, 1939) and* Things to be Remembered *(Unity, 1952) and has contributed a column to* Weekly Unity *since 1910.*

The Unity Treasure Chest *(Hawthorn, 1956) was designed by Sidney Feinberg and completely manufactured by American Book–Stratford Press, Inc. The body type is Caledonia, designed for the Linotype by W. A. Dwiggins, one of America's best-known typographers and designers.*

A HAWTHORN BOOK